Student
Activity
Workbook

College English & Communication

Sue C. Camp, Ed.D.
Broyhill School of Management
Gardner-Webb University
Boiling Springs, North Carolina

Marilyn L. Satterwhite
Business Division
Danville Area Community College
Danville, Illinois

 **Glencoe McGraw-Hill**

7th edition

New York, New York
Columbus, Ohio
Woodland Hills, California
Peoria, Illinois

Student Activity Workbook for *College English and Communication,*
Seventh Edition

Imprint 2000

Copyright © 1998 by The McGraw-Hill Companies, Inc. Printed in the United States of
America. All rights reserved. Copyright © 1992, 1987, 1982, 1975, 1969, 1964 by The
McGraw-Hill Companies, Inc. All rights reserved. Printed in the United States of America.
Except as permitted under the United States Copyright Act of 1976, no part of this publi-
cation may be reproduced or distributed in any form or by any means, or stored in a
database or retrieval system, without prior written permission of the publisher.

Send all inquiries to:

Glencoe/McGraw-Hill
21600 Oxnard St. Suite 500
Woodland Hills, CA 91367-4906

SBN 0-02-802173-8   SE

3 4 5 6 7 8 9 066 05 04 03 02 01 00

Contents

NOTES TO THE STUDENT

Developing the skills presented in your *College English and Communication* text requires practice. Reading and studying the text is an effective beginning, but to master those skills you must apply them—you must improve your use of language; listen and speak with confidence; prepare memos, letters, and reports; write, edit, and proofread correspondence. Remember that no matter what you want to accomplish and what specific skills you have, to succeed in business you need effective communication skills.

College English and Communication, Seventh Edition, offers you several formats for practicing those communication skills. Within the text, each section has Practical Application and Editing Practice activities; many sections also have Critical Thinking activities.

In addition to the opportunities within the text, *College English and Communication* also provides many additional practice situations in this *Student Activity Workbook for College English and Communication, Seventh Edition.* Use your developing communication skills and the references you have available as you continue your study of *College English and Communication.*

Remember that communication skills are not separate units to be studied and practiced individually and then stored away so that you can study another skill. Listening, speaking, reading, and writing are integrated skills. Two or three or even all four may be used in a single application. In the *Student Activity Workbook for College English and Communication,* you will use the building-block approach: Each succeeding chapter builds on those that came before. You will be asked to use all that you have learned—not only the skills in the current chapter—to complete the activities.

The *Student Activity Workbook for College English and Communication, Seventh Edition,* is organized and labeled to match the text. The workbook offers extensive and varied additional practice including short-answer, true/false, multiple choice, and narrative formats.

Understanding Communication. Chapter 1 of the text offers an introduction to the communication process—applied both to your personal life and to your business life. Chapter 1 in the activity workbook asks you to apply principles in the text to simulated business situations and to your own experiences.

Global, Electronic, and Ethical Communication. Chapter 2 introduces some of the technologies used to communicate globally and focuses on factors dealing with cultural diversity, ethics, and nondiscriminatory language in communication. Chapter 9 examines in detail the considerations for communicating electronically. Corresponding exercises in the activity workbook provide opportunities to apply the concepts covered in these chapters to realistic workplace situations.

Grammar, Punctuation, and Style. Chapters 3 and 4 in the text provide a thorough discussion of the principles of grammar, punctuation, and style. These chapters in the activity workbook give intensive application of these principles using business situations for the examples.

Reading for Understanding. Chapter 5 emphasizes the importance of reading in researching and retaining information and in writing and revising correspondence. The text and the workbook focus on reading strategies, vocabulary power, retention and comprehension, and note taking.

Oral Communication. Chapter 6 focuses on improving listening skills and on developing awareness of the importance of nonverbal communication. Chapter 8 of the text presents guidelines to help you speak effectively in one-to-one and group situations. Chapters 6 and 8 of the activity workbook offer situations that require you to apply specific listening and speaking skills related to listening strategies, nonverbal cues, pronunciation and enunciation, organization of ideas, telephone techniques, and development of an oral presentation.

The Craft of Writing. Chapter 7 in the text and the workbook uses a building-block approach in presenting the techniques for writing messages—moving from word choice and spelling to structuring phrases and clauses, writing sentences, and building paragraphs. Chapter 7 also will give you an understanding of revising, editing, and proofreading and the importance of these tasks in producing error-free communications. Developing your skills in proofreading and editing is not easy. First, you need to be able to spot a possible error. Next, you must decide if the situation really is an error. Finally, you must know how to correct the problem if an error exists. Another challenge is to find a better way to explain something. The workbook activities for Chapter 7 include practice in locating errors—first by category and then by document. You also have opportunities to rewrite messages for improvement.

Formatting Correspondence. Chapter 10 includes information on the purposes, types, styles, and writing techniques for memos. The workbook activities for Chapter 10 ask you to apply what you have learned about the purposes and formats for memos to writing and revising memos. Chapter 10 also asks you to demonstrate proficiency in formatting letters using different business letter styles.

Writing Business Correspondence. In Chapter 10 of the text and the activity workbook, you have the opportunity to plan, write, and revise memos and to format letters. Chapter 11 of the text and the activity workbook provides opportunities to apply all the writing techniques you've learned as you explore the various purposes and strategies for writing business letters.

Customer Service Communication. Chapter 12 discusses the importance of customer service communication in business. The accompanying work-book activities provide realistic business situations for practice in customer service communication.

Reports and Special Communications. Chapter 13 guides you through a number of other business communications—informal reports, formal reports, minutes of meetings, and news releases. Included in the Chapter 13 workbook activities are opportunities to explore the technology resources available to report writers.

Communication and Your Career. In Chapter 14 of both the text and the activity workbook, you apply all the communication skills you've developed in preparing for the job search, making your interviews more effective, and advancing in your career.

By a thorough study of your *College English and Communication* text and a careful application of the text principles to completing the exercises in the *Student Activity Workbook for College English and Communication*, you can develop the proficiency in writing, listening, speaking, and reading that you will need for career success.

NAME *Jaqueline Resende*　　DATE *2/5/02*　SCORE ____

 **SECTION 1.1**　　# EFFECTIVE COMMUNICATION IN EVERYDAY LIVING

A　Purposes of Communication

Indicate the most likely purpose of each of the following sentences—to inquire, to inform, to persuade, or to establish goodwill.

✓

1. What color are you going to paint your new house?　　1. *inquire* ____
2. The payment is due on the fifth of each month.　　2. *inform* ____
3. Thank you for your assistance at the fund-raiser.　　3. *good will* ____
4. Your new washer and dryer will last longer if you sign up for the service program.　　4. *persuade* ____
5. When will the shipment arrive?　　5. *inquire* ____
6. The generosity of your company is greatly appreciated.　　6. *good will* ____
7. We just purchased a new copier for the office.　　7. *inform* ____
8. You had better purchase the car today, if you want the special discount.　　8. *persuade* ____
9. Why is the fax machine not working?　　9. *inquire* ____
10. The office must be locked up when you go to lunch.　　10. *inform* ____

B　Giving Feedback

For each of the following situations, describe the type(s) of feedback the receiver should give. Indicate whether the feedback should be oral, written, or nonverbal, or a combination of these.

✓

1. You are meeting with your supervisor to discuss a sales report you are to compile for a meeting next week. Your supervisor is explaining what information is needed and how it should be presented. However, your supervisor has not been clear on several points. What feedback would you give your supervisor to show that you need clarification on the instructions?
   oral - explain Better

   1. ____

2. A coworker leaves a message on your voice mail. The coworker asks you to provide monthly sales figures for the last six months. What feedback would you give your coworker?
   oral

   2. ____

3. At the health clinic where you work, a patient asks you a question about tests that the doctor has ordered for the patient. What feedback would you give the patient?

Oral - talk directly to the doctor written list of directions.

3. ____

4. You work in the order department at a major electronics company. A customer asks you to make some changes to an order that she phoned in yesterday. The customer asks to receive confirmation that the order has been changed. What feedback should you give the customer?

Written / oral.

4. ____

5. A coworker who is also a friend of yours asks you to review a memo he wrote and to comment on the writing style. What feedback should you give your coworker?

oral / written

5. ____

C   Identify and Respond to Needs of the Receiver

Based on the following situations, identify which need of the receiver (esteem, physical, security, social, self-actualization) is not being met. Describe what could be done to meet that need.

1. Attendees at a one-day conference have not eaten since the 7:30 a.m. breakfast, and the noon luncheon program starts with an hour-long keynote speech.

Physical - hungry / tired / Room to hot / cold

1. ____

2. A new staff member is continually left to look after the office while the other staff members go to lunch together.

Social - self esteem Maybe be hired to work during lunch. speak up.

2. ____

3. A salesperson who frequently travels by car is hesitant to travel in unfamiliar surroundings, especially at night.

Security.

3. ____

4. The hardest working employee in the department has been passed over several times for recognition as employee of the month.

esteem, Security.

4. ____

D Analyzing Communication

In each of the following situations, identify the type of feedback the receiver would most likely give (oral, written, or nonverbal). In addition, explain your interpretation of the message. ✓

1. Sandy tells her student worker to make 100 copies of an eight-page test for an instructor, Mr. Luft. It is now 9:30 a.m., and Mr. Luft needs the tests by 10 a.m.

   Oral — will not be done by 10. Will need help.

   1. ____

2. A sales clerk is talking on the telephone to a customer as another customer walks up to the sales desk. The customer who walked up interrupts the sales clerk's conversation and asks for directions to another department.

   Oral

   2. ____

3. Nancy, an administrative assistant in a law office, receives a written note from Deanna, her supervisor, explaining the proper way to file documents.

   nonverbal-oral — may not understand the memo.

   3. ____

E Taking the Receiver's Background Into Account

In each of the following examples, determine the most appropriate way to communicate the message based on the receiver's background and the nature of the message. ✓

1. You are working with a new client who wants to purchase a house with assistance from your real estate company. The client has never purchased a house before and you must clearly explain all of the steps to be followed in detail.

   explain process
   ✓ off list.

   1. ____

2. A long-time friend has asked you for advice on a personal problem that has come up. You feel very strongly about this topic and know that your friend will be upset with your advice.

   explain it a positive feedback not too strong.

   2. ____

F Eliminating Barriers to Communication

For each of the following situations, identify any barriers to communication (physical, emotional, or language). List suggestions for overcoming or dealing with the barriers.

1. A training session is taking place in a room where the temperature is very warm.

   Barriers physical _____

   _____

   _____ 1. _____

2. An employee is having a difficult time concentrating on work because there is a rumor going around the office that employees are going to be laid off due to an upcoming merger with another company.

   emotional _____

   _____

   _____ 2. _____

3. A potential customer receives a sales letter that contains several misspelled words.

   language _____

   _____

   _____ 3. _____

G Responsibilities of the Sender and the Receiver

1. Briefly describe a situation in your life where miscommunication occurred, and describe how the miscommunication could have been avoided.

   _____

   _____

   _____

   _____ 1. _____

2. Describe a situation on the job where it would be important to maintain goodwill, and explain how you would accomplish this.

   _____

   _____

   _____

   _____ 2. _____

3. Describe a situation on the job where it would be important to maintain confidentiality, and explain how you would accomplish this.

   _____

   _____

   _____

   _____ 3. _____

THE COMMUNICATION SKILLS: LISTENING, SPEAKING, READING, AND WRITING

SECTION 1.2

A Interrelationship of Communication Skills

The four communication skills—listening, speaking, reading, and writing—are interconnected. In each of the following examples, one of the communication skills is featured. Explain how one or more of the other skills might be used in the situation to reinforce the primary skill.

✓

1. Listening to a coworker's concerns about completing an important project on time.

   listening → speaking (give advice)
   writing notes - to help her out.

   1. ___

2. Speaking to a customer about the differences between two computer products.

   speaking →
   listening - how is she going to use product.

   2. ___

3. Writing a report about the advantages and disadvantages of using electronic mail to communicate messages.

   Reading

   3. ___

4. Reading several books on conducting a job search to determine what strategies to use in finding a job.

   listening

   4. ___

5. Listening to your supervisor explain the preparations to be made for an upcoming meeting with clients from Japan.

   Speaking, Reading

   5. ___

B Reading and Writing

List five specific activities that would primarily require reading skills and five specific activities that would primarily require writing skills.

✓

READING

1. When you get a report.   1. ____
2. Homework   2. ____
3. Signs   3. ____
4. Cooking   4. ____
5. research.   5. ____

WRITING

1. letters.   1. ____
2. Advertising   2. ____
3. reports.   3. ____
4. E-mail   4. ____
5. message   5. ____

C Effective Communication

Indicate the communication skill or skills you would be most likely to use for each of the following situations. Explain why you would use the skill or skills.

✓

1. Researching material for a speech.
   Reading (note card).

   1. ____

2. Attending a sales presentation.
   listening
   reading
   speaking. (ask question).

   2. ____

3. Giving a friend directions to your new house.
   Speaking
   writing
   listening.

   3. ____

4. Explaining an assignment to a classmate.
   -Speaking
   -reading
   -listening

   4. ____

5. Helping a family member cope with a personal problem.
   Speaking
   listening

   5. ____

D Using the Four Communication Skills on the Job

Identify your career area and write a paragraph explaining how you might use each of the four communication skills on the job.

✓

YOUR CAREER AREA

Boston Market Inc.

USE OF COMMUNICATION SKILLS

- _writing - to take orders_
- _speaking_
- _listening_

E Combining the Communication Skills in Your Social, Educational, and Professional Lives

For each of the following situations, write one paragraph that explains how you would use a combination of communication skills to communicate.

✓

1. Communicating with a friend who lives six hours away.

social { - writing a letter to her.
- reading -
- listening - over the phone
- speaking over the phone

1. ____

2. Communicating with ten coworkers about the upcoming luncheon for your retiring supervisor.

professional { writing (memo - email)
listening (input etc).

2. ____

3. Communicating with a fellow student about a joint presentation the two of you will give in your speech class.

education { speaking
listening
reading
writing

3. ____

F Sensitivity in Communication

Sensitivity is the key to all effective communication. In the space provided next to each of the following phrases, write *S* if the phrase reflects sensitivity in business situations or *I* if it reflects insensitivity.

1. Considering *who* will be hearing or reading what you have to say   1. _I S_ ✓

2. Considering the needs of your audience   2. _S_

3. Interrupting a speaker   3. _I_

4. Changing the subject of discussion suddenly   4. _I_

5. Keeping your emotions under control   5. _S_

6. Using facial expressions and gestures that express a negative reaction to what the speaker is saying   6. _I_

7. Giving credit for others' contributions   7. _S I_

8. Giving incomplete information   8. _S_

9. Being punctual   9. _S_

10. Speaking in an almost inaudible voice   10. _I_

11. Giving a speaker your undivided attention and interest   11. _I S_

12. Reading a handout while someone is speaking   12. _I_

13. Taking into consideration what your audience already knows about the subject   13. _S_

14. Thinking about what your audience is interested in hearing   14. _S_

15. Not doing your fair share of work   15. _I_

16. Keeping your mind focused on the speaker's topic   16. _S_

SECTION 1.3 APPLYING YOUR COMMUNICATION SKILLS IN BUSINESS

A Using the Correct Tone

For each of the following communication situations, determine whether the tone should be formal or informal. ✓

1. Inform a friend about an upcoming career day at your college.

2. Discuss with your supervisor an idea for improving sales.

3. Write instructions for the company procedures manual on the proper way to format letters.

4. Give a presentation to the human relations committee at your company.

5. Discuss weekend plans with a coworker.

6. Write a letter to your senator describing your view on funding for education.

7. Present your findings on the cost efficiency of new computer equipment to your supervisor.

8. Inform staff members about plans for a new break room.

9. Write a letter responding to a customer's request.

10. Explain to your employer the reasons you decided to purchase a more expensive type of copy paper.

1. _Informal_ ____
2. _Formal_ ____
3. _formal_ ____
4. _formal_ ____
5. _informal_ ____
6. _formal_ ____
7. _formal_ ____
8. _informal_ ____
9. _formal_ ____
10. _formal_ ____

B Components of Business Communication

Indicate whether each of the following examples describes an external or an internal form of business communication. ✓

1. A memo from the sales manager to all salespeople in the office.

2. A staff meeting on ideas for decorating the new office.

3. A sales letter sent to prospective clients.

4. A telemarketing survey of local citizens.

5. A retreat for employees of the company to develop teamwork skills.

6. A newspaper ad for a paralegal position.

7. A sales pitch to a group of potential clients.

8. An office manager giving employees directions for dealing with problem clients.

1. _external_ ____
2. _internal_ ____
3. _external_ ____
4. _external_ ____
5. _internal_ ____
6. _external_ ____
7. _external_ ____
8. _internal_ ____

9. A memo from human resources about the new health care package.

10. A brochure explaining the new class offerings sent to current students.

✓

9. ___internal___ ___

10. ___external___ ___

C Flow of Communication Within an Organization

In a paragraph, describe how the tone of upward communication might differ from that of lateral or downward communication.

✓

_____
_____
_____
_____
_____
_____
_____
_____
_____
_____

D Upward, Lateral, and Downward Communication

Describe the upward, lateral, and downward communication that might occur in each of the following settings.

✓

1. A department meeting between the department chair and five full-time faculty members.

_____
_____
_____
_____
_____

1. ___

2. A classroom discussion between college students and the instructor on a specific topic.

_____
_____
_____
_____
_____

2. ___

3. An e-mail message sent by a staff member to all people on the production team whose members include both managers and staff employees.

_____
_____
_____
_____
_____

3. ___

02/06/2002

✓

4. A medical assistant with three years' experience explains office procedures to a newly hired medical assistant.

___
___
___
___
___

4. ___

5. An accountant in the finance department asks the benefits specialist in the human resources department about changes to the employee medical plan.

Casual Friendly

___
___
___
___

5. ___

E Applying the Six C's of Business Communication

Describe how you would apply the six C's of communication to each of the following situations.

✓

1. Setting up a sales appointment with a client.

- clear
- complete
- concise
- consistent
- correct.
- cortious

1. ___

2. Arranging for repair work to be done to the electrical wiring in your office.

___
___
___
___
___

2. ___

3. Giving a new worker instructions on sending out a mailing.

___
___
___
___

3. ___

4. Writing a status report to your supervisor about an ongoing project you are working on.

_____

_____

_____

_____

_____

_____   **4.** _____

5. Answering a telephone call from a patient about test results.

_____

_____

_____

_____

_____

_____   **5.** _____

F **Editing to Meet the Six C's of Communication**

Edit the following paragraph to reflect the six C's of communication. The edited paragraph should be clear, complete, concise, consistent, correct, and courteous.

> I am writing this letter to inform you that the shipment you ordered will be mailed to the address you requested on or before Wednesday. We could not get the shipment mailed any earlier due to processing problems at our plant. I hope this does not inconvenience you because we need your business and look forward to doing business with you in the future. If you have any questions or concerns about ~~this shipment wait until next tuesday to call so I have a chance to recover from the weekend.~~

This letter is to inform you that the shipment you ordered will be mailed to you on or before wedn. Were sorry about the delay and appreciate your business.

_____

_____

_____

_____

_____

_____

_____

ELECTRONIC COMMUNICATION

 Productivity in the Electronic Office

For each item in the chart, describe at least two ways some of the technologies intro-duced in Section 2.1 affect productivity in the electronic office.

	Productivity in the Electronic Office
Time	
Convenience	
Quality	

B **Advantages of Technology**

List four advantages of using a personal computer to type the minutes of the monthly company board meeting.   ✓

1. _____   ____
2. _____   ____
3. _____   ____
4. _____   ____

List four advantages of using voice mail to send and receive telephone messages.

1. _____   ____
2. _____   ____
3. _____   ____
4. _____   ____

C Using Business Communication Technology

In the space provided, describe how each form of technology assists communication in the electronic office.   ✓

1. Voice mail

_____

_____

_____

_____

_____   1. _____

2. Cellular phones

_____

_____

_____

_____   2. _____

3. Fax machines

_____

_____

_____

_____

_____   3. _____

4. Internet

_____

_____

_____

_____   4. _____

5. World Wide Web

_____

_____

_____

_____   5. _____

6. Modems

_____

_____

_____

_____   6. _____

✓

7. Electronic mail

_____
_____
_____
_____

7. ____

8. Personal computers

_____
_____
_____
_____

8. ____

9. Computerized information systems

_____
_____
_____
_____

9. ____

10. Laptop computers

_____
_____
_____
_____

10. ____

D Expanding Your Knowledge

Read the classified advertisement section of your local newspaper. Cut out one advertisement for each of the following areas: information processing, word processing, and telecommunications. What communication skills are required for each position?

✓

1. Information processing advertisement

_____
_____
_____
_____

1. ____

2. Word processing advertisement

_____
_____
_____
_____

2. ____

3. Telecommunications advertisement

_____
_____
_____
_____

3. ____

E Correcting Errors

On the lines provided, rewrite each sentence to eliminate any errors.   ✓

1. Technology has influenced teh way buzinesses communicate, especially with regard to productivity.

_____

_____

_____   1. _____

2. Voice mail allows business people to send and retrieve telphone messages at a convenient time.

_____

_____

_____   2. _____

3. Word procesing software eliminates the need for traditoional correction materials and retyping.

_____

_____

_____   3. _____

4. The Internet is a system of compouter networks that links computers form around the world.

_____

_____

_____   4. _____

5. Personal computers, computer networks, and voice mail are some of the technologies that help business people recieve and transmit information faster and more eficiently.

_____

_____

_____   5. _____

6. Technology is used to comunicate with people in both domestic and international lokations.

_____

_____

_____   6. _____

7. Cellular phones allow teh user to make and receive calls from almost any location, especially when traveling.

_____

_____

_____   7. _____

8. Electronic mail is a written massage that is typed and sent using the computer.

_____

_____

_____   8. _____

 **SECTION 2.2**

DOMESTIC AND INTERNATIONAL COMMUNICATION

A Taking Cultural Differences and Customs Into Account

The communication in each of the following situations could be improved. List the guideline for working with people from different cultural, religious, and ethnic groups that should be followed to improve the communication.   ✓

1. In Japan business cards are considered very important and should be treated with respect. While on a business trip to Japan to propose a new business arrangement, an American salesman wrote notes on the back of a Japanese business man's business card.

   _____

   _____

   _____   1. ____

2. A corporation's annual business meeting had to be rescheduled from its original date. The executive officer was surprised to learn that many stockholders who normally attend were refusing to come because the date fell on a Jewish holiday.

   _____

   _____

   _____   2. ____

3. Fred is talking with a potential client over dinner. Their server is an attractive looking Hispanic woman who has been slow to bring menus and to take their order. Fred makes a joke about the server possibly taking a siesta.

   _____

   _____

   _____   3. ____

4. While on a trip to France, Georgeanne decides to try out her newly acquired French vocabulary and accent in ordering from the menu. When her food arrives she discovers that it is not what she thought she had ordered.

   _____

   _____

   _____   4. ____

5. In Brazil business appointments are always scheduled at least two weeks in advance. Showing up without an appointment is frowned upon. An American business person, unaware of this custom, was traveling in Brazil and stopped by the offices of a potential client without having scheduled an appointment. The Brazilian business person was unable to meet with the American business person.

   _____

   _____

   _____   5. ____

B Domestic Communication

Throughout the United States different cultural and religious groups speak their traditional language and follow traditional customs and practices. Identify some cultural and traditional customs that people in your community practice. Describe some of these customs and practices.   ✓

_____

_____

_____

_____

_____

_____

C Calculating Time Differences

Using the time zone map on page 47 of your student text, calculate the time differences between the following pairs of cities.   ✓

1. Austin and Tokyo   **1.** _____ ____

2. Sydney and New York   **2.** _____ ____

3. Beijing and Los Angeles   **3.** _____ ____

4. Anchorage and London   **4.** _____ ____

5. Bombay and Cape Town   **5.** _____ ____

D Using Appropriate Language

Each of the following items violates one of the guidelines for using English in communicating with people in other countries. Revise each of the items to reflect sensitivity.   ✓

1. A penny saved is a penny earned.

_____   **1.** ____

2. Pardon my voice. I have a frog in my throat.

_____   **2.** ____

3. The manufacturing plant will be located a little ways outside the city.

_____   **3.** ____

4. There was a break in the negotiations.

_____   **4.** ____

5. That is a cool suit you are wearing.

_____   **5.** ____

6. Be sure to use your PIN number.

_____   **6.** ____

✓

7. The cost differences between the products are substantial, as I showed earlier in the visual aid.

_____   7. _____

8. Mr. Daniels is our policy wonk.

_____   8. _____

9. To add insult to injury, the negotiator was late in returning from lunch.

_____   9. _____

10. Have you boned up on the sales figures for the new product?

_____   10. _____

E Revising to Use Straightforward Language

Rewrite the following business messages intended for recipients in other countries. Be sure to replace clichés, slang, trendy terms, and abbreviations with straightforward language.

✓

1. The new computer program you sent to our office is really cool and we are putting it to good use.

_____
_____
_____   1. _____

2. I'm sure you will find the new printer to be wicked fast.

_____
_____
_____   2. _____

3. Everything here is right as rain and we hope your business is doing well too.

_____
_____
_____   3. _____

4. The IRS is auditing our business and we need some background materials on the project we did for you.

_____
_____
_____   4. _____

5. Our resident computer geek has agreed to look at the problem you are having with your computer equipment.

_____
_____
_____   5. _____

F Researching Information for an Overseas Trip

Make a list of the types of information to research before taking a business trip overseas. Write your answers in the spaces provided.

✓

1. _____

   _____   1. ____

2. _____

   _____   2. ____

3. _____

   _____   3. ____

4. _____

   _____   4. ____

G Demonstrating Knowledge of Other Cultures and Customs

Explain what you would do in each of the following situations based on your knowledge of other cultures and customs.

✓

1. You have arrived for a business meeting in Japan. During the conversation you notice that the Japanese business people have not made direct eye contact with you.

   _____

   _____   1. ____

2. A meeting has been scheduled by your Belgium customers on the Fourth of July.

   _____

   _____   2. ____

H Rewriting for Clarity

Rewrite each of the following figures of speech and clichés to use clearer wording. Write your answers in the spaces provided.

✓

1. A bird in the hand is worth two in the bush.

   _____

   _____   1. ____

2. Haste makes waste.

   _____

   _____   2. ____

3. You can't teach an old dog new tricks.

   _____

   _____   3. ____

4. Don't cry over spilt milk.

   _____

   _____   4. ____

 ETHICS AND PROFESSIONAL COURTESY IN
BUSINESS COMMUNICATION

 Demonstrating Ethical Behavior

The following situations involve unethical communication. Describe how each situation should be handled to achieve ethical communication. Write your answers in the space provided. ✓

1. When asked by a customer about the freshness of the flowers in the arrangements in the flower shop, the attendant replied, "The flowers will last about three days, which is the average length of time for an arrangement." What the attendant did not say was that the flowers will last ten days when they first arrive at the flower store from the supplier, but the store always sells the oldest flowers first.

_____

_____

_____ 1. _____

2. When asked about the quality of a former employee's work, the manager replied, "Anne does very sloppy work."

_____

_____

_____ 2. _____

3. In a televised newscast, the news media reports that the company you recently bought is responsible for polluting the environment. However, the report fails to mention that you are in the process of cleaning up the pollution caused by the previous owners.

_____

_____

_____ 3. _____

4. A nurse asked a famous singer for her autograph after the singer was admitted to the hospital for plastic surgery. The singer refused to give an autograph. When a reporter called to ask about the singer's condition, the nurse answered questions about the singer's surgery.

_____

_____

_____ 4. _____

5. The administrative assistant for the marketing manager at Apco Plastics has a friend who works at a rival company. When the assistant's friend calls and asks how things are going at work, the assistant reveals that a new line of products is behind schedule.

_____

_____

_____ 5. _____

6. Your supervisor has asked you to adjust sales figures in a report so that it appears that the amount of total sales is more than it actually is.

_____

_____

_____ 6. ____

7. A telephone caller contacts you at the bank where you work as a loan officer. The caller indicates he is an attorney for a customer of the bank and is calling to verify some account information that is needed for a meeting that afternoon. Your bank has a policy about not releasing information about customers' accounts without first getting permission from the customer.

_____

_____

_____ 7. ____

B Making Introductions

Describe what you would say in making introductions in each of the following situations. Write your answers in the space provided.

1. Introducing Gregory Green, a new marketing representative in the marketing department, to your supervisor, Mr. José Serna.

_____

_____ 1. ____

2. Introducing Gregory Green, a new employee in the marketing department, to a coworker in the marketing department, Nancy Touvell.

_____

_____ 2. ____

3. Introducing your supervisor, Ms. McNamara, to a potential client of the firm, Mr. Amala.

_____

_____ 3. ____

C Acknowledging Invitations and Thoughtful Actions

Describe what you would say to acknowledge the following invitations and thoughtful actions. Write your answers in the space provided.

1. You have been invited to the wedding reception of a coworker, but are unable to attend.

_____

_____ 1. ____

2. You have been invited to a surprise birthday party for a friend and will be able to attend. The invitation lists a phone number to which you may RSVP your reply.

_____

_____ 2. ____

✓

3. Your grandfather died and your coworkers sent a bouquet of flowers to the visitation.

_____

_____ **3.** _____

4. You receive a pen and pencil set from a business acquaintance to congratulate you on receiving a promotion.

_____

_____ **4.** _____

5. You receive an invitation to a party that you are able to attend and the invitation says "RSVP Regrets Only."

_____

_____ **5.** _____

D Code of Ethics

Write a code of ethics for business communicators using what you have learned in Section 2.3. Use the sample code of ethics in Figure 2.5 on page 53 of your student text as a guide.

_____

_____

_____

_____

_____

_____

_____

_____

_____

_____

_____

_____

_____

_____

_____

_____

_____

_____

_____

_____

_____

_____

_____

_____

E Selecting the Best Sentence

In each of the following pairs of sentences, one sentence is more specific. Select that sentence, and write its identifying letter on the line provided.   ✓

1. (a) Mr. Tiedje is a person with sound business principles.
   (b) Mr. Tiedje is a person who knows what is right.   1. _____ ____

2. (a) Our accountant is good at keeping information private.
   (b) Our accountant excels in maintaining confidentiality.   2. _____ ____

3. (a) An ethical person sticks with the facts.
   (b) An ethical person states facts instead of opinions.   3. _____ ____

4. (a) Ethical business communicators use objective
        language and verifiable information.
   (b) Ethical business communicators go with what they know.   4. _____ ____

5. (a) Confidential information should be released to authorized people only.
   (b) Confidential information should be kept secret from all but a few people.   5. _____ ____

6. (a) Professional courtesy means being polite.
   (b) Professional courtesy involves good manners and appropriate behavior.   6. _____ ____

7. (a) Deliberately withholding information is unethical.
   (b) Deliberately withholding information is not right.   7. _____ ____

8. (a) Ethics involves working toward the good of all rather than the good of
        some.
   (b) Ethics involves working toward the good of all rather than the good of
        a specialized group.   8. _____ ____

9. (a) A code of ethics for a business states rules to follow.
   (b) A code of ethics for a business states the goals of the group in terms of
        how the business operates.   9. _____ ____

10. (a) An RSVP notation on an invitation tells you to attend.
    (b) An RSVP notation on an invitation means you are expected to attend
         unless you reply that you are unable to attend.   10. _____ ____

 **SECTION 2.4** NONDISCRIMINATORY LANGUAGE

A **Avoiding Discrimination in Communication**

Rewrite each of the following sentences replacing gender-specific words with gender-neutral words.   ✓

1. The housewife is very good at baking cookies.

   _____

   _____   1. _____

2. The chairman of the board makes excellent decisions.

   _____

   _____   2. _____

3. The salesman had the highest rate of business for the month.

   _____

   _____   3. _____

4. The policeman was very helpful when our car broke down.

   _____

   _____   4. _____

5. The stewardess gave us excellent service.

   _____

   _____   5. _____

Rewrite each of the following sentences to use nondiscriminatory language. You may omit or replace words as needed.

1. The black student did surprisingly well on the exams.

   _____   1. _____

2. The well-informed Asian doctor explained the procedure.

   _____   2. _____

3. Elderly people are slow drivers.

   _____   3. _____

4. Her mother is crippled and uses a wheelchair.

   _____   4. _____

5. She teaches students who are diagnosed as morons.

   _____   5. _____

Rewrite each of the following sentences to eliminate stereotypes.

1. People who are overweight are lazy.

_____

_____ 1. _____

2. Many of our continuing education students are unwed mothers.

_____

_____ 2. _____

3. Of the two salespeople, Ms. Lawson is more inclined to be emotional than Mr. Gentry.

_____

_____ 3. _____

4. Some attorneys are ambulance chasers.

_____

_____ 4. _____

5. New Yorkers are rude.

_____

_____ 5. _____

B Avoiding Discriminatory Actions

Explain how you could improve the communication in the following situations.

1. A foreign exchange student is visiting your office and has a difficult time understanding the language. Your fellow office workers are trying to make the student understand what they are saying by talking louder.

_____

_____

_____ 1. _____

2. A long-time client who uses a wheelchair has come to your office for a meeting. Your new office assistant makes the comment that "it must be difficult to be tied to that chair." The client responds by saying he is tired of people saying that to him.

_____

_____

_____ 2. _____

3. A customer who is wearing a hearing aid asks for assistance in picking out a new blouse to wear to work. The clerk notices the hearing aid and asks the customer questions in an unusually loud voice to try and narrow down what type of blouse the customer wants.

_____

_____

_____ 3. _____

SECTION 3.1 LANGUAGE STRUCTURE

 Identifying Parts of Speech

Identify the words in parentheses in the following sentences. Use the following abbreviations: *N* (noun), *P* (pronoun), *V* (verb), *Adj* (adjective), *Adv* (adverb), *Prep* (preposition), *C* (conjunction), *I* (interjection).   ✓

1. (We) have interviewed (six) candidates (for) the position.   **1.** _____ _____

2. Several (of) my coworkers (commute) to work at least 12 miles one way.   **2.** _____ _____

3. All (full-time) employees are eligible (for) the dental plan.   **3.** _____ _____

4. Ms. Carsey is the (chairperson) for the (all-day) seminar.   **4.** _____ _____

5. Teresa is (scheduled) to visit many of (the) sales representatives (during) the next three weeks.   **5.** _____ _____

6. If (you) have a (question), please call Larry Sleva.   **6.** _____ _____

7. (Congratulations!) Completing your degree is (quite) an accomplishment.   **7.** _____ _____

8. (Craig Lawrence) manages the (branch) offices (in) Modesto and San Jose.   **8.** _____ _____

9. The (committee) will review the materials (and) submit (its) report (at) the next meeting.   **9.** _____ _____

10. Most of (our) employees have access (to) the Internet.   **10.** _____ _____

11. (I) was selected to be a member (of) a (jury).   **11.** _____ _____

12. Joan Miller (toured) the inventory warehouse (during) (her) visit to Tucson.   **12.** _____ _____

13. (Our) office manager (holds) a (weekly) status meeting for our department.   **13.** _____ _____

14. (Every) business person should (have) a style manual (for) reference.   **14.** _____ _____

15. Harry (or) Meg will contact (you) (soon) with information (about) the contract.   **15.** _____ _____

16. Within the next (few) days, we should (receive) (several) bids (for) the project.   **16.** _____ _____

17. (By) October, we will have (completed) the registration process for (new) customers.   **17.** _____ _____

18. (Our) customer hotline has been (flooded) with calls about our (latest) software.   **18.** _____ _____

19. Automated bank tellers will be (installed) at all our (branch) banks.   **19.** _____ _____

20. The enrollment period for the employee health (and) retirement plan is (always) in September.   **20.** _____ _____

21. (Attractive) visual aids (enhance) a presentation.

21. _____ ___

22. Although (they) (considered) the price (high), John and Rachel (placed) an order.

22. _____ ___

23. Stephanie will (review) the (completed) time sheets (before) they are (submitted) to the payroll department.

23. _____ ___

24. We (surely) need to request the (latest) version of the software program.

24. _____ ___

25. The company (immediately) hired a (consultant) to review the policies.

25. _____ ___

26. Diane (seems) happy (about) the reorganization.

26. _____ ___

27. We (almost) decided to take the (early) flight (to) Atlanta.

27. _____ ___

28. Margaret would not (agree) to modify the schedule, (nor) would she accept a change (in) the specifications.

28. _____ ___

29. (We) attended the travel convention (with) our supervisor (last) week.

29. _____ ___

30. (Yes!) I was (pleasantly) surprised (at) the news.

30. _____ ___

B Knowing Your Subjects

Underline the complete subject in each of the following sentences. Then, on the line provided, write the *simple subject* or the *compound subject*.

1. Elizabeth was named a senior partner in the firm.

1. _____ ___

2. By September 10, we will have completed the entire project.

2. _____ ___

3. Everyone in the Manufacturing Department has signed up for the company blood drive.

3. _____ ___

4. Susan and Marcus are the most recently hired employees.

4. _____ ___

5. Two to three years' experience in accounts payable is a requirement for the job opening.

5. _____ ___

6. Is Carol aware of the changes we made to the budget?

6. _____ ___

7. Dean and Marilyn are the chairpersons for the event.

7. _____ ___

8. Mark, Evan, or Denise will attend the seminar.

8. _____ ___

9. A new computer network will be installed this weekend.

9. _____ ___

10. I am responsible for purchasing the new computer equipment for our department.

10. _____ ___

11. All the assistants will take a training course to learn the new software package.

11. _____ ___

12. The top sales representative in each region will receive a 15 percent bonus.

12. _____ ___

13. You should request your passport at least two months before your overseas trip.

13. _____ ___

14. Alice's expertise in designing PowerPoint presentations makes her presentations attractive and dynamic.

14. _____ ___

✓

15. Have you discussed these procedures with
your supervisor?

15. _____ ____

16. Alice and Trevor are both skilled in giving presentations.

16. _____ ____

17. Excellent opportunities for advancement are available
in this industry.

17. _____ ____

18. The Internet and the World Wide Web are the two
most popular electronic resources for consumers.

18. _____ ____

19. For consumers, the Internet and the World Wide Web
are the two most popular electronic resources.

19. _____ ____

20. Only Thomas or Kathryn is authorized to sign off
on purchase orders.

20. _____ ____

21. In the library are the legal briefs for all our court cases.

21. _____ ____

22. Diane, Barbara, and Kent have been selected for
the management trainee program.

22. _____ ____

23. To whom should this package be delivered?

23. _____ ____

24. Revising your correspondence is easier when you
use a grammar checker.

24. _____ ____

25. Devon and Alana are on the executive search committee.

25. _____ ____

C Identifying Predicates

Underline the complete predicate in each of the following sentences. Then, on the line
provided, write the *simple predicate*.

✓

1. Matt and Chris registered for the time management
seminar.

1. _____ ____

2. An accounting firm has rented the office space next
to ours.

2. _____ ____

3. Advertising on the World Wide Web has increased
tremendously.

3. _____ ____

4. Mr. Corliss will arrive on Monday for the board meeting.

4. _____ ____

5. Jennifer called the clients about the change in the
tour dates.

5. _____ ____

6. Most of the employees enrolled with the health
maintenance organization.

6. _____ ____

7. Paul called about the change in the schedule.

7. _____ ____

8. The files for the Ocasek account are in the credenza
in my office.

8. _____ ____

9. I will attend the sales conference in August.

9. _____ ____

10. Both Jerry and Marie were recommended for promotion.

10. _____ ____

D Writing Sentences

On the lines provided, write the type of sentence indicated for each item. ✓

1. Declarative (makes a statement)

_____

_____

_____ **1.** _____

2. Interrogative (asks a question)

_____

_____

_____ **2.** _____

3. Imperative (states a command or request)

_____

_____

_____ **3.** _____

4. Exclamatory (expresses strong feeling)

_____

_____

_____ **4.** _____

E Identifying Clauses

Identify each of the following groups of words as *independent clauses* (sentences) or as *dependent clauses* incorrectly treated as sentences. Use the abbreviation *I* for independent clause and *D* for dependent clause. ✓

1. Sending messages using electronic mail. **1.** _____ _____

2. Using our electronic mail system, we can send messages quickly. **2.** _____ _____

3. When we heard the news of the merger. **3.** _____ _____

4. To attract more passengers during the slow season. **4.** _____ _____

5. Airlines often reduce their fares at the end of the summer. **5.** _____ _____

6. The human resources department offers an orientation session for new employees. **6.** _____ _____

7. Once we have examined your loan application. **7.** _____ _____

8. Dr. Cooke is scheduled to perform the surgery. **8.** _____ _____

9. This position offers you an excellent opportunity for advancement. **9.** _____ _____

10. Before we can make the recommendation. **10.** _____ _____

11. Whenever a patient is brought to the emergency room. **11.** _____ _____

12. They are scheduled to attend the luncheon meeting. **12.** _____ _____

13. If you have made an investment with this broker. **13.** _____ _____

14. Your company has been named the employer of the year. **14.** _____ _____

15. Both the chief executive officer and the president. **15.** _____ _____

F Using Phrases

On the lines provided, write a sentence that contains the phrase shown in parentheses.   ✓

1. Prepositional phrase (for two weeks)

_____

_____   **1.** _____

2. Infinitive phrase (to organize the information)

_____

_____   **2.** _____

3. Verb phrase (will be approved)

_____

_____   **3.** _____

4. Prepositional phrase (of the items)

_____

_____   **4.** _____

5. Infinitive phrase (to complete)

_____

_____   **5.** _____

6. Verb phrase (has asked)

_____

_____   **6.** _____

G Sentences or Fragments?

Which of the following are complete sentences, and which are fragments? At the right, circle *S* to indicate a complete sentence and *F* to indicate a fragment (incomplete sentence).   ✓

1. Melissa, our travel agent, made the arrangements for our trip.   **1.** S F _____

2. As you probably read in the company newsletter.   **2.** S F _____

3. If you plan to enroll in the database course.   **3.** S F _____

4. You and I will be in charge of the recycling committee.   **4.** S F _____

5. Two inventory analysts have reviewed the problem with our system.   **5.** S F _____

6. In response to your request for tuition reimbursement.   **6.** S F _____

7. So that we may better serve our customers.   **7.** S F _____

8. Greg made the announcement at our last status meeting   **8.** S F _____

9. Molly specified the type of desktop publishing software to order.   **9.** S F _____

10. Since the profit-sharing plan was started two years ago.   **10.** S F _____

H Changing Fragments to Sentences

Each of the following fragments is a dependent clause. For each fragment, add an independent clause to make the item a complete sentence. Write your answers on the lines provided.

✓

1. While Carlos writes the report

_____

_____ 1. _____

2. Because we completed the work ahead of schedule

_____

_____ 2. _____

3. Unless you are careful

_____

_____ 3. _____

4. When you receive approval for the trip

_____

_____ 4. _____

5. Before you interview for a position

_____

_____ 5. _____

I Proofreading Practice

Read the following paragraph from a memo to find any spelling errors. Write your corrections in the spaces provided.

✓

Beginning April 1, we will install a new security system in the building. Complte instalation should occur by the end of April. As part of the new system, we will install new magnetic card readers at all entrances. The new system will provide a more secure working environment, particularly in the evenings and on wekends. Entraces will lock and unlock automattically each day during working hourse. Please read the atached instructions for using the nwe system.

_____ _____
_____ _____
_____ _____
_____ _____
_____ _____
_____ _____
_____ _____

SECTION 3.2   NOUNS: PLURAL FORMS

A **Supplying Plurals**

In the space provided, write the plural of each of the following nouns.

1. company	1. _____	27. Mrs.	27. _____
2. politics	2. _____	28. deer	28. _____
3. wife	3. _____	29. scissors	29. _____
4. crisis	4. _____	30. half	30. _____
5. key	5. _____	31. Tseng	31. _____
6. tax	6. _____	32. class	32. _____
7. church	7. _____	33. attorney	33. _____
8. analysis	8. _____	34. Schauss	34. _____
9. potato	9. _____	35. video	35. _____
10. brother-in-law	10. _____	36. bulletin board	36. _____
11. McCarty	11. _____	37. proceeds	37. _____
12. Ms.	12. _____	38. territory	38. _____
13. 1990	13. _____	39. CPA	39. _____
14. hitch	14. _____	40. Sanchez	40. _____
15. motto	15. _____	41. woman	41. _____
16. child	16. _____	42. c.o.d.	42. _____
17. vice president	17. _____	43. service	43. _____
18. agenda	18. _____	44. timetable	44. _____
19. leaf	19. _____	45. money	45. _____
20. criterion	20. _____	46. Kusumoto	46. _____
21. chief of staff	21. _____	47. belief	47. _____
22. addendum	22. _____	48. Barry	48. _____
23. handful	23. _____	49. X ray	49. _____
24. Brooks	24. _____	50. staff	50. _____
25. salary	25. _____	51. zero	51. _____
26. notary public	26. _____	52. brush	52. _____

53. A and B	53. _____	57. CD	57. _____
54. Mr.	54. _____	58. Schwartz	58. _____
55. datum	55. _____	59. portfolio	59. _____
56. schedule	56. _____	60. alumnus	60. _____

B   Supplying Singulars

In the space provided, write the singular form of each of the following nouns.

1. diagnoses	1. _____	16. utilities	16. _____
2. appendixes	2. _____	17. series	17. _____
3. odds	3. _____	18. syntheses	18. _____
4. tomatoes	4. _____	19. shelves	19. _____
5. knives	5. _____	20. vetoes	20. _____
6. men	6. _____	21. CEOs	21. _____
7. curriculum	7. _____	22. ratios	22. _____
8. geese	8. _____	23. decisions	23. _____
9. bunches	9. _____	24. the Salters	24. _____
10. employees	10. _____	25. the Mmes. Stuart	25. _____
11. bases	11. _____	26. flights	26. _____
12. cargoes	12. _____	27. attorneys general	27. _____
13. aircraft	13. _____	28. curriculums	28. _____
14. chiefs	14. _____	29. plaintiffs	29. _____
15. policies	15. _____	30. lengths	30. _____

C   Knowing Your Plurals

For each noun enclosed in parentheses, write the plural form in the space provided.   ✓

1. Distribute two copies of the contract to the (Avery) at their home address.

1. _____ ____

2. The doctor will compare the (diagnosis) and then inform the patient about the course of treatment.

2. _____ ____

3. The (appendix) for the report contain detailed statistics.

3. _____ ____

4. Many electronic-mail programs allow you to post information on electronic (bulletin board).

4. _____ ____

5. Our staff has one paralegal assigned to assist two (attorney).

5. _____ ____

✓

6. The (notary public) are responsible for
   witnessing documents.   6. _____ _____

7. Were the (Gates) present at the shareholders' meeting?   7. _____ _____

8. Most of our computer (supply) are purchased wholesale.   8. _____ _____

9. Barry received two (B) in his courses this semester.   9. _____ _____

10. When you type this contract, place all page numbers
    in (parenthesis).   10. _____ _____

11. The (Mrs.) Fisher took the news of their father's
    death quite well.   11. _____ _____

12. When the temperature reaches the (90), the weather
    service will issue a heat advisory.   12. _____ _____

13. My two (sister-in-law) are partners in a real estate firm. 13. _____ _____

14. When the completed (survey) are returned,
    they will be tabulated.   14. _____ _____

15. The (Lucas) are interested in purchasing a condominium. 15. _____ _____

16. Both of the promotional (video) will be filmed
    at the studio.   16. _____ _____

17. The (Mr.) George and Kramer have been named
    to the board of directors.   17. _____ _____

18. I like to work for a company that makes all its
    (priority) clear to its employees.   18. _____ _____

19. As you know, Ms. Kumoto, the applicant meets
    all the (criterion) for the position.   19. _____ _____

20. Several large cities have constructed (stadium)
    for sports teams.   20. _____ _____

21. Both Jack and Patricia are in their early (thirty).   21. _____ _____

22. The (proceeds) from the charity auction will be used
    to fund cancer research.   22. _____ _____

23. Were the (Foster) members of the ad hoc committee?   23. _____ _____

24. Our investment broker advised us to have
    diversified stock (portfolio).   24. _____ _____

25. Needless to say, we discussed all these alternatives
    with both our (general manager).   25. _____ _____

D Proofreading for Plural Errors

Underline any errors in the use of plurals in the following sentences, and write your
correction on the lines provided. Write *OK* for any sentence that has no error.   ✓

1. At Ms. Andrew's request, all the editors in chief attended
   the financial seminar.   1. _____ _____

✓

2. The new library has facilitys for viewing videotapes and searching the Internet.

2. _____ ____

3. Let me know by Thursday if the Jones's are able to attend the seminar.

3. _____ ____

4. The spouse's of employees are always invited to attend the company's social functions.

4. _____ ____

5. I called Mr. and Mrs. Lopez today and discovered that the Lopezs have been on vacation all week.

5. _____ ____

6. The doctor advised me to get a new prescription for my contact lenses.

6. _____ ____

7. According to the shareholders' report, the Mrs. Johnson own nearly 38 percent of the company stock.

7. _____ ____

8. Due to staffing changes, our sales force will have to cover larger territorys next year.

8. _____ ____

9. All the children in the day care center have parents who work full-time jobs.

9. _____ ____

10. We are having a special sale this month on all pianoes in stock.

10. _____ ____

11. My brother-in-laws are scheduled to testify in court on behalf of the plaintiffes in the case.

11. _____ ____

12. The agendums for the staff meetings are posted on the bulletin board.

12. _____ ____

13. Both the Haggartyes and the Dunbars took photoes of the event.

13. _____ ____

14. Based on two separate analysis conducted by specialists, we have decided to manufacture the product.

14. _____ ____

15. Of the 12 CPA's in our firm, only 3 are interested in working overseas.

15. _____ ____

E Editing for Accuracy

Underline any errors in the use of plurals in the following paragraphs from a memo. Write your corrections on the lines provided.

✓

Beginning May 1, the Human Resources Department will offer a series of workshopes called "Quality: Every Employee's Goal." The purpose of the workshops is to help all personnel share in the rewards of error-free products here at Douglas Industrys. All employees are encouraged to attend the three sessiones, which will be held on Tuesdays and Thursdayes. Included as guest speakers are two vice president's from subsidiaries and several consultants from major citys across the country.

_____ ____
_____ ____
_____ ____
_____ ____
_____ ____
_____ ____
_____ ____
_____ ____
_____ ____

Please join us for these informative workshopes. Each session will begin at 1 p.m. in the main conference room.

_____ ____
_____ ____

SECTION 3.3 NOUNS AND PRONOUNS: POSSESSIVE FORMS

A Possessive Case of Nouns

In the space provided, write the correct possessive form of the nouns in parentheses. ✓

1. (Justine) coursework in computers
2. Lloyd (Burns) loan application
3. our (supervisor) office
4. the (Hopkins) account
5. three (week) vacation
6. her (coach) encouragement
7. (Dallas) airport
8. the (managers) meeting
9. his (brother-in-law) law firm
10. our (children) health
11. (Andrew and Kelly) house
12. my (advisor) recommendation
13. the (attorney general) opinions
14. Ms. (Sanchez) request
15. both (witnesses) testimony
16. the (vice president) promotion
17. a (witness) testimony
18. her (doctor) diagnosis
19. all (salesclerks) commissions
20. the (company) retirement plan
21. (Ross) portfolio
22. a (consultant) fees
23. several (consultants) fees
24. both (women) ideas
25. almost one (month) interest
26. most (advisors) recommendations
27. the (associate) clients
28. (Bob and Constance) restaurant
29. an (operator) decision
30. the (vice presidents) unanimous vote

1. _____ _____
2. _____ _____
3. _____ _____
4. _____ _____
5. _____ _____
6. _____ _____
7. _____ _____
8. _____ _____
9. _____ _____
10. _____ _____
11. _____ _____
12. _____ _____
13. _____ _____
14. _____ _____
15. _____ _____
16. _____ _____
17. _____ _____
18. _____ _____
19. _____ _____
20. _____ _____
21. _____ _____
22. _____ _____
23. _____ _____
24. _____ _____
25. _____ _____
26. _____ _____
27. _____ _____
28. _____ _____
29. _____ _____
30. _____ _____

B Possessive Case of Nouns and Pronouns

On the line at the right, write the correct possessive form of each word in parentheses. ✓

1. While the company's sales have increased,
   (it) costs have also increased.

   1. _____ ____

2. (Brenda DeNova) resignation came as a surprise to us.

   2. _____ ____

3. Can you tell me (who) coat is in the closet?

   3. _____ ____

4. Our (boss) management style is to use a team approach
   to solving problems.

   4. _____ ____

5. (Ken and Deborah) travel agency was named the local
   business of the year.

   5. _____ ____

6. The (Schauss) airline reservations were verified by
   computer.

   6. _____ ____

7. Daniel is the person (who) hard work won the contract
   for our company.

   7. _____ ____

8. Each (accountant) office will be equipped with a laser
   printer.

   8. _____ ____

9. (They) reasons for not supporting the proposal are
   well known.

   9. _____ ____

10. (Manuel and John) sons both work as interns at
    Riverside Memorial Hospital.

    10. _____ ____

11. Did you know that they are responsible for over
    35 percent of the (company) product line?

    11. _____ ____

12. Your certificate of deposit has earned nearly
    nine (month) interest.

    12. _____ ____

13. The (Marx) children have all received their vaccinations.

    13. _____ ____

14. My project seems rather tedious; on the other hand,
    (you) appears more interesting.

    14. _____ ____

15. My (stepfather) family is having a reunion this August
    in St. Louis.

    15. _____ ____

16. (Ellen Sykes) presentation is the next item on the agenda.

    16. _____ ____

17. Of course, an (employer) hiring policy must be fair in
    every detail.

    17. _____ ____

18. According to CNN, the Senate will announce (it) decision
    later today.

    18. _____ ____

19. Members of the (men) and (women) basketball teams
    must sign up for physicals.

    19. _____ ____

20. Our manager approved (Eric) traveling to New Orleans.

    20. _____ ____

21. I have only one (hour) work to finish before I begin
    writing the report.

    21. _____ ____

22. What is your opinion of the (consultant) proposal?

    22. _____ ____

23. (Everett & Perkins) stock price has risen dramatically
    since the announcement.

    23. _____ ____

✓

24. Of all the presentations, (Ms. Jennings) was the
most informative.

24. _____ ____

25. (Lois) computer will be upgraded to one that has fax
capability.

25. _____ ____

C Proofreading for Possessive Errors

Underline any possessive errors in the following sentences, and write your corrections
on the lines provided. Write *OK* for any sentence that has no error.

✓

1. After one year in operation, Scott's and Tom's business is
doing better than anyone had expected.

1. _____ ____

2. Both of Darlene projects are ahead of schedule.

2. _____ ____

3. Most of the patients have completed their insurance
forms.

3. _____ ____

4. I think that the cellular phone is her's, isn't it?

4. _____ ____

5. All managers are responsible for submitting they're
expense reports on time.

5. _____ ____

6. Patrick is always editing everybody's else reports.

6. _____ ____

7. Several applicant's résumés have been forwarded to
Mr. Dean for review.

7. _____ ____

8. Each employees' workstation is equipped with a modem.

8. _____ ____

9. Both of the managers congratulated us on our
presentation.

9. _____ ____

10. Unfortunately, we do not know whose responsible for
this excellent suggestion.

10. _____ ____

11. Yes, there is a copy of the companys' annual financial
report in the conference room.

11. _____ ____

12. One of the medical assistants timecards is incomplete.

12. _____ ____

13. The only reason for there delaying there decision is the
concern about the applicant's experience.

13. _____ ____

14. Marvins' suggestion for purchasing software is a good
one.

14. _____ ____

15. The responsibility for completing projects on
schedule and within budget is strictly your's.

15. _____ ____

16. Our paralegals are involved in preparing briefs for the
firms' clients.

16. _____ ____

17. The marketing department outlined they're plan for the
sales campaign.

17. _____ ____

18. As you requested, we are examining you're proposal
more closely.

18. _____ ____

19. Most of the medical assistants received they're training at Concord College.

19. _____ _____

20. The insurance investigator said that the Walshes claim was valid.

20. _____ _____

D Editing for Accuracy

Underline any errors in the following sentences, and write your corrections on the lines provided. Write *OK* for any sentence that has no error.   ✓

1. Ms. Connollys' speech was the keynote address at the conference.

1. _____ _____

2. Kathryn said that the team members was responsible for meeting the deadline.

2. _____ _____

3. As of October 3, we had exceeded our sales projections for this year.

3. _____ _____

4. Does Mr. Baxter think its necessary to get several bids for the project?

4. _____ _____

5. Have you received Ms. Closs' credit report?

5. _____ _____

6. If I was the patient, I would consult someone for a second opinion.

6. _____ _____

7. Our you sure that the audit is scheduled for next week?

7. _____ _____

8. Their may be a very good reason for Dianes' objection.

8. _____ _____

9. Yes, we received you're travel request for next month.

9. _____ _____

10. Once we rise enough funds, we will be able to construct a new facility.

10. _____ _____

E Proofreading for Errors

Underline any errors in the following paragraphs, and write your corrections on the lines provided.   ✓

    We need to help all our employee's use there time more efficiently. One way to make better use of our time is to understand each others jobs so that we can work as a team. Therefore, any employee whose interested may register for team-building sessions during work hours. If your interested in finding out more about the sessions offered and how to register for them, call Debbie Payne in the Human Resources Department, or ask for Debbies' assistant, Clara Farrell.

    The sessions will be held each Tuesday and Thursday in Septmber. A session lasts too hours. Participants will be divided into teams and given tasks to accomplish. At the end of a session, each team will assess it's performance.

_____ _____
_____ _____
_____ _____
_____ _____
_____ _____
_____ _____
_____ _____
_____ _____
_____ _____
_____ _____
_____ _____

PRONOUNS: NOMINATIVE AND OBJECTIVE FORMS

A **Nominative Case or Objective Case?**

Circle *N* if the nominative form of a pronoun would correctly complete a sentence.
Circle *O* if the objective form would be correct.   ✓

1. Do you know whether it was _____ who prepared this report?   1. N O _____

2. We would prefer to have Naomi, rather than _____ head the team.   2. N O _____

3. Two manager trainees, Susan and _____, could not attend yesterday's seminar.   3. N O _____

4. _____will you recommend for the new position?   4. N O _____

5. In Joyce's opinion, the new sales manager will be Tom, Deborah, or _____.   5. N O _____

6. As you know, it was _____ who developed the Internet site for our company.   6. N O _____

7. To _____ does this laptop computer belong?   7. N O _____

8. Alex, _____ you know is my manager, will also have to approve the budget.   8. N O _____

9. The best computer programmer at Ferris Communications is probably _____.   9. N O _____

10. Yes, all _____ customer service representatives have exceeded our goals.   10. N O _____

11. Marianne is as much an expert in Web page design as _____.   11. N O _____

12. Give Claudia and _____ all the legal briefs for the Morgan case.   12. N O _____

13. With _____ are you attending the luncheon?   13. N O _____

14. If I were _____, then I would certainly apply for the position.   14. N O _____

15. Did both financial analysts, Chris and _____, work on last year's budget report?   15. N O _____

16. Roger, do you know whether it was _____ who designed these brochures?   16. N O _____

17. Our new sales representatives are Steve and _____.   17. N O _____

18. Leroy, I would recommend that _____ be appointed treasurer.   18. N O _____

19. As you directed, we made reservations for Mark, Brenda, and _____.   19. N O _____

20. Our financial advisor and _____ recommended we contact a tax attorney.   20. N O _____

21. It was kind of you to invite Carole and _____ to the luncheon.   21. N O _____

22. Assign this task to _____ has the most experience with database software.   22. N O _____

23. As soon as Joanna and _____ arrive, we will leave for the seminar.   23. N O _____

24. Fred asked _____ to get bids from three different vendors.   24. N O _____

25. When Roberta heard Bruce's voice on the answering machine,
    she thought him to be _____ .   25. N O _____

26. The president congratulated _____ two regional sales managers on
    opening several new accounts.   26. N O _____

27. Rosa and _____ would like to delay the meeting until the results of the
    research are presented.   27. N O _____

28. _____ will you recommend to handle the project?

28. N O _____

29. _____ is responsible for taking the patient's vital signs?

29. N O _____

30. Yes, I would recommend Jacob rather than _____.

30. N O _____

B Supplying Pronouns

Which case of the pronouns *I, he, she, we, they, them, who,* or *whoever* correctly completes the following sentences? Write the correct pronoun in each sentence on the line provided.

✓

1. Renee is a trainee _____ is surely going to be a very successful customer service representative.

1. _____ _____

2. If Brad had asked Jamie and _____, we would surely have driven him to the airport.

2. _____ _____

3. Ask either of the nursing assistants, Maria or _____, to help you assess the patients.

3. _____ _____

4. Both attorneys, Lisa and _____, specialize in estate law.

4. _____ _____

5. Yes, you are correct: Faye and _____ are leaving for Los Angeles on Tuesday.

5. _____ _____

6. The Celasco Publishing Company always gives a bonus to _____ exceeds sales quotas.

6. _____ _____

7. Loretta said, "I enjoy working with _____ I respect."

7. _____ _____

8. Two of the assistants, Jessica Baxter and _____, will be transferring to our Omaha office.

8. _____ _____

9. _____ is the new personnel manager?

9. _____ _____

10. If _____ pays the bill within 10 days, you may allow a 5 percent discount.

10. _____ _____

11. Send _____ a copy of the latest software manual.

11. _____ _____

12. Invite _____ is interested to attend the series of wellness workshops at the hospital.

12. _____ _____

13. Most of the designs that were approved were created by Kate and _____.

13. _____ _____

14. Who is the keynote speaker for the seminar, Gary Albertson or _____?

14. _____ _____

15. Ms. Fisher recommends only those consultants _____ she knows are qualified.

15. _____ _____

16. _____ pays within 15 days will receive a 2 percent discount.

16. _____ _____

17. Offer a special vacation package to _____ responds to our newspaper advertisement.

17. _____ _____

18. Both insurance agents, Anne Talmadge and _____, have reviewed the policies for us.

18. _____ _____

19. Given the increase in our business during the past six months, _____ will have to hire additional staff members.

19. _____ _____

✓

20. Mike Lee, _____ is our insurance agent, is retiring this year.

20. _____ _____

21. Lynn, please give Courtney and _____ your new address and telephone number before you leave.

21. _____ _____

22. _____ will staff the blood pressure booth at the health fair?

22. _____ _____

23. Who do you think is more likely to be promoted, Russell or _____?

23. _____ _____

24. _____ shall I say is providing the samples for the sales kits?

24. _____ _____

25. Fax information about our stock options to Ms. Salters and _____ this afternoon.

25. _____ _____

26. We do not know _____ placed the order.

26. _____ _____

27. At the videoconference, Marsha sat between Randy and _____.

27. _____ _____

28. If you were hiring the consultant, _____ would you select?

28. _____ _____

29. Can you think of anyone _____ would be able to work overtime this weekend?

29. _____ _____

30. Perhaps it was _____ who took the photographs.

30. _____ _____

C Proofreading for Pronoun Errors

Underline any pronoun errors in the following sentences, and write your corrections on the lines provided. Write *OK* for any sentence that has no error.

✓

1. They will contact we financial managers when the consultant arrives.

1. _____ _____

2. In your opinion, would Serena and her work well together on the task force?

2. _____ _____

3. Ms. Hastings offered both of them, Alan and she, a bonus for their exceptional sales.

3. _____ _____

4. Between you and I, all employees should have access to the Internet.

4. _____ _____

5. How could he blame either you or me for the error?

5. _____ _____

6. Julia seems to prefer the work on the Internet site as much as him.

6. _____ _____

7. Ask Mr. Lewis if us travel agents may order copies of this reference manual.

7. _____ _____

8. No, I did not arrange a meeting with the marketing consultant who Ms. Delgado recommended.

8. _____ _____

9. Finally, the issue was resolved by my supervisor, his assistant, and me.

9. _____ _____

10. Marcus, who you met at the sales meeting, will surely be our new regional vice president.

10. _____ _____

11. Between you and me, Bill should award the contract to the supplier who is best equipped to handle the job.

11. _____ ____

12. The two employees recognized for their outstanding service are Gary and her.

12. _____ ____

13. Was it him who was responsible for negotiating the new contract?

13. _____ ____

14. Ms. Pomery appointed both Jerry and I to the production team.

14. _____ ____

15. Ask whether it was him who recommended we purchase new computers.

15. _____ ____

16. Yes, Yvonne has more accounting experience than me.

16. _____ ____

17. Our new paralegal will work with Deborah and myself on the Maxwell case.

17. _____ ____

18. When I first answered the telephone, I thought Robert to be him.

18. _____ ____

19. The accountants who work best under pressure are José and me.

19. _____ ____

20. If I could choose, I would much prefer to work with Maxwell than with she.

20. _____ ____

21. As you know, all invoices over $500 must be approved by both Ms. Tate and he.

21. _____ ____

22. They might have avoided this problem if they had first checked with we programmers.

22. _____ ____

23. Georgette congratulated Karen and I on winning the design award.

23. _____ ____

24. Until we develop an Internet site for our company, our competitors will have an advantage over us.

24. _____ ____

25. To be honest, I wasn't sure that it was him.

25. _____ ____

26. The most talented analyst in the accounting department is her.

26. _____ ____

27. Would you like to join Amy and I for lunch tomorrow?

27. _____ ____

28. The new medical assistant has been extremely helpful to both Carol and I.

28. _____ ____

29. The ability to critically evaluate applicants' skills and experience is important to the success of we human resource managers.

29. _____ ____

30. Do you think that both the president and her will attend the dedication ceremony?

30. _____ ____

D Who Did What?

For each of the following sentences, select the pronoun in parentheses that best completes the sentence. ✓

1. (Who, Whom) is the staff member responsible for updating the information on our Internet site?

1. _____ _____

2. Do you know (who, whom) we should contact for information about the change in tax laws?

2. _____ _____

3. (Whoever, Whomever) we hire for the teaching position must have at least four years of teaching experience.

3. _____ _____

4. Give this assignment to (whoever, whomever) has the lightest workload.

4. _____ _____

5. Jillian is the laboratory technician (who, whom) is responsible for analyzing the blood samples.

5. _____ _____

E Editing Practice

Underline any errors in the following sentences, and write your corrections on the lines provided. Write *OK* for any sentence that has no error. ✓

1. Ms. Douglas said that she always relies on we inventory analysts to double-check the production reports.

1. _____ _____

2. Patrick and I had expected the Mitchell's to submit a bid for the entire project.

2. _____ _____

3. Diana asked all sales representatives to submit there expense reports by the fifth of each month.

3. _____ _____

4. Ms. Destefano reminded us to be sure not to leave important legal documents laying on our desks.

4. _____ _____

5. Did you know that the city planner is Carrie Bullock, not her?

5. _____ _____

6. Jennifer attending the meeting certainly was a surprise to all of us.

6. _____ _____

7. As you know, us tax preparers are always very busy at this time of the year.

7. _____ _____

8. According to Michael, the most useful software package that we have is the one recommended by Lisa and he.

8. _____ _____

9. Mr. Parrish, the assistant sales manager, said, "If I was in charge of the sales meeting, I would have each marketing manager conduct a presentation."

9. _____ _____

10. Just for a moment, I mistook James Kirby to be him.

10. _____ _____

11. The human resources department has several training videoes to use for orientation seminars for new employees.

11. _____ _____

12. Please ask either Michelle or he to create the PowerPoint slides for the presentation.

12. _____ _____

13. According to the new medical plan, hourly employees receive the same benefits as us.

13. _____ ____

14. The attornies for the plaintiff presented new evidence in the case.

14. _____ ____

15. Us medical assistants would like to attend a one-day seminar on dealing with hospice patients.

15. _____ ____

16. Give the latest supply of the catalogs to Carl and I.

16. _____ ____

17. Most job applicants have brought portfolioes of their work to job interviews.

17. _____ ____

18. Based on sales figures for last year, our new offices in Asia have allowed we to expand our markets by 10 percent.

18. _____ ____

19. If you were me, would you apply for the job opening in the accounting department?

19. _____ ____

20. Do you know whether Dr. Camillo and him have scheduled the surgery for tomorrow?

20. _____ ____

F Proofreading for Accuracy

Underline any errors in the following memo, and write your corrections in the spaces provided. Assume that names of people are spelled correctly. ✓

MEMO TO:	Tony Reeves	_____ ____
FROM:	Gwen Trivett	_____ ____
DATE:	Febuary 19, \<YEAR\>	_____ ____
SUBJECT:	Presentation Software Packages	_____ ____

Tony, as you know, us are in the process of selecting a presentation software package for our sales staff to use in presenting are products to customers. Marshall Danvers and me has reviewed them, and we would like you to do the same. As the senior member of the sales staff, your opinion will be valuable.

_____ ____
_____ ____
_____ ____
_____ ____
_____ ____
_____ ____
_____ ____

Attached are copys of both presentation software packages. Please return your comments on both packages to me by Febuary 25.

_____ ____
_____ ____
_____ ____

Attachments

SECTION 3.5   VERBS

A Principal Parts

On the lines provided, write the past tense, the past participle, and the present participle for each of the following verbs.

PRESENT	PAST	PAST PARTICIPLE	PRESENT PARTICIPLE	✓
1. prepare	_____	_____	_____	**1.** ____
2. listen	_____	_____	_____	**2.** ____
3. enjoy	_____	_____	_____	**3.** ____
4. call	_____	_____	_____	**4.** ____
5. need	_____	_____	_____	**5.** ____
6. drop	_____	_____	_____	**6.** ____
7. enter	_____	_____	_____	**7.** ____
8. start	_____	_____	_____	**8.** ____
9. greet	_____	_____	_____	**9.** ____
10. try	_____	_____	_____	**10.** ____
11. attend	_____	_____	_____	**11.** ____
12. occur	_____	_____	_____	**12.** ____
13. die	_____	_____	_____	**13.** ____
14. fill	_____	_____	_____	**14.** ____
15. type	_____	_____	_____	**15.** ____

B Writing Skill

For each of the following verbs, write a sentence using the form of the verb described in parentheses.   ✓

1. offer (present perfect)

_____   **1.** ____

2. present (past)

_____   **2.** ____

3. check (present)

_____   3. ____

4. try (present progressive)

_____   4. ____

5. fix (past)

_____   5. ____

6. agree (present perfect)

_____   6. ____

7. install (future)

_____   7. ____

8. consider (past)

_____   8. ____

9. finish (present perfect)

_____   9. ____

10. travel (past)

_____   10. ____

C Energizing Sentences

Underline the verb or the verb phrase in each of the following sentences. Then write the main verb in the space provided.

1. Do you agree with the proposal?   1. _____ ____

2. We are concerned about the costs.   2. _____ ____

3. The medical records department has been processing a large volume of patient charts.   3. _____ ____

4. Our new automated recordkeeping system makes processing documents much easier.   4. _____ ____

5. Yes, Ms. Huang should have received the test results by now.   5. _____ ____

6. Several of the paralegals have been working overtime this month.   6. _____ ____

7. Have you seen the Web page for our closest competitor?   7. _____ ____

8. Roxanne often calls her sales manager in the afternoon.   8. _____ ____

9. Today, she has already called twice.   9. _____ ____

10. Your travel request has been approved.   10. _____ ____

11. This year, our region has almost exceeded the company's all-time sales record.   11. _____ ____

12. By the end of the year, we will surely have broken the record.   12. _____ ____

✓

13. Franklin should have applied for the new accounting
    position.   13. _____ ____

14. He is the most skilled accountant in our department.   14. _____ ____

15. Based on the feedback from the survey, we should make
    more of an effort to accommodate customers' needs.   15. _____ ____

16. As a result, we have improved our customer service
    procedures.   16. _____ ____

17. The new pension plan was being discussed at the board
    meeting.   17. _____ ____

18. All board members unanimously approved the pension
    plan.   18. _____ ____

19. We will fly to Seattle for the computer conference.   19. _____ ____

20. Our flight to Seattle is scheduled for 8:20 a.m. tomorrow.   20. _____ ____

21. We should arrive at the airport no later than 7 a.m.   21. _____ ____

22. Have you written your performance goals for next year?   22. _____ ____

23. You should work with your supervisor to develop
    your goals.   23. _____ ____

24. All performance goals should be submitted to the human
    resources director by March 15.   24. _____ ____

25. Has the invoice for the computer equipment been
    paid yet?   25. _____ ____

D Principal Parts

On the lines provided, write the past tense, the past participle, and the present
participle for each of the following verbs.

PRESENT	PAST	PAST PARTICIPLE	PRESENT PARTICIPLE	✓
1. grow	_____	_____	_____	1. ____
2. go	_____	_____	_____	2. ____
3. give	_____	_____	_____	3. ____
4. forget	_____	_____	_____	4. ____
5. fly	_____	_____	_____	5. ____
6. fall	_____	_____	_____	6. ____
7. eat	_____	_____	_____	7. ____
8. drive	_____	_____	_____	8. ____
9. do	_____	_____	_____	9. ____
10. come	_____	_____	_____	10. ____

PRESENT	PAST	PAST PARTICIPLE	PRESENT PARTICIPLE	✓
11. choose	_____	_____	_____	**11.** ___
12. bring	_____	_____	_____	**12.** ___
13. break	_____	_____	_____	**13.** ___
14. begin	_____	_____	_____	**14.** ___
15. am	_____	_____	_____	**15.** ___
16. know	_____	_____	_____	**16.** ___
17. lay	_____	_____	_____	**17.** ___
18. leave	_____	_____	_____	**18.** ___
19. lie	_____	_____	_____	**19.** ___
20. pay	_____	_____	_____	**20.** ___
21. rise	_____	_____	_____	**21.** ___
22. see	_____	_____	_____	**22.** ___
23. send	_____	_____	_____	**23.** ___
24. sit	_____	_____	_____	**24.** ___
25. speak	_____	_____	_____	**25.** ___
26. stand	_____	_____	_____	**26.** ___
27. take	_____	_____	_____	**27.** ___
28. tell	_____	_____	_____	**28.** ___
29. wear	_____	_____	_____	**29.** ___
30. write	_____	_____	_____	**30.** ___

E Finding Errors

Underline any verb errors in the following sentences, and write your corrections on the lines provided. Write *OK* for any sentence that has no error.   ✓

1. Has Monica began the analysis for Mr. Santos?   **1.** _____ ___

2. If the price of the company stock raises, we will buy more shares.   **2.** _____ ___

3. As you know, we grown all our flowers in the greenhouse.   **3.** _____ ___

4. Please lie the catalogs on the desk next to the copier.   **4.** _____ ___

5. Had we knew about the delay, we would have made other shipping arrangements.   **5.** _____ ___

6. We have drove that route to work before.   **6.** _____ ___

7. The attorney has been speaking for almost 20 minutes.   **7.** _____ ___

8. Brad and Katsue have went to the training session.   **8.** _____ ___

✓

9. Have you chose the car you wish to buy?

9. _____ ____

10. If Diego was here, you could ask him yourself.

10. _____ ____

11. As the speaker approached the podium, we rised to greet him.

11. _____ ____

12. Most of the guests have finished eaten their meals.

12. _____ ____

13. Admissions to the hospital have fell by 5 percent the last six months.

13. _____ ____

14. We have broken the existing sales record for the second straight year.

14. _____ ____

15. At every meeting Colleen acts as if she was in charge.

15. _____ ____

F Choosing the Correct Verb

On the line provided, write the verb in parentheses that correctly completes each sentence.

✓

1. The patient should (lie, lay) on his back for a week.

1. _____ ____

2. You'll find the CD-ROM (laying, lying) on the shelf above the computer.

2. _____ ____

3. The samples were (sitting, setting) on the counter.

3. _____ ____

4. Please (set, sit) the room temperature at a more comfortable level.

4. _____ ____

5. Somewhere in Murray's office (lays, lies) the spreadsheets that Gwen needs.

5. _____ ____

6. Yes, Lauren, I remember where you (lay, laid) the report.

6. _____ ____

7. It is polite to (rise, raise) to greet a visitor.

7. _____ ____

8. Warehouse employees should use the hydraulic lift to (raise, rise) the pallets.

8. _____ ____

9. The cargo plane carrying the shipment is (sitting, setting) on the runway.

9. _____ ____

10. To fit the copy on the page, you should (sit, set) wider margins.

10. _____ ____

11. Due to the heavy rains, the water level in the reservoir has (raised, risen) two feet.

11. _____ ____

12. Tell the carpenters to (lie, lay) the lumber beside the construction trailer.

12. _____ ____

13. Remember to (raise, rise) that point at the next status meeting.

13. _____ ____

14. Last year's project files have (laid, lain) in the storage room for months.

14. _____ ____

15. The telephone company has (lain, laid) the fiber optic cables for the new office building.

15. _____ ____

16. Please (sit, set) the printer to the right of the computer monitor.

16. _____ ____

17. Ask Giancarlo to (lie, lay) the design boards on the conference table.

17. _____ ____

18. Use a level to check that you have (lay, laid) the bricks correctly.

18. _____ ____

19. We have (sat, sit) around long enough; let's get back to work.

19. _____ ____

20. Do you know where Jonathon has (lain, laid) the entry forms?

20. _____ ____

G Transitive, Intransitive, or "Being"?

Underline the verb or the verb phrase in each of the following sentences. Then, at the right, circle *T* if the verb is transitive, *I* if the verb is intransitive, or *B* if the verb is a "being" verb. ✓

1. Dwayne will assist us with the blueprints.

1. T I B ____

2. Estrella was interviewed by Mr. Salvi last week.

2. T I B ____

3. She is the leading candidate for the sales position.

3. T I B ____

4. Luis has been a software specialist for the past three years.

4. T I B ____

5. I have applied for my passport.

5. T I B ____

6. Shirley will be traveling to Europe next month on business.

6. T I B ____

7. In my opinion, the bank should be open on Sundays.

7. T I B ____

8. Noah's advertising campaign has become a great success.

8. T I B ____

9. Our instructor encouraged us to apply for internships.

9. T I B ____

10. As of next week, Charlotte will be in charge of the Desktop Publishing Department.

10. T I B ____

11. We asked our financial planner for his opinion on the investment.

11. T I B ____

12. Tomorrow we will mail the invitations to the open house.

12. T I B ____

13. The senior pharmacist has the weekend off.

13. T I B ____

14. Of course, we are confident about the plan.

14. T I B ____

15. My father-in-law was admitted to the hospital last night.

15. T I B ____

16. On February 5, Mr. Mahon will have been with the company for 15 years.

16. T I B ____

17. Antonio bought his car a year ago.

17. T I B ____

18. Yes, the developer's fee has changed.

18. T I B ____

19. Of all the accountants, only Nurjani is a CPA.

19. T I B ____

20. Did Mr. and Mrs. Jacobs return all copies of the contract?

20. T I B ____

SECTION 3.6   PREDICATE AGREEMENT

A   Singular or Plural Verbs and Pronouns?

Circle *S* if a singular verb or pronoun would correctly complete a sentence. Circle *P* if a plural would be correct.   ✓

1. All paralegals _____ been informed of the change in assignments.   **1.** S P _____

2. Do you know if he and Jerry _____ planning to attend the opening performance?   **2.** S P _____

3. As reported in the newspaper, our company _____ planning to expand its facilities.   **3.** S P _____

4. Yes, all the desktop publishing operators _____ familiar with the new page
   layout software.   **4.** S P _____

5. Where _____ the original copy of the Olson contract?   **5.** S P _____

6. The fire department _____ responded to a record number of automobile
   accidents this month.   **6.** S P _____

7. A great number of accidents _____ reported during the recent tornado season.   **7.** S P _____

8. Members of the jury _____ reviewing the evidence.   **8.** S P _____

9. The jury _____ reached a verdict.   **9.** S P _____

10. Eugene Webster and Roberta Todd _____ responsible for entering customers'
    flight reservations on the computer.   **10.** S P _____

11. Ask Jerome if he wants to order _____ book for the library.   **11.** S P _____

12. Our manager, as well as the two sales representatives, _____ compiling
    the yearly sales report.   **12.** S P _____

13. Did you know that over 500 people _____ visited our Web site so
    far this month?   **13.** S P _____

14. The tax attorney _____ working on documentation to support the claims
    for deductions.   **14.** S P _____

15. Does Angela have the cost estimates for _____ products?   **15.** S P _____

16. Nearly two-thirds of our operating budget _____ used for print advertisements.   **16.** S P _____

17. Our most dependable supplier _____ Maxwell Printing.   **17.** S P _____

18. When _____ we supposed to receive the final order of laser printers?   **18.** S P _____

19. If either Sally or Jeanette calls, please give _____ this message.   **19.** S P _____

20. Perhaps Carmen can explain why both of _____ printers were ordered.   **20.** S P _____

21. _____ Rob contacted all the project managers?   **21.** S P _____

22. Call the managers to inform _____ of the change.   **22.** S P _____

23. We _____ all the specifications for the software.   **23.** S P _____

24. Do you know if Anna _____ a candidate for the position?   **24.** S P _____

25. Most of the salespeople _____ enthusiastic about the product.   **25.** S P _____

B Selecting the Correct Verb

For each of the following sentences, choose the correct verb in parentheses. Write your answers on the lines provided.   ✓

1. Mr. and Mrs. Wesley (is, are) planning to update their wills.

    1. _____ _____

2. The committee chairperson (is, are) responsible for setting the agenda.

    2. _____ _____

3. Doug Ramsay (has, have) asked Mr. Alden for approval to travel to the sales conference in San Francisco.

    3. _____ _____

4. On the CD-ROM (is, are) the latest version of the browser software.

    4. _____ _____

5. The restaurant critic reported that (there is, there are) several restaurants willing to honor gift certificates from their competitors.

    5. _____ _____

6. According to Patrick, the criteria for the decision (is, are) sound.

    6. _____ _____

7. One-third of the proceeds from the sale of the CD-ROM (has, have) been donated to charity.

    7. _____ _____

8. A number of students (has, have) applied for the four-year scholarship.

    8. _____ _____

9. There (is, are) several options for the legal counsel to consider before the case goes to trial.

    9. _____ _____

10. At least two-thirds of our employees (agree, agrees) with the restructuring plan.

    10. _____ _____

11. Either our accountant or our tax attorney (file, filed) the extension for our income tax return.

    11. _____ _____

12. Our franchise is one of those restaurants that (has, have) special family value meals.

    12. _____ _____

13. Do you know whether the new laboratories (has, have) been inspected?

    13. _____ _____

14. Tessa is the only one of the nurses who (has, have) more than fifteen years of service with the hospital.

    14. _____ _____

15. Neither the attorney nor the paralegals (has, have) contacted the clients.

    15. _____ _____

16. (Is, Are) the blueprints for the Greiner project attached to the latest draft of the site plans?

    16. _____ _____

17. The architect and the builder (disagree, disagrees) on where to install the water purification system.

    17. _____ _____

18. (There is, There are) only one way to resolve the dispute.

    18. _____ _____

19. The number of Web page designers (has, have) increased dramatically during the last two years.

    19. _____ _____

20. Members of the committee (is, are) debating the proposal to offer stock options to employees.

    20. _____ _____

C Predicate Agreement With Compound Subjects

Circle *S* if a singular verb would correctly complete a sentence. Circle *P* if a plural verb would be correct. ✓

1. Aerobics, swimming, and weight training—all _____ available at the Easton Athletic Club.
1. S P _____

2. The heating contractor told me that neither the condensing unit nor the air filter _____ causing the problem.
2. S P _____

3. Both stocks and bonds _____ wise choices for long-term investments.
3. S P _____

4. Surprisingly, neither Bruce nor Carmen _____ interested in learning how to use the presentation software.
4. S P _____

5. Every geologist and every engineer _____ required to complete a course in handling hazardous materials.
5. S P _____

6. According to Tonya, fuel economy and safety features _____ the most important factors to consider in selecting a new car.
6. S P _____

7. Each assistant and supervisor _____ received training on how to use the new Internet browser.
7. S P _____

8. According to Ms. Stevens, neither Mitch nor Connie _____ completed the CPA exam.
8. S P _____

9. Swimming and walking _____ recommended activities for individuals who are overweight.
9. S P _____

10. Neither the engineer nor the technicians _____ checked the test results.
10. S P _____

11. The accident investigator and the claims adjuster _____ estimated the cost of repairing the two vehicles.
11. S P _____

12. Either underscoring or italics _____ used to indicate the title of a book or newspaper.
12. S P _____

13. Yes, my husband and I _____ interested in purchasing stock options without a broker.
13. S P _____

14. If either the school board or the voters _____ in favor of the voucher plan, we will place the measure on the ballot.
14. S P _____

15. Of course, every management trainee in our headquarters _____ been given training in how to use the new spreadsheet software.
15. S P _____

D Proofreading for Agreement Errors

Underline any errors in the following sentences, and write your corrections on the lines provided. Write *OK* for any sentence that has no error. ✓

1. If either Marie or Elena have an interest in working on the company's Web site, ask them to speak with the department manager.
1. _____ _____

2. Every employee is expected to do their part to promote a stress-free work environment.
2. _____ _____

3. Have Michael completed his drafting course yet?

3. _____ ____

4. The marketing manager, along with two assistants, are responsible for compiling the sales kits for our products.

4. _____ ____

5. Annette don't know yet about the new procedure for processing insurance claims.

5. _____ ____

6. Of course, each employee may contribute funds to their flexible spending account to pay for medical expenses.

6. _____ ____

7. Every one of these compact disc players are on sale for the next two weeks.

7. _____ ____

8. All the fire extinguishers in our building has been inspected by the fire department.

8. _____ ____

9. Anyone who are interested may volunteer to participate in the community walkathon.

9. _____ ____

10. The automatic settings on these camcorders makes it very convenient for recording events.

10. _____ ____

11. Dr. Catalfino and Dr. Farber, the new internists at Brevard Memorial, is planning to open a medical practice together.

11. _____ ____

12. Gerard, where are the charts for the patients who were admitted this morning?

12. _____ ____

13. Each supervisor is required to meet weekly with his staff members.

13. _____ ____

14. There is several factors to consider before we can approve the purchase of a new computer operating system.

14. _____ ____

15. Are you sure there was some other computer diskettes in the storage cabinet?

15. _____ ____

16. Was Eleanor employed at RPG Packaging Corporation at the same time you were there?

16. _____ ____

17. Each sales representative who meets their sales goal will receive a 10 percent bonus.

17. _____ ____

18. Most of our assembly workers, of course, are against the change in production methods.

18. _____ ____

19. Monica, where are the results of the stress tests that Dr. Stoffer have been looking for?

19. _____ ____

20. Our videoconference with the satellite offices in Hong Kong and Amsterdam are scheduled for tomorrow at 2 p.m. our time.

20. _____ ____

21. The primary cause for the delays in the past year were our inability to hire the staff we needed.

21. _____ ____

22. We are pleased to announce that Mark Dodson have accepted the position of vice president of advertising.

22. _____ ____

23. Gainesville Home Furnishings, Inc., is one of the furniture manufacturers that has been looking to expand into the East Coast market.

23. _____ ____

✓

24. The original contract, as well as two copies, were mailed to the marketing consultant.

24. _____ ____

25. Many a school principal and teacher have protested the use of school vouchers.

25. _____ ____

26. There's only two positions in the inventory department that have not been filled.

26. _____ ____

27. A great number of Internet sites on Web page design is available to businesses and individuals.

27. _____ ____

28. Is this software program one of the two that was recommended for use with our computerized inventory system?

28. _____ ____

29. Either Vincent's father-in-law or his two brothers is going to invest in the franchise with him.

29. _____ ____

30. Each computer technician said that they would like to receive additional training so that they may better serve our customers.

30. _____ ____

E Editing Practice

Underline any errors in the following sentences, and write your corrections on the lines provided. Write *OK* for any sentence that has no error.

✓

1. Nearly two-thirds of the staff members in our headquarters office has volunteered to donate for the blood drive.

1. _____ ____

2. Many a travel agent and an airline reservations clerk have used this software.

2. _____ ____

3. Neither Ms. Cutler's nor Mr. Kosta's assistant know the telephone number of the hotel where the convention is being held.

3. _____ ____

4. On the conference table is the questionnaires that were completed by all staff members.

4. _____ ____

5. You may request a list of approved suppliers from the Purchasing Department.

5. _____ ____

6. Two-thirds of the inventory for that software package have been reserved to fill backorders.

6. _____ ____

7. Do you know whether everyone has already submitted their updated personal information forms to the Human Resources Department?

7. _____ ____

8. Call Shannon and tell her that there is two software consultants waiting in the reception area.

8. _____ ____

9. Here's more completed insurance forms to be processed.

9. _____ ____

10. We asked each vice president to give us their opinion of the proposed improvements to our automated banking machines.

10. _____ ____

11. Yes, Indika and myself will send the forms to everyone
on our client list.

11. _____ _____

12. Corinne mentioned that Paul increasing his sales so
dramatically surprised Mr. Orrville.

12. _____ _____

13. Mr. Wozniak, here's the names of the five candidates for
the marketing position.

13. _____ _____

14. A list of recommended computer consultants is posted in
the newsletter.

14. _____ _____

15. As I indicated, the major distinctions between our product
and our closest competitor's is described in this report.

15. _____ _____

16. Although these are only draft copies of the contracts,
do not leave them laying around on your desk overnight.

16. _____ _____

17. Ms. Ikawa asked Sean and I to chair the design meeting
for the Dunstin project.

17. _____ _____

18. As you know, customer's comment cards are available
at the front desk of the hotel.

18. _____ _____

19. Shawna said that Grant and she are happy in their new
jobs in the admissions office at the university.

19. _____ _____

20. Of course, we will has appropriate company representatives
attend the dedication ceremony for the new building.

20. _____ _____

21. If the Avilas agree to the sellers' purchase price, we may
be able to close the sale by the end of October.

21. _____ _____

22. According to the article in the company newsletter, it will
be him, not her, who will be the next director of nursing.

22. _____ _____

23. Yes, us regional managers should meet to discuss all these
issues at our next quarterly meeting.

23. _____ _____

24. Does Lorraine know that their is a good possibility for
advancement in that position?

24. _____ _____

25. Who does Linda wish to speak with, Quentin or her?

25. _____ _____

F Proofreading Application

Underline any errors in the following paragraph, and write your corrections in the spaces provided. ✓

Anna Garofalo and Gaylord Jewell, the vice president's
of the new division, has spoke with a representative of
the leasing company that owns the site of are new
distribution center. According to the companys' report,
Monroe Kosisko is the only person who understand all
the systems of the new facility. As you know, Monroe
have been an important resource person for us since we
first began looking for a new site for the distribution
center. Since then, Monroe has gained the confidence of
every member of our staff who he has met.

_____ _____
_____ _____
_____ _____
_____ _____
_____ _____
_____ _____
_____ _____
_____ _____
_____ _____
_____ _____

SECTION 3.7 ADJECTIVES

A Comparing Adjectives

On the lines provided, write the comparative and superlative forms of the adjectives
listed at the left. ✓

POSITIVE	COMPARATIVE	SUPERLATIVE	
1. good	_____	_____	**1.** ____
2. reasonable	_____	_____	**2.** ____
3. large	_____	_____	**3.** ____
4. many	_____	_____	**4.** ____
5. practical	_____	_____	**5.** ____
6. angry	_____	_____	**6.** ____
7. important	_____	_____	**7.** ____
8. much	_____	_____	**8.** ____
9. sharp	_____	_____	**9.** ____
10. tactful	_____	_____	**10.** ____
11. lively	_____	_____	**11.** ____
12. important	_____	_____	**12.** ____
13. bad	_____	_____	**13.** ____
14. wide	_____	_____	**14.** ____
15. profitable	_____	_____	**15.** ____
16. thin	_____	_____	**16.** ____
17. loud	_____	_____	**17.** ____
18. beneficial	_____	_____	**18.** ____
19. up-to-date	_____	_____	**19.** ____
20. fine	_____	_____	**20.** ____
21. strong	_____	_____	**21.** ____
22. cautious	_____	_____	**22.** ____
23. complete	_____	_____	**23.** ____
24. little	_____	_____	**24.** ____

B Proofreading for Adjective Errors

Underline any errors in the following sentences, and write your corrections on the lines provided. Write *OK* for any sentence that has no error. ✓

1. After comparing the two software programs, Bethany said that the first was certainly good but the second was definitely the best.

   1. _____ ____

2. Yes, writing this competitive analysis should be more easy than conducting the research.

   2. _____ ____

3. You should purchase a computer with these kind of options.

   3. _____ ____

4. Please request more bigger banquet rooms for the convention.

   4. _____ ____

5. We would like to invest in tax free bonds as one form of retirement savings.

   5. _____ ____

6. Ask Deanne if them transcripts are the ones Mr. Regan wanted to review.

   6. _____ ____

7. This supply of plasma must be shipped to the regional trauma center by the most fastest method.

   7. _____ ____

8. Our vacation time seems short every year.

   8. _____ ____

9. These cellular phones seem to be more smaller than the ones we recently purchased from our supplier.

   9. _____ ____

10. Whom do you consider to be the most creative computer programmer—Franklin or Kathryn?

    10. _____ ____

11. Would Brenda prefer to have one of them ergonomic keyboards for her computer?

    11. _____ ____

12. Neither of the three surgical nurses has signed up for the critical care seminar.

    12. _____ ____

13. We preferred the second video because the sound was clearer and the situations were more realistic.

    13. _____ ____

14. My new supervisor, Joanne Sleva, knows more about our manufacturing process than any manager in the division.

    14. _____ ____

15. Vernon and I like both ergonomic keyboards, but the less expensive one seems to have the most features.

    15. _____ ____

16. Festival Food Service, Inc., has signed a three year contract to be the food service provider at all five of our buildings.

    16. _____ ____

17. Beth is definitely the most ambitious of any of our sales representatives.

    17. _____ ____

18. Our new distribution center in Harrisburg is more automated than any distribution facility in the country.

    18. _____ ____

19. Marty has more experience in probate law than anyone else with our firm.

    19. _____ ____

20. Jana's approach to troubleshooting problems with computer software is certainly most unique.

    20. _____ ____

✓

21. We reviewed carefully all the bids that the construction firms submitted and agreed that the bid from Randall Construction was the better one.

21. _____ ____

22. These computer monitors seem to be more larger than the ones we recently bought.

22. _____ ____

23. As you can see from the report, Samuel has provided a comprehensive, up to date analysis of market trends in travel and tourism.

23. _____ ____

24. Of course, my being nominated for the outstanding employee of the year award was the most biggest surprise of my career.

24. _____ ____

25. The judge granted the defense attorney a 15 minute recess to confer with the defendant.

25. _____ ____

C Editing Practice

Underline any errors in the following sentences, and write your corrections on the lines provided. Write *OK* for any sentence that has no error.

✓

1. According to the monthly timesheets, Teresa works more hours of overtime than anyone on the surgical staff.

1. _____ ____

2. According to the newspaper article, the board of directors for the animal shelter have voted to expand the facility.

2. _____ ____

3. The attorney generals for all fifty states met in Atlanta for their annual conference.

3. _____ ____

4. Victor, is there any other instructions you would like to give Jeff before the presentation?

4. _____ ____

5. The city manager recommended that the new city treasurer should be her.

5. _____ ____

6. Our fall line of childrens' clothing will be shipped to the distributor on June 5.

6. _____ ____

7. Who's the client who requested that the date of the deposition be changed?

7. _____ ____

8. We were real excited about the announcement that we would form a joint venture with an investment company in Malaysia.

8. _____ ____

9. Yes, the revised version of the user's manual is much more clear, in my opinion.

9. _____ ____

10. Being that the school board has approved the measure by a five-to-one vote, we will enact a voucher program for all city schools.

10. _____ ____

11. Deborah has come to depend upon Priscilla for advice on how to advance on the job.

11. _____ ____

12. Linda placed an order for a new computer hard drive for Courtney and myself.

12. _____ ___

13. Do you know who's design was chosen for the new company logo?

13. _____ ___

14. Sondra did not feel good, so she went to her doctor for a checkup.

14. _____ ___

15. Is the electrical wiring in our new building in compliance with the city's updated fire code?

15. _____ ___

16. We will send the sample CD-ROM to whomever requests one.

16. _____ ___

17. Kelsey is the accountant which is in charge of the budget committee.

17. _____ ___

18. Ms. Terleski said that neither she nor Mr. Osborne are in favor of moving the headquarters to Cincinnati.

18. _____ ___

19. To be honest, I do not like working on these kind of rush projects.

19. _____ ___

20. Does California have more severe types of weather than any state in the continental United States?

20. _____ ___

D Proofreading Application

Correct any errors in the following letter, and write your answers on the lines provided. ✓

Dear Ms. Franklin:

_____ ___

    Thank you for your leter of October 10 requesting information about Central Carolina Bank's home-equity loans.

_____ ___
_____ ___
_____ ___

    Over the past year, as mortgage rates has fallen under 10 percent, the rates charged by major credit cards have not. With more major credit cards, you likely pay form 18 to 21 percent interest on your balance. With an home-equity loan from Central Carolina Bank, you can borrow money for only 8¾ percent interest! In addition, the interest you pays on your loan is tax-deductible. The interest you pay on your credit cards is not tax-deductible.

_____ ___
_____ ___
_____ ___
_____ ___
_____ ___
_____ ___
_____ ___
_____ ___

    To learn more about the benefits of a home equity loan from Central Carolina Bank, please call I at 910-555-6265 to schedule an appointment. You'll be real glad you did!

_____ ___
_____ ___
_____ ___

Sincerely,

_____ ___

SECTION 3.8   ADVERBS _____

A   Forming Adverbs

On the lines provided, write the adverb forms of the adjectives in the left column.

ADJECTIVE	ADVERB	✓	ADJECTIVE	ADVERB	✓
1. abrupt	1. _____	____	21. persuasive	21. _____	____
2. absolute	2. _____	____	22. possible	22. _____	____
3. actual	3. _____	____	23. practical	23. _____	____
4. apparent	4. _____	____	24. precise	24. _____	____
5. busy	5. _____	____	25. professional	25. _____	____
6. careful	6. _____	____	26. prompt	26. _____	____
7. competent	7. _____	____	27. quiet	27. _____	____
8. complete	8. _____	____	28. real	28. _____	____
9. confident	9. _____	____	29. responsible	29. _____	____
10. convenient	10. _____	____	30. satisfactory	30. _____	____
11. direct	11. _____	____	31. scarce	31. _____	____
12. entire	12. _____	____	32. sole	32. _____	____
13. equal	13. _____	____	33. specific	33. _____	____
14. happy	14. _____	____	34. steady	34. _____	____
15. honest	15. _____	____	35. true	35. _____	____
16. immediate	16. _____	____	36. trustworthy	36. _____	____
17. inefficient	17. _____	____	37. universal	37. _____	____
18. legal	18. _____	____	38. unnecessary	38. _____	____
19. mutual	19. _____	____	39. visible	39. _____	____
20. obvious	20. _____	____	40. whole	40. _____	____

B   Proofreading for Adverb Errors

Underline any errors in the following sentences, and write your corrections on the lines provided. Write *OK* for any sentence that has no error.   ✓

1. Clarke and I only know about the potential closing of the
   Chesapeake fishery; no one else knows about it.   1. _____ ____

2. If you really don't feel good, Shauntel, you should see your doctor.

2. _____ ____

3. Ms. Woolfe always seems somewhat anxiously right before the monthly status meeting.

3. _____ ____

4. Our company guarantees that the air-filtration system will work satisfactory, so there's no risk in signing the contract.

4. _____ ____

5. We received the Sanchezes' offer for the property, but we never received confirmation from the mortgage company.

5. _____ ____

6. Did you read in the newspaper where the two largest Internet providers are forming a joint partnership?

6. _____ ____

7. When I heard Ms. Trudeau speak at the conference, her voice sounded very differently.

7. _____ ____

8. You will be able to save your documents more fast when you upgrade the memory on your computer.

8. _____ ____

9. We put Evan and Laurie in charge of the Safeway account because they work very good together.

9. _____ ____

10. The city council wants to build a sports arena along the riverfront in the worst way.

10. _____ ____

11. We will, naturally, be glad to reimburse you for the total purchase price; please submit your invoice to our credit department.

11. _____ ____

12. To be honest, I think that Gary's plan to annex the property is practically.

12. _____ ____

13. Please be sure that all the operating rooms are cleaned complete before you and your staff leave for the day.

13. _____ ____

14. Joanne and Peter are upset only about bonuses awarded to executives, not to middle managers.

14. _____ ____

15. The judge must sure have meant to give the jury different instructions regarding the defendant's testimony.

15. _____ ____

16. Ramona Ortiz, an experienced investor, advised strong against buying stock in Maxwell Pharmaceuticals at its present high price.

16. _____ ____

17. The software designer said that this program is exceptionally well designed and that it should meet our needs for many, many years.

17. _____ ____

18. Sidney and I, as directors of the recycling committee, feel badly about the mix-up in labeling the displays donated by area organizations.

18. _____ ____

19. Given the lengthy approval process, I can't hardly believe that the project has been authorized.

19. _____ ____

20. Yesterday Alonzo and Marie received some real exciting news about their patent application.

20. _____ ____

C Editing Practice

Underline any errors in the following sentences, and write your corrections on the lines provided. Write *OK* for any sentence that has no error.   ✓

1. Our customer surveys indicate that sales of computer games increased some during the summer.

    1. _____ ____

2. Neither the attorney nor the investigator were aware of the change in the court date.

    2. _____ ____

3. Have you noticed that this purifier helps to make the air smell freshly?

    3. _____ ____

4. One purpose of the team-building workshops is to help employees develop more productive working relationships with each other.

    4. _____ ____

5. This new compact camcorder is definitely the best model of any that we have sold.

    5. _____ ____

6. Don't Louis or Suzanne usually request the software upgrades?

    6. _____ ____

7. Is Friday and Saturday the only two days that the symphony will perform the conductor's new composition?

    7. _____ ____

8. Only one witnesses testimony was heard this morning.

    8. _____ ____

9. During the winter season, we generally like to advertise these kind of vacation getaways.

    9. _____ ____

10. Be sure to read these contracts very careful before you approve them, Carolyn.

    10. _____ ____

11. Didn't you say that we need another sales representative in California in the worst way?

    11. _____ ____

12. The advertisement claims that this toothpaste will whiten teeth better than any brand.

    12. _____ ____

13. Most of us agree that Gail is a real loyal supervisor who cares about her staff.

    13. _____ ____

14. Yes, Randall, Mr. Koblentz was very satisfied with all them designs that you sent him.

    14. _____ ____

15. Yesterday there was only two support specialists handling calls to the software hotline.

    15. _____ ____

D Proofreading Practice

Some of the following sentences contain spelling errors, possessive errors, or vocabulary errors. Underline the error in each sentence, and write your correction in the space provided. Write *OK* for any sentence that has no error.   ✓

1. According to the official reports, the accident occured two miles north of the airport.

    1. _____ ____

2. Alicia calculated the cost estamates carefully before submitting them to the manufacturing coordinator.

2. _____ ____

3. The Payne family recomended that we take a vacation to Hawaii.

3. _____ ____

4. Aparently, it was Mr. Rigney's decision to delay the shipment until the order was complete.

4. _____ ____

5. Although we expect 250 guests for the reception, the accommodations at the West Side Hotel will easily meet our needs.

5. _____ ____

6. In my opinion you are all ready overstaffed for this project and may end up with little profit.

6. _____ ____

7. Send these copies to the Ms. Richters; then ask each sister to sign and return one of the contracts.

7. _____ ____

8. The commercial showing families working together to construct a neighborhood park is our's.

8. _____ ____

9. Since we purchased the jet ski, we have spent most every weekend at the lake.

9. _____ ____

10. The companies plan is to discontinue its less profitable lines and concentrate on its most successful products.

10. _____ ____

11. Lloyd maybe appointed to the design team that is working on the construction plans for the arena.

11. _____ ____

12. Earl ordered a new devise that is supposed to sense even the slightest amounts of smoke in the air.

12. _____ ____

13. Is it necessary to include payment with my order, or will the company bill me later?

13. _____ ____

14. I am not certain weather Ms. Kagami plans to return to the Tokyo office after next week.

14. _____ ____

15. We need to reserve the main conferance room for an all-day videoconference with our manufacturing team in Indonesia.

15. _____ ____

E Correcting Errors

Correct any errors in the following memo, and write your answers on the lines provided. ✓

MEMO TO: Customer Service Representatives

_____ ____

FROM: Janet Vascura

_____ ____

DATE: May 16, <YEAR>

_____ ____

SUBJECT: Results of Customer Survey

_____ ____

Attached are the results of the survey that was sent to our customer's the beginning of April. In the survey, us asked customers to comment honest on our products and our service. As you can see from the results, our customers noted us four our outstanding service in all categorys in the questionnaire.

_____ ____
_____ ____
_____ ____
_____ ____
_____ ____
_____ ____

You are all to be congratulated for your hard work and dedicasion in handling customer's questions and requests.

_____ ____
_____ ____

SECTION 3.9   PREPOSITIONS _____

A The Correct Preposition

On the lines provided, write the correct prepositions to be used after the following words.

                          ✓   ✓

1. abide (a decision)	1. _____ ____	16. correspond (match)	16. _____ ____
2. accompanied (item)	2. _____ ____	17. deal	17. _____ ____
3. agree (a person)	3. _____ ____	18. depend	18. _____ ____
4. agree (a thing)	4. _____ ____	19. different	19. _____ ____
5. attend (listen)	5. _____ ____	20. discrepancy (one thing)	20. _____ ____
6. attend (wait on)	6. _____ ____	21. enter (agreements)	21. _____ ____
7. beneficial	7. _____ ____	22. identical	22. _____ ____
8. buy	8. _____ ____	23. independent	23. _____ ____
9. compare (likeness)	9. _____ ____	24. inferior	24. _____ ____
10. compliance	10. _____ ____	25. plan	25. _____ ____
11. comply	11. _____ ____	26. profit	26. _____ ____
12. confide (place confidence)	12. _____ ____	27. retroactive	27. _____ ____
13. conform	13. _____ ____	28. speak (tell something)	28. _____ ____
14. consist (make up)	14. _____ ____	29. speak (discuss with)	29. _____ ____
15. convenient (near)	15. _____ ____	30. wait (customer)	30. _____ ____

B Proofreading for Preposition Errors

Underline any preposition errors in the following sentences, and write your corrections on the lines provided. Write *OK* for any sentence that has no error. ✓

1. As you know, Serena and I agree in the plan to expand our sales territory.

    1. _____ ____

2. Did you notice that there is an obvious discrepancy in the sales estimates submitted by Juan and the sales estimates submitted by Angela?

    2. _____ ____

3. Surprisingly, the two parties agreed with the judge's suggestion to work with a mediator.

    3. _____ ____

4. In regard with our request, the order will be shipped next week.

    4. _____ ____

5. Never let yourself remain angry at someone for long.

5. _____ ____

6. The sales kits were distributed equally between the five regional managers.

6. _____ ____

7. Make sure our department vacation policy is in compliance with the recent updates.

7. _____ ____

8. As we anticipated, the Jackson bid is almost identical to the Centofani bid.

8. _____ ____

9. The salary increase for all staff personnel will be retroactive from March.

9. _____ ____

10. All of the stockholders received a copy of the company's annual report.

10. _____ ____

11. We expect to complete the upgrade to the computer network inside of the week.

11. _____ ____

12. See if you can get some extra catalogs from Emily.

12. _____ ____

13. Our new headquarters building will be located opposite to the statehouse.

13. _____ ____

14. The recommendations in the second proposal were quite different than the ones originally submitted.

14. _____ ____

15. The new reservations manager will be selected from among these seven candidates.

15. _____ ____

16. This incentive plan will be beneficial of both sales and marketing personnel.

16. _____ ____

17. Our new banquet facilities are convenient to weddings and business receptions.

17. _____ ____

18. We will enter in an exclusive contract with DiYanna Distribution.

18. _____ ____

19. When you see Aaron, please ask him if he knows where Ms. Gonzales went to.

19. _____ ____

20. This modem is different than the others.

20. _____ ____

21. Yes, we agreed with the board's recommendation.

21. _____ ____

22. Are you conversant to this new database software?

22. _____ ____

23. Duane and Stacey are planning on applying for the medical assistant position.

23. _____ ____

24. Of course, these procedures can be adapted to the needs of each department.

24. _____ ____

25. We have adapted for the change in our operating procedures.

25. _____ ____

C Editing Practice

Underline any errors in the following sentences, and write your corrections on the lines provided. Write *OK* for any sentence that has no error. ✓

1. We were pleased to hear about you accepting the transfer to our department.

1. _____ ____

✓

2. As you know, these kind of pagers have just been approved for sale.

2. _____ ____

3. In the supply room is the paper and the envelopes that must be delivered to the Word Processing Department.

3. _____ ____

4. As indicated earlier, the firm of Rothman & Savino represent us in this lawsuit.

4. _____ ____

5. Aaron and I agree that the number of responses to the classified ad are very gratifying.

5. _____ ____

6. Are they the consultants whom Ms. Spradlin chose to complete the market research?

6. _____ ____

7. There's only two other companies that manufacture these kinds of diskettes.

7. _____ ____

8. Yes, either Dennis or Julia are scheduled to prepare the presentation for the sales meeting.

8. _____ ____

9. Ms. Kanise was sure impressed when she saw the increase in sales and decrease in overhead expenses.

9. _____ ____

10. All the nurses except Helen and I attended the Infection Control seminar.

10. _____ ____

11. Of course, I would of stayed later to complete the report if I had known about the deadline.

11. _____ ____

12. Frank was some unprepared for the increase in demand for the upgraded computers.

12. _____ ____

13. Don't Cassandra know that the new billing system will not be in effect until February 1?

13. _____ ____

14. In our opinion, there new store should be very successful.

14. _____ ____

15. The Marcus's purchased a condominium near the shopping center.

15. _____ ____

16. Jun Koo, as everyone knows, manages the Inventory Department very good.

16. _____ ____

17. Every corporate manager at Zettler Electronics Company was asked to reduce his staff by 20 percent.

17. _____ ____

18. Only one of the printers whom we consulted were able to meet our tight schedule.

18. _____ ____

19. Before you make the flight reservations for you and I, check the flight information on the Internet.

19. _____ ____

20. Two of our technicians, Mr. Nourai and her, will conduct software training for all employees.

20. _____ ____

21. Have you been able to find the reason for the discrepancy in the two accounts?

21. _____ ____

22. We plan on provide upgraded computers with modems for all employees.

22. _____ ____

D   Testing Your Writing Skill

Each of the following expressions contains a preposition. Use each of the expressions correctly in a sentence. Write your answers on the lines provided.   ✓

1. adapted to

_____

_____   1. ____

2. consist of

_____

_____   2. ____

3. depend on

_____

_____   3. ____

4. part with

_____

_____   4. ____

5. speak to

_____

_____   5. ____

E   Proofreading Practice

Correct any errors in the following paragraphs from a memo. Write your corrections on the lines provided.   ✓

Christine Hernandez and I are planning on offering a seminar that is specifically designed to meet the needs of aspiring graphic designers. We would like for you to review the enclosed materials in regards to this proposed seminar.

As you will see, Christine and myself estimate that we will have about 200 attendees. We are planning on charging each attendee $75 for registration and materials. Our tentative schedule includes guest speakers. Beside some of the area's most successful graphic designers, we will have the president's of two of Chicago's most prestigious design firms.

Christine and me have not yet decided where the seminar will be held at, but we will select a site inside of the next two weeks. If you or your assistant need any additional copies of the enclosed agenda, you may get more off Jeanne Leland in the Conferences and Exhibits Department.

 **SECTION 3.10** CONJUNCTIONS

A Classifying Conjunctions

Underline each conjunction in the following sentences. Then, on the line at the right, label each conjunction as *coordinating, correlative,* or *subordinating.* ✓

1. Before Juanita processes the orders, ask her to double-check the account numbers.

    1. _____ ____

2. We hired additional staff members for our Phoenix, Boston, and Detroit offices.

    2. _____ ____

3. Spencer acts as if he were personally responsible for acquiring the Landau account.

    3. _____ ____

4. Warren or Ramona will update our Web site.

    4. _____ ____

5. Warren and Ramona are updating our Web site.

    5. _____ ____

6. Not only Peggy but also Angelo will conduct the seminar

    6. _____ ____

7. Whenever you have time, please review the brochure.

    7. _____ ____

8. The Morrises wanted to vacation in Canada, but their children wanted to vacation in Florida.

    8. _____ ____

9. Although we have compared several models of computers, we have not yet decided which model to purchase.

    9. _____ ____

10. Please proofread these invoices whenever you have time.

    10. _____ ____

11. Both the customer service representatives and the programmers are responsible for our excellent service record.

    11. _____ ____

12. As soon as you complete your analysis, contact the client in Spain.

    12. _____ ____

13. The landscaping company planted trees, flowers, and shrubs outside the mall.

    13. _____ ____

14. You may make flight reservations with a travel agency or with the airline.

    14. _____ ____

15. Neither the attorney nor the paralegal had a copy of the contract.

    15. _____ ____

B Proofreading for Conjunction Errors

Underline any conjunction errors in the following sentences, and write your corrections on the lines provided. Write *OK* for any sentence that has no error. ✓

1. The primary reason for inviting Ms. Latisha is because she is considered an expert on investments.

    1. _____ ____

2. All purchase orders over $250 must be approved by Marvin or by Arlene.

    2. _____ ____

✓

3. This policy covers neither fire or flood damage.

3. _____ _____

4. During the meeting we not only agreed to produce the candidate's campaign advertisements but also to conduct the press conferences.

4. _____ _____

5. They will have only two weeks to conduct the training seminars, and they are certain that they will get the job done on time.

5. _____ _____

6. Product testers were selected because of their ability to be objective nor impartial.

6. _____ _____

7. We were specifically instructed either to send the completed form to the Personnel Department or calling Personnel with the information.

7. _____ _____

8. Although the surgery was successful, the patient was still apprehensive.

8. _____ _____

9. You may transfer the funds either by telephone and by computer.

9. _____ _____

10. Keenen said that he will go to the presentation with you and that he might be late.

10. _____ _____

11. The company was successful before it became famous.

11. _____ _____

12. Glen answered the questions quickly, correctly, or authoritatively.

12. _____ _____

13. Do not register for the conference except you are sure Mr. Cummings will approve the travel expense.

13. _____ _____

14. The reason for the change in the itinerary is that the flight has been delayed.

14. _____ _____

15. When she returned from her trip, Ms. Torres looked like she was very tired.

15. _____ _____

16. The new promotional campaign will stress our high-quality products and our outstanding service.

16. _____ _____

17. Being that our department is understaffed, we are all working overtime.

17. _____ _____

18. Even though Dominic pretends like he is shy, he is really quite outgoing.

18. _____ _____

19. Darnell has always enjoyed both writing advertising copy and demonstrating new products for customers.

19. _____ _____

20. I especially enjoyed the speaker's lively manner but her interesting anecdotes.

20. _____ _____

21. Like Ms. Levakis said, change is the only thing that's constant in business.

21. _____ _____

22. Patients may not receive aspirin without written permission from their doctors.

22. _____ _____

23. Both Dean and I enjoy taking photographs and jogging.

23. _____ _____

24. Philip Whitacre is the manager which is responsible.

24. _____ _____

25. Each of the laboratory technicians is experienced in analyzing blood samples and to identify blood types.

25. _____ _____

NAME _____

C Selecting the Correct Conjunction

On the line at the right, write the conjunction that would correctly complete each sentence. Some answers may vary.   ✓

1. Jason was surprised at the news, _____ he tried to remain calm.

1. _____ _____

2. Sometimes Rebekah acts _____ she were solely responsible for the success of the new product line.

2. _____ _____

3. Yes, I'm certain _____ Allegra is responsible for getting the invoices approved in a timely manner.

3. _____ _____

4. Kendra and Damon work well as a team, _____ you said they would.

4. _____ _____

5. We will not reassign any operating room personnel _____ Dr. Waite gives his approval.

5. _____ _____

6. _____ you specified, we have reinvested your stock dividend.

6. _____ _____

7. Do you know _____ Dr. Melrose has left?

7. _____ _____

8. As Heidi Simon explained, the reason we are advertising on the World Wide Web is _____ most of our customers are Internet users.

8. _____ _____

9. _____ I conducted the research, I investigated appropriate sites on the Internet.

9. _____ _____

10. The store was closed, _____ Leslie did not seem to mind.

10. _____ _____

D Writing Skill

For each of the following conjunctions, write a sentence that uses the conjunction. Write your answers on the lines provided.   ✓

1. although

_____
_____ _____

2. before

_____
_____ _____

3. even if

_____
_____ _____

4. since

_____
_____ _____

5. that

_____   ___

6. unless

_____   ___

7. until

_____   ___

8. either . . . or

_____   ___

9. whether

_____   ___

10. while

_____   ___

E Proofreading Practice

Proofread the following memo and correct any errors. Write your corrections on the lines provided. Assume that names of people are correct.

MEMO TO:	All Employees	_____ ___
FROM:	Dwayne Calder, Presidant	_____ ___
DATE:	September 5, <YEAR>	_____ ___
SUBJECT:	Cost-Saving Measures	_____ ___

As we all know, this year have been very challenging for hospitals. For the past few weeks, we been asking employees for they're suggestions for cutting budgets and streamlining procedures without compromising patient care. Thanks to all of you that submitted suggestions for consideration.

Beginning September 15, managers from all departments will meet to review the suggestions and to recommend actions to be taken.

Being that this will be a hospital-wide initiative, we would appreciate your cooperation in this matter.

SECTION 4.1 SENTENCE ENDERS

A Punctuating Correctly

On the lines provided, indicate whether periods, question marks, or exclamation points are needed at the points marked by parentheses. If none of these marks is needed, write *None*. ✓

1. Congratulations( ) You certainly earned your promotion to general manager.

   1. _____ _____

2. Frank asked why the sales were down for the last quarter( )

   2. _____ _____

3. Reynaldo called both Ralph and Jeremy, didn't he( )

   3. _____ _____

4. Will you please enter the figures and have the computer generate a graph( )

   4. _____ _____

5. The service was horrible; I'll starve before I go to that restaurant again( )

   5. _____ _____

6. Haley, do you think that Mark and Melinda will buy that house( )

   6. _____ _____

7. At our next staff meeting, we will discuss the following:
   1. E-mail policies( )
   2. Voice mail courtesy( )
   3. Fax cover sheets( )

   7. _____ _____
      _____ _____
      _____ _____

8. At the next staff meeting, we will discuss:
   1. E-mail policies( )
   2. Voice mail courtesy( )
   3. Fax cover sheets( )

   8. _____ _____
      _____ _____
      _____ _____

9. Have you already mailed your application( ) check( ) room deposit( )

   9. _____ _____
      _____ _____
      _____ _____

10. May we have your decision by August 1( )

    10. _____ _____

11. Good luck( )We wish you the best in your college career.

    11. _____ _____

12. Mr. Nelson made the recommendation, didn't he( )

    12. _____ _____

13. Has the new manager met with all the supervisors yet( )

    13. _____ _____

14. What a superb idea( ) Who suggested it?

    14. _____ _____

15. George asked who would be driving the tour bus( ) when it left for New York.

    15. _____ _____

16. Are each of the camp instructors trained in CPR( )

    16. _____ _____

17. After smelling smoke, Margaret shouted, "Call 911( )"

    17. _____ _____

18. Answering all questions(,) truthfully is the best strategy.   18. _____ ____

19. The base price of the computer is $1900(.) Software is priced separately.   19. _____ ____

20. Can the PowerPoint slides be updated in two hours for the 10:30 presentation( )?   20. _____ ____

21. Fred had questioned the possibility of mailing the report by noon( ).   21. _____ ____

22. My expenses were $975(.) for the trip.   22. _____ ____

23. Her new business will be located at 1831 South Harrison Blvd.( )   23. _____ ____

24. Has Miquel finished the estimates for the mall construction( )?   24. _____ ____

25. After graduation she plans to work for Office Systems, Inc(.)   25. _____ ____

B Punctuation Practice

Insert periods, question marks, and exclamation points as needed in the following sentences. Write *OK* beside correct sentences.   ✓

1. Mrs. Dakis asked if I could watch her children until 1:30 a.m.   1. OK

2. Jason M. Raduly III will be our guest speaker for the seminar .   2. .

3. Karel asked if I could work next Saturday   3. .

4. Surveyed employees are interested in (1) health insurance, (2) life insurance, and (3) dental insurance.   4. OK

5. Surveyed employees are interested in:

   1. Health insurance   5. →

   2. Life insurance   →

   3. Dental insurance   →

6. Surveyed employees are interested in the following insurance coverage:

   1. Health insurance   6. →

   2. Life insurance   →

   3. Dental insurance   →

7. Surveyed employees are interested in the following insurance coverage:

   1. Approximately 95 percent want health insurance   7. →

   2. At least 80 percent want life insurance   →

   3. About 60 percent want dental insurance   .

✓

8. The executive asked why the report did not include last
month's figures

8. _⊘_ _____

9. When is Madeline going to Jacksonville, Miami, and Tampa?

9. _OK_ _____

10. Congratulations, Ms. Graybill, on getting us the biggest
contract in our company's history

10. _⊘_ _____

C   Proofreading for Verb Errors

Underline each error in the following sentences, and write your corrections on the lines
provided. Write *OK* for any sentence that has no error.   ✓

1. ~~Does~~ *Do* Darlene and Patricia want to update the software
immediately?

1. ____*Do*____ _____

2. Florence raised a question concerning the dates of
the conference.

2. _OK_ _____

3. Is it true that neither Dana nor Joellen <u>have</u> *has* confirmed
seats on the flights?

3. ____*has*____ _____

4. If the supervisor leaves you in charge, you should strive
to achieve company goals.

4. _Ok_ _____

5. Gracie ~~seen~~ *saw* the carpet and paint samples, hasn't she?

5. ____*saw*____ _____

6. Only one of the applicants who ~~was~~ *has* interviewed have
completed community college.

6. ____*has*____ _____

7. Have Leigh, Nelson, and Ginger ~~went~~ *gone* to the warehouse?

7. ____*gone*____ _____

8. That same issue has been <u>risen</u> *raised* by five different
departments.

8. _*raised*_ _____

9. Is either Mike or Emily available to proofread the report?

9. ____*Ok*____ _____

10. If I ~~was~~ *were* president, I <u>would</u> promote Sue to vice president.

10. ____*were*____ _____

11. The computer disk with the inventory figures <u>have</u> *has*
been misplaced.

11. ____*has*____ _____

12. Baxter ~~done~~ *did* an excellent job in recruiting our new
nursing assistants.

12. ____*did*____ _____

13. The prime acreage for development lays just north
of the city.

13. _____ _____

14. ~~Have~~ *has* all our club members did their volunteer work for
this month?

14. ____*has*____ _____

15. As most of you are aware, the new building that *has* been
under construction <u>was</u> damaged during the storm.

15. ____*has*____ _____

16. Moira and Steven has already reviewed the advertising
copy for the new brochure.

16. ____*have*____ _____

17. At the next board meeting we will rise the issue of
expanding the incentive plan to include all employees.

17. _*with raise*_ _____

18. Jared <u>had</u> *has* began his research before he received the
notice about the cancellation of the project.

18. ____*has*____ _____

D Punctuation Application

In the following memo, strike through exclamation points, periods, and question marks that are incorrectly used. Write the correct punctuation beside the incorrect punctuation. Remember not to overuse the exclamation point.

✓

MEMO TO: Sean Templeton

FROM: Dawn Blevins

DATE: June 30, <YEAR>

SUBJECT: Patrelli Account

Congratulations? Winning the Patrelli account from our competition is quite a feather in your cap? Ms. Harrelson, our new marketing vice president, called just as soon as she saw the order! She asked me if you did anything spectacular to convince Mr. Patrelli to buy from us?

Your outstanding PowerPoint slide presentation definitely made an impression on Mr. Patrelli. The information on the slides was clear and placed attractively! When you quickly and accurately answered his questions, he was favorably impressed and felt confident that you knew your product! Also, when you used our spreadsheet program to predict his profits at the various prices, I saw his expression change from negative to positive?

You certainly did your homework for this presentation? Thanks for your hard work in obtaining this account.

SECTION 4.2 COMMAS

 Correcting Comma Errors

Underline any errors in the use of commas in the following sentences, and write your corrections on the lines provided. Write *omit comma* for commas that are not needed, and write *OK* for any sentence that is correct.   ✓

1. Hilary S. Miller, M.D., has been instrumental in developing standards for pediatric medicine.

    1. Miller, MD, ____

2. Being concerned about the public relations aspect of the project, we asked Mr. Marvin his opinion on our strategies.

    2. OK ____

3. Erin Mathison, who worked with us for ten years, opened her own accounting firm.

    3. OK ____

4. Do you know, what the speed of the modems is on our new computers?

    4. ____

5. Only those taxpayers, who wrote a letter with their tax returns, should be eligible for a refund.

    5. OK ____

6. A copy of your passport should be mailed directly to your tour director, not to me.

    6. ____

7. The man, whom you met this morning, donated one of his kidneys to his son.

    7. OK ____

8. July 4, 1996 marked the two hundredth anniversary of our country.

    8. ____

9. Is she planning to go to Dallas, Texas in two weeks?

    9. ____

10. By October 2018 we will have paid off the mortgage on our beautiful, well-constructed home.

    10. ____

11. Construction on the mall, which was to be completed August 14, was delayed because of bad weather.

    11. OK ____

12. Lamont who is planning to be a sports broadcaster is a communications major.

    12. ____

13. Thank you Peggy for being a competent assistant.

    13. ____

14. His chronic absenteeism, in my opinion, will keep him from getting a promotion.

    14. ____

15. Larry approves all major expenditures, and he co-signs any check over $5000.

    15. ____

16. Craig spoke, and Marcus listened.

    16. ____

17. Darius, Lydia, and Susanna will attend the first session.

    17. ____

18. You may apply for the loan in person, over the telephone or by computer.

18. _____ ____

19. Exercise equipment, workout clothes, athletic shoes, etc. will be included in our fall sale.

19. _____ ____

20. To be a successful job candidate you must be confident and well prepared.

20. _____ ____

21. As soon as you complete the form return it to the Human Resources Department.

21. _____ ____

22. For more information on our products please visit our Web site.

22. _____ ____

23. An effective strategy in my opinion would be to advertise on the Internet.

23. _____ ____

24. Our latest franchise will open on Monday August 15.

24. _____ ____

25. Three of the candidates for the customer service position, currently work in the Inventory Management Department.

25. _____ ____

B More Comma Errors

Underline any errors in the use of commas in the following sentences, and write your corrections on the lines provided. Write *omit comma* for commas that are not needed, and write *OK* for any sentence that is correct.

1. Danielle will take a course in literature, or a course in composition.

1. _____ ____

2. Mr. Felter has enclosed for your approval, several proofs for the advertising campaign.

2. _____ ____

3. Have you signed up for the company's new retirement plan)Meg?

3. _____ ____

4. Change our address to 5,500 Belmont Place.

4. _____ ____

5. Alex set up the computer in his office, and installed six software packages.

5. _____ ____

6. Les agreed, but Mary disagreed.

6. _____ ____

7. We plan to use many advertising methods: newspapers, magazines, radio, Internet etc.

7. _____ ____

8. Ms. Hill flew to Dallas, drove to Houston, and then flew to San Antonio.

8. _____ ____

9. Kyle, Wendy, and Abe, have demonstrated their willingness to work on this dangerous project.

9. _____ ____

10. Improving production efficiency for the compact disks, will be difficult without buying new equipment.

10. _____ ____

11. Disks, paper, ribbons, etc. are big sellers because we have the best prices in town.

11. _____ ____

12. Knowing that the price of coffee would probably increase John bought 20 cases that will be delivered next week.

12. _____ ____

2/8/02

✓

13. Before you meet with your new client, study his stock portfolio and his recent purchases.

13. ___OK___ ___

14. No, your prescription will not be ready until after 5 p.m. today.

14. _____ ___

15. Matthew flew to Atlanta, where he met with several detectives.

15. ___OK___ ___

16. Leah is in charge of the promotions for the trade show, and Faina is responsible for the displays.

16. _____ ___

17. Before we purchase the property, we would like a structural engineer to inspect the building.

17. _____ ___

18. Our house is located at 1,674 Delmar Avenue.

18. _____ ___

19. Have you told Mr. Wells, Ms. Cortez, and Mr. Thornton, about the meeting?

19. _____ ___

20. After we present the proposed development plan, the city council will vote on the proposal.

20. _____ ___

21. Although we were aware of the upcoming merger, we were surprised by the sudden announcement.

21. _____ ___

22. Our newest staff member, Geneva Mansfield, graduated *from Champion College in January.*

22. _____ ___

23. The most recent school operating levy, which was on the November ballot, was defeated.

23. _____ ___

24. My new laptop computer weighs 2 pounds, 8 ounces.

24. _____ ___

25. Lawrence Tyrell, Ph.D. is the new superintendent of schools for our district.

25. _____ ___

26. Our computer network specialists will attend training sessions at Software Solutions, Inc., in Darlington, Michigan.

26. _____ ___

27. Brenna is an enthusiastic, dynamic salesperson.

27. _____ ___

28. You may have noticed, Mr. Engle, that next year's budget is based on conservative sales estimates.

28. _____ ___

29. The first issue of *Computer Times* magazine will be published on April 5, 1999.

29. _____ ___

30. On March 16, 34 owners of dealerships in the tri-state area will tour our manufacturing plant.

30. _____ ___

31. In February, 1999, we will move to our new headquarters facility in Groveport.

31. _____ ___

32. Brendan Carle, who is our legal counsel, advised us to seek a compromise with the complainant.

32. _____ ___

33. To receive a free copy of our catalog, simply complete and mail the enclosed self-addressed postcard.

33. _____ ___

34. Obviously we are curious to find out who will be elected as the next state senator for our district.

34. _____ _____

35. We have, at your suggestion, installed video monitors at all the store entrances.

35. _____ _____

C Pronoun Review

Underline any errors in pronoun use in the following sentences, and write your corrections on the lines provided. Write *OK* for any sentence that has no error.   ✓

1. Since Anna has taken more software courses than me, Mr. Kline will probably choose her for the position.

1. _____ _____

2. Do you know whom was responsible for checking his references?

2. _____ _____

3. Give this faster computer to whoever you think needs it most.

3. _____ _____

4. Both of us were asked to discuss these issues with Ms. Helms and him next Friday.

4. _____ _____

5. David assigned Internet addresses to the new employees, William and she.

5. _____ _____

6. Between you and me, I don't think that the paint color matches the carpet.

6. _____ _____

7. Does anyone know who Mrs. Oberlin has promoted to office manager?

7. _____ _____

8. If I were her, I would ask about the status of the report.

8. _____ _____

9. Of course, I knew immediately that it was him when I heard his voice.

9. _____ _____

10. Mr. Jasper doesn't know to whom he should address the letter.

10. _____ _____

11. Jason, as well as me, approved purchasing the microwave.

11. _____ _____

12. Do you know whom has been selected to receive the cost effectiveness award?

12. _____ _____

13. Do you think that the new company car will be given to us or to they?

13. _____ _____

14. She arranged a meeting with we computer operators for noon today.

14. _____ _____

15. Please give Nancy and I the specifications as soon as they are available.

15. _____ _____

16. Jane gave Margaret and we free passes to attend the hockey game.

16. _____ _____

17. I left a message for Ellen Masters, but her has not returned my call.

17. _____ _____

18. Most of our customers are business people whom have dealt with our company for a number of years.

18. _____ _____

✓

19. Between you and I, the cost estimates for the proposal
    are too high.   19. _____ ____

20. It must have been him who ordered the new projection
    equipment for the conference room.   20. _____ ____

21. Wallace and I will oversee the move to the new building. 21. _____ ____

22. Whom will make the arrangements for the house closing
    on the property—the buyer broker or the Realtor?   22. _____ ____

23. The Albreckts invited my husband and I to vacation
    with them in Florida.   23. _____ ____

24. Mr. Shimota plans to schedule a meeting with they
    this afternoon to discuss the progress on the Lawrence
    account.   24. _____ ____

25. Megan Spencer, who we consider our top designer,
    has been promoted to the position of design director.   25. _____ ____

D Predicate Agreement Review

Underline any errors in predicate agreement in the following sentences, and write your
corrections on the lines provided. Write *OK* for any sentence that is correct.   ✓

1. Each of the supervisors was asked to provide a list
   of needed repairs.   1. _____ ____

2. There is plenty of suggestions but no realistic solutions
   to the problems.   2. _____ ____

3. The specifications that they gave us for the wheelchair
   access ramp were accurate.   3. _____ ____

4. Does he know whether Wanda or Patrick is the manager
   for the Forest City branch?   4. _____ ____

5. Which government regulations affects the transport of
   goods across state lines?   5. _____ ____

6. Doesn't Earl and Henry know that the article must be
   released to the media this afternoon?   6. _____ ____

7. In which office is the scanner and the fax machine?   7. _____ ____

8. Obviously, neither Geraldo nor Julianna want to
   withdraw from this experiment at such a critical time.   8. _____ ____

9. Ms. Mullins is one of those executives who demands as
   much of themselves as they demand of others.   9. _____ ____

10. Yes, John told me that there was only two weeks left to
    apply for the job.   10. _____ ____

11. Sarah's manager, as well as all managers in this region,
    were traveling to the international meeting in Denmark.   11. _____ ____

12. Neither Elizabeth nor Susan mind staffing the company
    exhibit at the county fair.   12. _____ ____

Assume that the following letter is correct except that there are too many commas. Underline each comma that is not needed, along with the word before and after the unneeded comma. Be sure to check all parts of the letter, not just the body, for errors. ✓

July 23, <YEAR>

Mr. H. David Tarragon
Strategic Investments Company
2298 Fifth Avenue
New York, NY, 10012

Dear Mr. Tarragon:

    Enclosed, is a transfer rollover request form dated today and signed by my client, Rebecca Annette Turpish. In our meeting today, she asked that this rollover take place immediately; thus, please process this request, as soon as possible.

    Note, that this is a transfer to a new 403(b) plan, and that no amount should be withheld for tax purposes. A new 403(b) account has been established, with World Wide Investment Company, for the purpose of receiving these funds. All checks should be made payable to World Wide Investment Company FBO of Rebecca Annette Turpish, and forwarded to the address below:

                Mr. Lane S. Williams
                Park Circle Investment Services
                Post Office Box 249
                Shelby, NC, 28150

    This letter is to serve as an official acceptance of these funds on behalf of my firm. Please contact me, at 704-555-8238, with any questions that you may have. Thank you, Mr. Tarragon, for your help with this transaction.

Sincerely,

(Mr.) Lane S. Williams, Branch Manager
Registered Principal
Investment Consultant
Authorized Signature of Acceptance

scc
Enclosure

 **SECTION 4.3**   SEMICOLONS, COLONS,
AND DASHES

 Using Semicolons, Colons, and Dashes Correctly

On the lines provided, indicate whether semicolons, colons, or dashes are needed at the
points marked by parentheses. If none of these marks is needed, write *None*.   ✓

1. Note the coding by shape for highway signs( ) octagon
   for STOP, rectangle for information, and triangle
   for yield.   1. _____ _____

2. The enclosed brochure describes the following modes
   of tour transportation( ) air-conditioned motor coach,
   train, or plane.   2. _____ _____

3. When you mark your ballot for committee members,
   indicate the term of service( ) namely, one year, two
   years, or five years.   3. _____ _____

4. Partial payment is required when you make reservations
   for the cruise( ) you may, however, pay by check or
   credit card.   4. _____ _____

5. The British spelling of several words is different from
   the American spelling( ) for example, *labour, theatre,* and
   criticise.   5. _____ _____

6. When the elevator got stuck between floors, Sheila( )
   no, it was Roberta( ) used the emergency telephone to
   call a security officer.   6. _____ _____

7. The following products are our best sellers( ) cellular
   phones, fax machines, and cordless telephones.   7. _____ _____

8. Monitors, laser printers, modems, and microphones( )
   these items will be discounted by 25 percent during
   our Labor Day sale.   8. _____ _____

9. The reasons for upgrading our in-store advertising
   displays are to( ) attract attention, emphasize seasonal
   merchandise, and target special age groups.   9. _____ _____

10. Our refund policy applies to purchases made throughout
    the year( ) Every returned item must be accompanied
    by the original sales receipt.   10. _____ _____

11. Plan your research paper( ) that is, prepare a tentative
    outline before you go to the library.   11. _____ _____

12. Marty Rubin excelled in his studies( ) and graduated
    with honors.   12. _____ _____

13. Tanya is our patient advocate( ) she is the person who
    values your constructive comments.   13. _____ _____

14. Please order these items for delivery before our noon
    rush tomorrow( ) napkins, paper cups, straws, and
    sandwich bags.   14. _____ _____

15. The purpose of each trip must be noted on the
expense account( ) moreover, a receipt must
accompany each expense over $10.

15. _____ ____

B   More Semicolons, Colons, and Dashes

On the lines provided, indicate whether semicolons, colons, or dashes are needed at the
points marked by parentheses. If none of these marks is needed, write *None*.

1. Let's draft the report before lunch( ) we'll begin
editing it about 1:30 p.m.

1. _____ ____

2. Let's draft the report before lunch( ) and begin editing
it about 1:30 p.m.

2. _____ ____

3. Remember( ) Drive carefully because the snow has made
the roads treacherous.

3. _____ ____

4. Address the envelope as follows( ) Mrs. W. H. Champion,
243 Edins Road, St. Louis, MO 63132.

4. _____ ____

5. Ms. Susan Lane( ) she's our vice president for
communications( ) is extremely talented.

5. _____ ____

6. The two brands of computers were equivalent; therefore,
we looked at our next important consideration( ) cost.

6. _____ ____

7. You will receive coupons worth $25( ) only good credit
customers receive them.

7. _____ ____

8. Charles reached his sales quota two months early( )
quite a feat for someone without previous sales
experience.

8. _____ ____

9. Your tour price covers the following( ) two meals per day,
all transportation, transfers, and two plays.

9. _____ ____

10. Lee selected the carpet and paint( ) a horrible
combination of colors.

10. _____ ____

C   Punctuation Checkup

Underline any punctuation errors in the following sentences, and write your
corrections on the lines provided. Write *OK* for any sentence that has no error.

1. The infomercial has been especially effective in
increasing orders—extremely effective!

1. _____ ____

2. Has our Marketing Department considered seasonal
discounts? special floor displays? direct-mail advertising?

2. _____ ____

3. Dennis Rutledge hired a new lab assistant, he seems
competent and friendly.

3. _____ ____

4. First, brainstorm the new advertisement—do you
generally do that—then begin the design process.

4. _____ ____

5. It is important: that we review the procedures manual
carefully, revise it as necessary, and print and
distribute copies to all employees.

5. _____ ____

✓

6. Capstone Electronics will introduce a new laptop computer next week, it will be in retail stores within the month.

6. _____ ____

7. Our best cameras have been sold; we should, however, receive a big shipment before the holiday season.

7. _____ ____

8. This product is unique—not only in design, but also in function.

8. _____ ____

9. For no extra charge, you will receive with your order: a box of high-quality disks and a cleaning kit.

9. _____ ____

10. Please send your completed loan application to: the Personal Loan Department.

10. _____ ____

11. Following this simple procedure—have you tried it yet—will surely save you time.

11. _____ ____

12. If you want more information on financial planning, read Chapter III. of this book.

12. _____ ____

13. Sales representatives must meet certain requirements to apply for the sales management position, for instance, they must have at least three years' experience.

13. _____ ____

14. Congratulations. The Board of Directors applauds your willingness to head the volunteer staff at the homeless shelter.

14. _____ ____

15. Fred Gatlin is retiring this year, isn't he.

15. _____ ____

16. You must pay for the conference by October 5 to receive the discount; please include your check for $75.00 with your registration form.

16. _____ ____

17. Ms. Trexler asked why the computers had not been tagged with inventory numbers?

17. _____ ____

18. Mr. Mason called to say that he would not be in the office today, his flight from Detroit was canceled because of the weather.

18. _____ ____

19. Several people have already registered for the training session for our updated software, including: Steve Billings, Virginia Holtz, and Tanya Geiger.

19. _____ ____

20. Ms. Stansbury has reviewed your proposal, she will make a decision within ten days.

20. _____ ____

21. Will you please make the travel arrangements for the sales conference in Brussels?

21. _____ ____

22. Based on our research Mr. Wentworth we should upgrade our computers in all departments of the hospital.

22. _____ ____

23. Should we ship these packages for overnight delivery or for two-day delivery.

23. _____ ____

24. When Kathy returned from the conference she shared the information she obtained about distance learning.

24. _____ ____

D Adjective and Adverb Review

Underline any errors in adjective and adverb use in the following sentences, and write your corrections on the lines provided. Write *OK* for any sentence that is correct. ✓

1. Because of increased demand for our services, we must hire a considerable larger staff of software specialists.

    1. _____ ____

2. Charleston, South Carolina, is probably more famous than any city in that state.

    2. _____ ____

3. A midnight view from the eighty second floor is impressive.

    3. _____ ____

4. Jamal was more determined to excel than any other student.

    4. _____ ____

5. Wallid wrote and recorded an excellent self instructional tape for international visitors to Cairo.

    5. _____ ____

6. Pablo Martinez was the best of the two golfers our company entered in the industrial league golf competition.

    6. _____ ____

7. Having considered the three candidates, I believe the best one was the community college student.

    7. _____ ____

8. Selling that large parcel of land will give you a real big commission.

    8. _____ ____

9. Donnis now realizes that not finishing her degree was the worse career mistake that she has ever made.

    9. _____ ____

10. Our communications tower is the tallest of any communications tower in the county.

    10. _____ ____

E Punctuation Application

Most offices use electronic mail as a convenient way to communicate easily and quickly. Even though electronic mail is often considered an informal communication method, messages should still be correct. Underline any punctuation errors, and insert needed punctuation in the body of the following electronic-mail message. ✓

As part of our ongoing training program we are pleased to offer the following mini courses Memo Writing, International Communication, Introductory PowerPoint, and Advanced PowerPoint. All employees are encouraged to participate there is no charge.

_____
_____
_____
_____

The courses will be taught simultaneously on Monday Tuesday and Thursday nights from 6:30 to 9:30 therefore each employee can take only one course at a time. Depending on demand, the courses will be repeated the first two weeks of next month.

_____
_____
_____
_____

All courses run for two weeks and they begin Monday February 1. Please sign up by return e-mail Your registration will be confirmed by e-mail within two days. Register today Classes are limited to the first 15 people who request them.

_____
_____
_____

 **SECTION 4.4**

QUOTATION MARKS, PARENTHESES, AND APOSTROPHES

A Punctuating Correctly

Underline any errors in the use of quotation marks, parentheses, and apostrophes in the following sentences. Write your corrections on the lines provided. Write *OK* for any sentence that is correct.   ✓

1. Make your reservations as soon as possible (many people will be traveling to Myrtle Beach during July.)

    1. _____ ____

2. Kim wouldnt have missed her plane if the weather had been clear.

    2. _____ ____

3. The so-called management consultant submitted a report that embarrassed the person who hired him.

    3. _____ ____

4. "The price of coffee," according to the article, will not be affected by the drought in Brazil."

    4. _____ ____

5. According to the article, "The price of coffee will not be affected by the drought in Brazil."

    5. _____ ____

6. The hospital spokesperson said, "Our doctors can't afford to pay these exorbitant malpractice insurance premiums"!

    6. _____ ____

7. "Its an environment in which creative people thrive," the recruiter said proudly.

    7. _____ ____

8. When the jewelry is delivered (have you called the messenger yet)? please ask the messenger to get a signed receipt.

    8. _____ ____

9. His interesting video, "Buying and Selling Real Estate for Fun and Profit", has many tips for enthusiastic entrepreneurs.

    9. _____ ____

10. At the next meeting (April 4 or 5), we will discuss the need to implement a more sophisticated computer security system.

    10. _____ ____

11. When completing the application, use black ink to mark with X's all the boxes that apply.

    11. _____ ____

12. "All requests for new expenses must be submitted before August 5," according to the e-mail, "in addition, each new expense must be justified."

    12. _____ ____

13. Nancy announced "that after graduation she would seek a marketing position in the southeastern part of the United States."

    13. _____ ____

14. James specifically said, "Send the checks by UPS;" therefore, we followed his instructions.

    14. _____ ____

15. All of the equipment will be delivered by June 15 (our fiscal year ends June 30), therefore, we will claim the cost this year as a capital expense.

15. _____ ____

16. The following items will be on sale next week (look for our full-page ad in Sundays newspaper): televisions, portable CD players, microwave ovens, and luggage.

16. _____ ____

17. Order extra copies (Just call our toll-free number) for a fraction of the original cost.

17. _____ ____

18. The branch managers dont know that tomorrow's meeting has been rescheduled for Friday.

18. _____ ____

19. We will send you (and the other cardholders in your family, of course,) your new cards by September 1.

19. _____ ____

20. Label each package "Fragile", David, and take them to the post office immediately.

20. _____ ____

21. The headline for the full-page ad will read, "Now's the time to plan for retirement".

21. _____ ____

22. Below the headline the copy will read as follows: "Buy brand names for nearly 60 percent off list prices"!

22. _____ ____

23. His so-called "dedicated employee" called in sick today to play in the golf tournament.

23. _____ ____

24. Mr. Kalton asked, "Who's available to help me plan our company picnic?"

24. _____ ____

25. "Will it be possible to pay for the computer by credit card" asked Ms. Chung?

25. _____ ____

26. Let's ask Ruth "whether the computers will be delivered by November 8."

26. _____ ____

27. You should buy a scanner (a device that enters images or text into your computer) to reproduce pictures of available homes for advertising purposes.

27. _____ ____

28. When you land on Maui, (your tickets are enclosed) a tour guide will meet you at the airport.

28. _____ ____

29. "All the news that's fit to print," is the slogan of *The New York Times*.

29. _____ ____

30. When Jack received the award, did he actually ask, "Are you sure that there isn't some mistake?"

30. _____ ____

B Proofreading for Punctuation

Test your skill at finding errors in the following sentences. Underline each error, and write your correction on the line provided. Write *OK* for any sentence that is correct. ✓

1. Elizabeth Thomas is working in the Greensboro branch, isn't she.

1. _____ ____

2. All the members of our technical support staff are knowledgeable, and eager to help customers solve their problems.

2. _____ ____

✓

3. Our new restaurant (the one in the Haywood Mall), is
   expected to gross about $750,000 a year.   3. _____ _____

4. Raquel S. Perez, Ph.D. is the number-one candidate for
   the product research position.   4. _____ _____

5. "If you need more time," said Mrs. Denver, We will
   extend your deadline by one week".   5. _____ _____

6. Because Ms. Rochester is out of town (she's in Austin,
   Texas,) Mr. Rubin will help process your loan application. 6. _____ _____

7. Lettuce, tomatoes, cucumbers, carrots, dressing, these
   are the basic ingredients for a tossed salad.   7. _____ _____

8. The former manager of our Marketing Division, is now
   on a retainer as a consultant.   8. _____ _____

9. Remember; It is important to call 911 immediately when
   an emergency situation occurs.   9. _____ _____

10. Josh, Millie and Preston will coordinate shipping during
    the peak holiday season.   10. _____ _____

11. Prices of most products continue to rise prices of
    calculators and other electronic goods, however, have
    been steadily declining.   11. _____ _____

12. Joseph he's our public relations director will give us
    instructions on how to deal with the media.   12. _____ _____

13. Most employees take work-related courses. Because of
    the company's full reimbursement policy.   13. _____ _____

14. If we finalize our report before the deadline—it's
    January 15, isn't it—we have a good chance of winning
    this cost reduction incentive.   14. _____ _____

15. It seems that many many errors are overlooked when
    documents are proofread.   15. _____ _____

16. Before Mr. Dewey returns from his vacation, let's finish
    the Campbell advertising proposal.   16. _____ _____

17. Nearly 90 percent of the targeted market who
    responded to our questionnaire, have indicated an
    interest in Saturday banking.   17. _____ _____

18. In the back of this building, is a parking garage facility
    that provides security around the clock.   18. _____ _____

19. Cathy's responsibilities include: supervising employees,
    ordering merchandise, and dealing with dissatisfied
    customers.   19. _____ _____

20. Our investment strategy as you know is to be
    conservative as we increase our many portfolios.   20. _____ _____

21. Like many physicians Dr. Hanna Johnson has
    difficulty collecting overdue bills.   21. _____ _____

22. Two decorators estimate that the cost of refurbishing our offices should not exceed $7,000.00.

22. _____ ____

23. The primary goals of these daytime seminars are to: develop employees' communication skills and to teach them basic accounting procedures.

23. _____ ____

24. The order was shipped last Friday, however, because Monday was a holiday, it was not delivered here until Tuesday.

24. _____ ____

25. Mr. Castor—he's the person in charge of mail distribution.—will explain the delays in shipping parcels.

25. _____ ____

C Punctuation Application

Add quotation marks, parentheses, and apostrophes that are needed in the following memo. Underline any punctuation errors; then insert punctuation marks where needed.

MEMO TO: Dexter Philips

FROM: Joyce Meade

DATE: September 5, <YEAR>

SUBJECT: Policy Manual

Thank you for all the time that you spent developing our new policy manual. I sent it to Gaither Printing the company you recommended early this morning.

Lewis Gaither, the owner, promised that we would have the proofs no later than September 30. Mr. Gaither didnt give me a time frame for printing the manual, but he wont do the final printing until you and I have had an opportunity to check the proofs. He said that putting the manual on disk made the printing so much faster and easier. He also said, Thanks for using software that was compatible with ours.

You completed the policy manual in record time less than two months and improved both the design and the content.

Thanks again, Dexter, for a job well done!

SECTION 4.5 CAPITALIZATION

A Correcting Capitalization Errors

Underline any capitalization errors in the following sentences, and write your corrections on the lines provided. Write *OK* for any sentence that is correct. ✓

1. Karen Wray wrote to The Internal Revenue Service about her tax situation, but the IRS has not replied yet.

    1. _____ ____

2. Dorothea Merks is retiring from AT&T on December 30.

    2. _____ ____

3. Yes, Social Security No. 041-45-6882 was printed on all of his bank statements.

    3. _____ ____

4. Barbara Stansbury recommended that I reread "Buying And Selling Real Estate," which was written by Cedric S. Webber, Ph.D.

    4. _____ ____

5. We agreed to purchase 35 Davis Electronics Computers and Printers.

    5. _____ ____

6. I volunteered to pick up Mr. Wellsley at the Airport at 6:30 a.m. tomorrow.

    6. _____ ____

7. You should call Ms. Dinero, the Manager of our branch store in Dalton, Georgia.

    7. _____ ____

8. The new auditorium at the High School in Austin, Texas, is being completed by Jaymar Construction company.

    8. _____ ____

9. Although we manufacture the scuba equipment in the north, almost 80 percent of it is sold in the south.

    9. _____ ____

10. Nathan Winters is a Vice President of Scofield Jewelry Stores in Tallahassee, Florida.

    10. _____ ____

11. In an effort to improve outpatient services, we met with the Staff and a group of hospital Volunteers.

    11. _____ ____

12. Ms. Sanford said that she read Chapter 2, "Midwives and their Responsibilities," but disagreed with the content.

    12. _____ ____

13. Store managers in the mall report that Fall sales, which included the back-to-school merchandise, were much lower than anticipated.

    13. _____ ____

14. Cathy Bennett, who is a tax attorney, holds an official position with the American Bar association.

    14. _____ ____

15. Our conference for Sales Representatives who have met their quotas is scheduled at the Four Seasons Resort on Maui.

    15. _____ ____

16. This dispute will be resolved at the federal Communications Commission's hearing on November 13.

    16. _____ ____

17. One of the subsidiaries of our Corporation distributes Bost Bakery's breads, cakes, and pies throughout the southeast.

17. _____ _____

18. At a press conference at the White House, the president discussed his plan to reduce violent crime.

18. _____ _____

19. Ask Mr. O'leary to meet with us on Friday.

19. _____ _____

20. Jeanne won first prize, which was a three-week cruise to several Pacific Islands.

20. _____ _____

21. Consumers rely on Government safety standards to protect them.

21. _____ _____

22. Our tour will take us to the Empire State Building, which is one of the tallest buildings in New York city.

22. _____ _____

23. Several Canadian Companies, most of them in Toronto or Montreal, are among our primary suppliers.

23. _____ _____

24. During the conference, please visit our hospitality suite in the Ashley Suites Hotel one block North of the Jacksonville Convention Center.

24. _____ _____

25. In addition to increasing the number of employees in several Departments, we are also enlarging our manufacturing facilities at all our locations.

25. _____ _____

B Preposition and Conjunction Review

Underline any preposition or conjunction errors in the following sentences, and write your corrections on the lines provided. Write *OK* for any sentence that has no error.

1. You cannot get a passport without you submit your birth certificate or some other acceptable proof of citizenship.

1. _____ _____

2. He decided to make an A in the course, but he made an A.

2. _____ _____

3. Have you received any more information as regards the two industries that are planning to locate here?

3. _____ _____

4. Dana should have called the doctor as soon as she became ill.

4. _____ _____

5. Do you feel like we were right to disagree with his decision?

5. _____ _____

6. Divide the prize money between the three people who tied for first place.

6. _____ _____

7. "The incentive pay plan is retroactive to July 1," Ms. Loftis explained.

7. _____ _____

8. Dr. Strokanof said that he can't help but think that the computer has a virus.

8. _____ _____

9. You should contact Anne Settlemeyer in regards to your insurance coverage.

9. _____ _____

10. Does Ms. Orsini plan on traveling by commercial or private plane?

10. _____ _____

✓

11. The safe is in back of the large pictures in Dr. Kennedy's library.

11. _____ _____

12. Ms. Lowe does not know much about driving a forklift, and she is eager to learn if she gets the job.

12. _____ _____

13. The Texas rancher said, "No cowboy likes to part from comfortable boots."

13. _____ _____

14. Yesterday, Mildred Poston copied the files off of my disk.

14. _____ _____

15. The janitor discarded the files in the box besides the trash can.

15. _____ _____

16. Without Ben's approval, I cannot agree with these new policies.

16. _____ _____

17. Her actions were justified, but I think she should have been more patient.

17. _____ _____

18. Stephen, do you know where my laptop is at?

18. _____ _____

19. Peyton's strategy is different than Wexler's strategy, but both are acceptable.

19. _____ _____

20. After lunch, please take all the outdated magazines off of the table in the reception area.

20. _____ _____

C Detecting Punctuation Errors

Underline any punctuation errors in the following sentences, and write your corrections on the lines provided. Write *OK* for any sentence that is correct.

✓

1. Twin boys. I know that you are both excited about your new arrivals.

1. _____ _____

2. To complete the wiring and installation of the fiber-optic cable on time, (the deadline is May 25) we must work overtime every week until that date.

2. _____ _____

3. When Ms. Wong heard the ridiculous price that had been quoted, she exclaimed, "How unfair."

3. _____ _____

4. My staff assistant works long hours," Ms. Baxter argued, "and he deserves a generous increase in pay."

4. _____ _____

5. One customer asked whether the store brands were as good as the national brands?

5. _____ _____

6. During our annual August car sale, you can buy the car of your choice now, and begin making payments in January.

6. _____ _____

7. Lucy handles all domestic shipments, Ethel and Fred handle all international shipments.

7. _____ _____

8. The instructions read as follows, Have each form signed by an officer of the company; also, have each signature notarized. All forms must be received by May 10.

8. _____ _____

9. Milk, bread, and sugar, these are the items that most grocery shoppers buy regularly.

9. _____ ____

10. Have you considered renting a safe deposit box at First City Bank—our rates are most reasonable—to store all your important personal documents?

10. _____ ____

D Proofreading Application

The following letter contains a variety of errors. Underline each error, and write the corrections in the spaces provided. If a line has no errors, write *OK*.   ✓

Dear Ms. Dermont:

As you reported to us, the January Statement of your credit card had several unauthorized charges. These charges are listed below;

National Airlines	$ 839.00
Holiday Rental Cars	233.46
Morgan Manor Inn	659.20
	$1,731.66

National Airlines	$ 489.00
Mountain Inn Restaurant	138.78
	$ 627.78

Each charge in the first group of charges were simply a duplicate charge for an expenditure that you actually made. All charges in the second group was for expenditures that you didnt make.

Your account has been adjusted in two separate entries; one for $1,731.66 and the other for $4,627.78. These adjustments will appear on your march Statement.

Thank you for calling this matter to our attention. Because all of these charges were made by the same firm that had access to your credit card number, you asked that we issue you a new credit card with a different number? You should receive your new card within five business days.

This matter has been turned over to the fraud department of our Company. Mr. Spears, supervisor of that Department, will be contacting you soon.

Sincerely,

SECTION 4.6 ABBREVIATIONS

A Identifying Abbreviations

In the space provided, write out the words that are abbreviated. Use a dictionary if needed. ✓

1. M.D.	_____	**1.** ____
2. D.V.M.	_____	**2.** ____
3. ACLU	_____	**3.** ____
4. A.A.	_____	**4.** ____
5. ROTC	_____	**5.** ____
6. TDD	_____	**6.** ____
7. TOEFL	_____	**7.** ____
8. USDA	_____	**8.** ____
9. VDT	_____	**9.** ____
10. APB	_____	**10.** ____
11. AMA	_____	**11.** ____
12. ATM	_____	**12.** ____
13. COD	_____	**13.** ____
14. ET	_____	**14.** ____
15. EDT	_____	**15.** ____
16. SPF	_____	**16.** ____
17. UPC	_____	**17.** ____
18. WATS	_____	**18.** ____
19. PS	_____	**19.** ____
20. RDA	_____	**20.** ____

B Abbreviation Errors

Underline any abbreviation errors in the following sentences, and write your corrections on the lines provided. Write *OK* for any sentence that is correct. ✓

1. Frieda F. Brown, Ph.D., has resigned from her teaching responsibilities to devote full time to her counseling practice.

1. _____ ____

2. Because there is no direct flight to Little Rock, you will have to change planes in Saint Louis.

2. _____ ____

3. Special weather bulletins were issued from C.B.S. and N.B.C. during the hurricane.

3. _____ _____

4. Please change my address in Scottsdale to 1922 Harrison Boulevard, N.W.

4. _____ _____

5. Have a courier service deliver the contracts to Mister Alex D. Rosenberg, 823 East 58 St., by noon.

5. _____ _____

6. Have you met Kennedy Sewell, Jr., the owner of Bagels and Stuff, Inc.?

6. _____ _____

7. Our accountant called the I.R.S. to verify that she had applied the tax code correctly when completing our tax returns.

7. _____ _____

8. In an effort to serve our clients better, we opened an office in Pt. Washington earlier this month.

8. _____ _____

9. The personnel director said that we must make any desired changes in our fringe benefits by Oct. 15.

9. _____ _____

10. Although most of our restaurants are located in the SW part of the state, we plan to expand as soon as we sell more franchises.

10. _____ _____

11. Heloise Reyes, MD, has volunteered two weeks of her time per year to practice medicine in a foreign country.

11. _____ _____

12. We do a great deal of business with S. Street Medical Supply Company on DeKalb St.

12. _____ _____

13. Because next Fri. is a holiday, all copy for Sunday's classified ad section must be received by Tues., July 1.

13. _____ _____

14. Each piece of luggage must weigh less than 45 lbs!

14. _____ _____

15. What is the invoice no. printed in the upper right-hand corner?

15. _____ _____

16. The papyrus drawing, which measures 10 by 15 in, will be matted and framed.

16. _____ _____

17. Benita's flight from Fairbanks has been delayed because of snow; it is now scheduled to leave at 11:45 p.m., instead of 11:45 a.m.

17. _____ _____

18. Our next two investment seminars will be held in Philadelphia and NYC.

18. _____ _____

19. The water tank, which has a capacity of 20,000 gal, has been inspected and approved.

19. _____ _____

20. Companies in the U.S. are helping Eastern European nations rebuild their economies.

20. _____ _____

21. We ordered extra copies of the USDA booklets that we consider helpful.

21. _____ _____

22. Amber canned 44 qts. of green beans and froze 12 doz. ears of corn.

22. _____ _____

23. According to the UPI reports, O.P.E.C. members are arguing over the current price of their crude oil.

23. _____ _____

✓

24. In the financial community, an address on Wall St. is prestigious.

24. _____ ____

25. Bonds issued by the Government National Mortgage Association are especially popular among investors; these bonds are known as GNMAs (pronounced Ginnie Maes).

25. _____ ____

C Forming Plurals and Possessives

In each sentence write the correct plural or possessive form of the word enclosed in parentheses.

✓

1. Each (supervisor) accident report must be signed and dated before it is submitted to me.

1. _____ ____

2. Our lab completed (analysis) to determine what made the fabric fade.

2. _____ ____

3. Jason Van Zandt suggested that his two (daughter-in-law) join their spouses in working for the family business.

3. _____ ____

4. Most (instructor) offices have been wired for immediate connection to the Internet.

4. _____ ____

5. The consultant recorded all of the (nurse) concerns, suggestions, and recommendations.

5. _____ ____

6. Have the (Mr.) Zander received copies of the offer to purchase the land that they inherited from their father?

6. _____ ____

7. To improve the air quality, the air conditioning duct work and filters have been replaced in (Dan and Steve) office.

7. _____ ____

8. The (editor in chief) of two major newspapers decided not to publish the story because they felt the source was unreliable.

8. _____ ____

9. Both of the (Davis) signatures must be on the tax refund check before it can be cashed.

9. _____ ____

10. (Lynn) finishing her project early gave her time to help me with the Vanguard proposal.

10. _____ ____

D Plural and Possessive Review

Correct any errors in plural and possessive use in the following sentences. Underline each error, and write your correction in the space provided. Write *OK* for any sentence that is correct.

✓

1. Harry and William's bonuses were the two highest in our company's history.

1. _____ ____

2. Of course, most of they're losses were covered by insurance.

2. _____ ____

3. Her companys' profit sharing plan increased by 14 percent last year.

3. _____ ____

4. Dillon planning for the conference made our jobs much easier.

4. _____ ____

5. The theme of our fashion show is "Fashion for Professional Woman."

5. _____ ____

6. For the last three months, each departments' profit report indicated a downward trend.

6. _____ ____

7. Husbands and wifes of full-time employees are eligible for insurance coverage.

7. _____ ____

8. Copies of all the thesis have been placed in the library.

8. _____ ____

9. All of the c.o.d.'s will be shipped tomorrow.

9. _____ ____

10. Dean asked both Ms. Berkleys to wait in the reception area until the detectives arrived.

10. _____ ____

E Proofreading Application

There are five errors in the following memo. Underline the errors, and write the corrections in the spaces provided. If a line is correct, write *OK*.

✓

MEMO TO: Adrianna Cortez, Human Resource Manager

_____ ____

FROM: Nina Westin Brookshire

_____ ____

DATE: October 5, <YEAR>

_____ ____

SUBJECT: Insurance Coverage

_____ ____

Please add my husband, John Robert Brookshire, Sr. to my health coverage plan. It is my understanding that an additional $65 per month will be withheld from my check to cover his insurance. You indicated that this additional amount will be took from my check beginning with the Nov. 15 payroll.

_____ ____
_____ ____
_____ ____
_____ ____
_____ ____
_____ ____

Also, please enroll both of us in the dental and vision insurance programs that will become available Jan. 1. According to the information package distributed, the additional coverage cost of $20.00 per month will also be deducted. This deduction will begin with my December payroll check.

_____ ____
_____ ____
_____ ____
_____ ____
_____ ____

SECTION 4.7   NUMBERS

 **Using Numbers Correctly**

Underline any errors in the following sentences, and write your corrections on the lines provided. Write *OK* for any sentence that has no error. ✓

1. By August 1st at the latest, we will have all campus computers connected to the Internet.

   1. _____ ____

2. We will have special programs for all age groups to celebrate our church's 125th anniversary.

   2. _____ ____

3. Our strategic plan has a list of objectives that must be reached by the year 2,005.

   3. _____ ____

4. Postage expenses exceeded the budgeted amount by $250.00.

   4. _____ ____

5. During the next ten years, we plan to increase on-campus enrollment by thirty-five percent.

   5. _____ ____

6. Sales projections indicate an increase of from twelve to fifteen percent in the northwestern part of the country.

   6. _____ ____

7. Mr. Edwards, I will have the report finished by late afternoon on the fifth of September or by early morning on the sixth.

   7. _____ ____

8. On June 5, 24 of our secretaries will attend a special conference on improving electronic communications.

   8. _____ ____

9. 89 percent of hospital patients report that they were pleased with the human relations skills of our nursing staff.

   9. _____ ____

10. During our sidewalk sale, we are selling beach attire at 2/3s off the original price.

  10. _____ ____

11. The 911 dispatcher sent the paramedics to 1801 86 Street.

  11. _____ ____

12. About 1/3 of the area coffee shops have already raised their prices because of the increased cost of coffee from Brazil.

  12. _____ ____

13. A one-year subscription to our magazine is $20.00; a two-year subscription costs $36.

  13. _____ ____

14. Jasper estimated a total cost of one thousand dollars to repair the storm damage.

  14. _____ ____

15. According to my calendar, the meeting with Mr. McDermott is scheduled at ten a.m. tomorrow.

  15. _____ ____

B Numbers Review

Underline any errors in the following sentences, and write your corrections on the lines provided. Write *OK* for any sentence that has no error.

✓

1. We began our plant's operation on April 5th, 1996.

1. _____ ____

2. Each mug will cost $.85 to produce.

2. _____ ____

3. This antique desk was made during the 19th century.

3. _____ ____

4. Reporters estimated that the crowd for the cycling event was several 1000 people.

4. _____ ____

5. Twelve ounce soft drinks cost $.60, and the family size costs $1.59.

5. _____ ____

6. Our health insurance deductible is $500.00 per individual covered.

6. _____ ____

7. Our Birmingham headquarters has moved to 21,600 Main Street.

7. _____ ____

8. After a lengthy discussion, Rhyne Printing reduced their printing charges for 5,000 6-page brochures to a more reasonable amount.

8. _____ ____

9. The capacity of each container is only 3 quarts 3 pints.

9. _____ ____

10. 100 new environmental centers will be completely operational by 2001.

10. _____ ____

11. During last year, Heath Printing and Packaging had an operating income of $6,000,000 and income from other sources of $800,000.

11. _____ ____

12. By 2003 we forecast annual revenues of $5 to $5.5 million.

12. _____ ____

13. For most cleaning needs, you should add two quarts of water to two and a half cups of concentrated liquid Magic Cleaner.

13. _____ ____

14. Your first house payment of $648.22 is due on the 1st of April.

14. _____ ____

15. During the 1990's our company built its first plant, which was located near the Houston airport.

15. _____ ____

16. Paul ordered 5 10-gallon drums for mixing the chemicals.

16. _____ ____

17. On April 25 our second day-care center opened on 7th Street.

17. _____ ____

18. Each capsule contains one hundred percent of the recommended daily requirement of vitamins and minerals.

18. _____ ____

19. 500 copies of these sales flyers will be placed on cars during the high school football game Friday night.

19. _____ ____

20. His portfolio management fee is .6 percent; is that acceptable?

20. _____ ____

Punctuation Review

Review punctuation usage by underlining the errors in the following sentences and writing your corrections on the lines provided. Write *OK* for any sentence that is correct.   ✓

1. Our offices in Raleigh, Durham and Greensboro will soon be merged into one district office.

     1. _____ ____

2. The person who should be named to head the Shipping Department, is Patricia Devinney; she has the most experience and is a superior manager.

     2. _____ ____

3. Doris Muldowney will write the proposal, however, she cannot begin it until Monday.

     3. _____ ____

4. Molly Chang, the manager of our Hong Kong office will be visiting the United States during the month of August.

     4. _____ ____

5. The Country Garden Landscaping Company of Nashville, Tennessee had the best layout for the company picnic area.

     5. _____ ____

6. Dr. Negbenebor wrote a comprehensive authoritative book about economics.

     6. _____ ____

7. The three accountants' monthly reports for January and February are on the hard drive of my computer, Sam.

     7. _____ ____

8. Ms. Wilson carefully reviews every customers loan application and credit history.

     8. _____ ____

9. Two of the people, who were selected for the training program, are Lauren Ramsey and Ken Walters.

     9. _____ ____

10. Among the topics that must be discussed are the following: schedules, deadlines, and suppliers.

     10. _____ ____

11. Cindy McKinney asked, "Does anyone have any information about a company called Valley Tree Surgeons, Inc."?

     11. _____ ____

12. Mr. Vandretti will need a projector and a remote-control unit (are they already in the auditorium?) for this mornings meeting.

     12. _____ ____

13. Quality, dependability, service, these are the reasons customers cited for buying our computers.

     13. _____ ____

14. Lander Millsap, Ph.D. is the company's expert on international trade.

     14. _____ ____

15. Thomas Reeves is the sales manager at Security and Alarm Company, Inc., isn't he.

     15. _____ ____

D Editing Practice

Underline any errors in the following sentences, and write your corrections on the lines provided. Write *OK* for any sentence that is correct.   ✓

1. I faxed a purchase order today, we should receive the merchandise within ten days.

1. _____ _____

2. The cost of moving my family from New York to San Francisco, was approximately $4,000.

2. _____ _____

3. The sales report as you know compares actual sales with estimated sales for the past quarter.

3. _____ _____

4. Brian Nelson or Jill Turner have final approval on all purchasing agreements.

4. _____ _____

5. Ask someone from maintenance to have all them empty cartons taken to the recycling facility.

5. _____ _____

6. The Hudson's made their hotel reservations six months ago.

6. _____ _____

7. Everyone except you and I has donated blood today; let's go donate now.

7. _____ _____

8. We keep all patient's files on microfilm indefinitely.

8. _____ _____

9. All reports indicate that the new division performed well during its first three months of operation.

9. _____ _____

10. The police officers want a statement from everyone who seen the accident.

10. _____ _____

E Proofreading for Accuracy

The following copy is the text of an e-mail message that you typed yesterday afternoon. Before sending the e-mail, you decide to proofread it. Underline each error and write your corrections in the spaces provided. If a line has no errors, write *OK*.   ✓

Alan you asked that I give you an update on
the latest sales figures before you leave for
Japan. The following figures are based on
preliminary reports; $2,348,826.00 within the
U.S. and $1,498,382.00 in our international market.

These figures represent an increase of fourteen
percent over the same period last year. Sam and
me are quite pleased and have projected even better
figures for next quarter. We feel that we should
explore the possibility of doing business in 2
more countries by the end of the year, and will
have a proposal for that expansion on your desk
by Jan. 15th.

BASICS OF READING _____

A Adjust Your Reading Rate to Your Purpose

For each of the following situations, decide if you should read for specific data, for
retention or analysis, or for checking and copying.   ✓

1. Proofreading a production report you typed.   1. _____ ____

2. Reading a user's manual for a new software program. 2. _____ ____

3. Reading a journal to learn background information
   about a new product.   3. _____ ____

4. Looking up a company's telephone number in the
   Yellow Pages.   4. _____ ____

5. Reading the instructions for the new copier.   5. _____ ____

6. Verifying that information on the computer screen
   matches handwritten copy.   6. _____ ____

7. Looking for a specific person's name in a newspaper article. 7. _____ ____

8. Checking invoices for accuracy.   8. _____ ____

9. Reading a pamphlet that describes your new
   job responsibilities.   9. _____ ____

10. Looking up a topic in an encyclopedia.   10. _____ ____

B Test Your Reading Retention

Read the following article on a business-related topic. Then answer the questions that
follow.

> Managing diversity is an important issue for businesses. To attract and retain
> qualified employees and to work with customers around the world, businesses
> need to address the interests and needs of diverse groups. Managing diversity
> includes recognizing and understanding differences in gender, culture, ethnic
> background, age, and physical ability.
>
> To attract and retain a diverse workforce, businesses must recognize and accommo-
> date differences in employees' lifestyles and cultures. For example, the increase in
> the number of women and ethnic minorities in the workforce has led businesses to
> offer a variety of options to employees. Offering flexible work schedules, providing
> assistance with child and parent care, and presenting cultural-awareness courses
> are some ways businesses address diversity in the workforce.
>
> Managing diversity also extends to attracting and retaining customers. In the age
> of the Internet and electronic mail, businesses come in contact with people of
> different cultural and ethnic backgrounds every day. To compete on a global basis,
> businesses must develop an understanding of, and respect for, cultural differences.
> This awareness involves learning and accommodating the business customs and
> cultural beliefs of customers in other countries.

1. What is the main idea of the article?

_____

_____

_____   1. _____

2. What are the two main reasons for managing diversity in the workplace?

_____

_____

_____   2. _____

3. What does managing diversity involve?

_____

_____

_____   3. _____

4. List examples of ways that businesses address diversity in the workforce.

_____

_____

_____   4. _____

5. List examples of what business can do to increase their understanding of, and respect for, cultural differences.

_____

_____

_____   5. _____

C Checking Copy for Accuracy

Compare the items in List A with the items in List B. Write *match* if the items in both columns match. Write *do not match* if the items do not match.   ✓

LIST A	LIST B		
1. Electronic Mail	Electronc Mail	1. _____	___
2. PKT0386147	PKT0386147	2. _____	___
3. Spreadsheet Program	Spreadshet Program	3. _____	___
4. Word processing	Word precesing	4. _____	___
5. McIlvaine Industries	MCIlvaine Industries	5. _____	___
6. Sales Estimates	Sales Estimates	6. _____	___
7. 600,743,983.32	600,743,938.32	7. _____	___
8. August 28, 1998	August 28, 1998	8. _____	___
9. Account 3489-345	Account 3498-345	9. _____	___
10. Phone # 919-555-3852	Phone # 919-555-3852	10. _____	___

 IMPROVING
VOCABULARY POWER

 Using the Dictionary

Look up each of the following words in a dictionary. List the definitions, synonyms, and inflectional forms and derivatives for each word on the lines provided.   ✓

1. compensation

   definition: _____

   _____ _____

   synonyms: _____ _____

   inflectional forms and derivatives: _____ _____

2. disparate

   definition: _____

   _____ _____

   synonyms: _____ _____

   inflectional forms and derivatives: _____ _____

3. query (verb)

   definition: _____

   _____ _____

   synonyms: _____ _____

   inflectional forms and derivatives: _____ _____

4. reciprocate

   definition: _____

   _____ _____

   synonyms: _____ _____

   inflectional forms and derivatives: _____ _____

5. survey (verb)

   definition: _____

   _____ _____

   synonyms: _____ _____

   inflectional forms and derivatives: _____ _____

6. tangible

   definition: _____

   _____ _____

   synonyms: _____ _____

   inflectional forms and derivatives: _____ _____

B Substituting Synonyms

Read the following memo. Look up the definition for each underlined word, and substitute an appropriate synonym for the word. Write your answers on the lines provided. ✓

MEMO TO: Naomi Sugino

FROM: Mary Kay Kisor

DATE: July 12, <YEAR>

SUBJECT: Additions to Office Procedures Manual

As you prepare the office procedures manual, please be sure to include the following guidelines:

- Before making <u>impetuous</u> decisions, always consult a customer service representative first.

- All new hiring decisions should be kept <u>surreptitious</u> until a public announcement has been made.

- When <u>ascribing</u> job instructions on a page layout form, specify the type of word processing software to be used.

- When dealing with an irate customer, make sure to retain your <u>equanimity</u>.

- If you are being <u>bothered</u> by a coworker, report the incident immediately to your supervisor.

Thank you for your attention to these topics. Based on your past performance, I am confident that the new office procedures manual will be complete and accurate.

C Using New Words

Look up the definition of each of the following words in a dictionary. Then use each word correctly in a sentence. Write the definitions and sentences on the lines provided. ✓

1. ergonomics

definition: _____

_____

_____

2. nuisance

definition: _____

_____

_____

3. alternative (noun)

definition: _____ ____

_____ ____

_____

4. expenditure

definition: _____ ____

_____ ____

_____

5. zeal

definition: _____ ____

_____ ____

_____

6. asset

definition: _____ ____

_____ ____

_____

7. fiscal (adjective)

definition: _____ ____

_____ ____

_____

8. substantial

definition: _____ ____

_____ ____

_____

9. freelance (adjective)

definition: _____ ____

_____ ____

_____

10. criteria

definition: _____ ____

_____ ____

_____

Systematic Vocabulary Building

For the next four weeks, add to your vocabulary five new words each week. Detach this page and place it in a notebook for ready reference.

Week 1	New Word	Definition	Synonyms
1			
2			
3			
4			
5			
Week 2			
1			
2			
3			
4			
5			
Week 3			
1			
2			
3			
4			
5			
Week 4			
1			
2			
3			
4			
5			

 STRATEGIES FOR COMPREHENDING
AND RETAINING CONTENT

 Improving Reading Comprehension

Read the following passage. Take notes on the passage, making sure to identify the
main idea and supporting points in each paragraph. Write your notes on the lines
provided. ✓

> Businesses use periodic reports to track certain types of information at specific
> intervals. Such reports may be prepared daily, weekly, monthly, quarterly, or annu-
> ally. Sales reports, financial reports, and inventory reports are some examples of
> periodic reports used in business.
>
> Periodic reports may be prepared in one of two ways. A report writer may use
> preprinted forms that provide blank spaces for recording information. Another
> option is to use a template form on the computer. All the report writer needs to
> do is enter the data in the appropriate places on the template. Either way, the
> use of preexisting forms ensures that essential information will be included and
> reduces the amount of time needed to prepare periodic reports.

PARAGRAPH 1
Main idea: _____
_____
_____ ____

Supporting points: _____
_____
_____
_____
_____
_____ ____

PARAGRAPH 2
Main idea: _____
_____ ____

Supporting points: _____
_____
_____
_____
_____
_____ ____

B Selecting Reading Strategies

For each of the following situations, determine what reading strategies you should use to comprehend and retain information. Write your answers on the lines provided.

1. You are a printing assistant at D & D Printing Company. Your supervisor has asked you to read and summarize an article on the new color process for offset printing. Your summary will be distributed to all staff members. What reading strategies would you use to comprehend and retain the information?

   _____

   _____

   _____

   _____

   _____ _____

2. As a customer service representative for Woodbine Software Company, you answer telephone and e-mail requests from customers regarding software they purchased from Woodbine. Today you received a 12-page description of the latest software packages released by Woodbine. This software will be shipped to customers in two days, so you must quickly familiarize yourself with the information. What reading strategies would you use to comprehend and retain the information?

   _____

   _____

   _____

   _____

   _____ _____

C Achieving Variety in Word Usage

It is easy to develop the habit of using the same word over and over. In the following expressions, substitute other words for the much overused words *check* and *nice*.

1. check the date
2. check the account balance
3. check the appendices
4. check the itinerary
5. check the dictionary
6. nice person
7. nice time
8. nice weather
9. nice work
10. nice outfit

1. _____ _____
2. _____ _____
3. _____ _____
4. _____ _____
5. _____ _____
6. _____ _____
7. _____ _____
8. _____ _____
9. _____ _____
10. _____ _____

D **Identifying Ideas**

Read the following passage and make an outline that lists the main idea and supporting points in the passage. Write your outline on the lines provided.

THE JOB SEARCH

When conducting a job search the important thing to remember is that you are selling a product—yourself—to prospective employers. Making yourself marketable involves preparing a résumé, writing a letter of application, and preparing for an interview.

One of the first things you should do before looking for a job is prepare a professional looking résumé. A résumé includes information such as your name, address, education experience, previous work experience, honors, and references. Often your résumé is the only information an employer has to judge you on before the first interview. For this reason, it is extremely important that your résumé be complete yet concise.

Another item you need when applying for most jobs is a letter of application. This letter tells the employer which job you are interested in, highlights some of your best qualities, and encourages the employer to contact you for an interview. The first paragraph of your application letter is especially important because it must grab the employer's attention and invite him or her to read further. The body of your letter must highlight your best qualities and provide supporting examples. The closing must convince the employer to call you for an interview

When called for an interview, be sure to dress professionally. First impressions can be lasting impressions, and you want to make a positive first impression with the employer. Address the employer in a courteous and professional manner. In response to the employer's questions, give concise, honest answers that highlight your strengths and abilities. After the interview, send a follow-up letter that thanks the employer for talking with you and highlights your assets.

Throughout the job search, remember to present your product—yourself—in the best possible light. Whether you are preparing your résumé, writing a letter of application, or interviewing for a job, be concise yet thorough. Always maintain a positive attitude. Remember: The job you apply for just may become yours. ✓

_____
_____
_____
_____
_____
_____
_____
_____
_____
_____
_____
_____

 **SECTION 5.4**   EFFECTIVE NOTE TAKING
WHILE READING

 Taking Notes

Read the following passage. Take notes on the passage using the guidelines for taking notes found on pages 277 and 278 of your textbook.   ✓

Many business people underestimate the importance of building and maintaining goodwill when they write letters to customers and clients. Business letters written to people outside your organization should do two things: keep the reader's needs in mind, and present a favorable image of the organization.

For each business letter you write, think of the overall effect your writing will have on the reader. The letter should create an impression of a friendly organization that cares about its customers and clients. Also, the letter should express genuine interest in the reader. You can convey goodwill in your letters by anticipating questions the reader might have, such as describing the warranty offered with a product. Another way to promote goodwill is to include information that will interest the reader. For example, you might enclose with the letter an article, a brochure, or a catalog that provides more detailed information.

Letters influence what people think about an organization. What you say and how you say it influences how the reader will react to the message. Even if you are writing a letter that answers no to a customer's request, you should use positive wording and the you-attitude. In this way you help to create a favorable view of your organization.

_____
_____
_____
_____
_____
_____
_____
_____
_____
_____
_____
_____
_____
_____
_____
_____
_____
_____

B Using Secondary Sources

Select two topics from the following list that you would like to research. For each topic locate three secondary sources. Take notes from each source using the guidelines for note cards found on page 278 of your textbook.   ✓

electronic mail   videoconference   entrepreneurship
cellular phones   World Wide Web   voice mail

_____
_____
_____
_____
_____
_____
_____
_____
_____
_____
_____
_____

C Prioritizing Your Reading

Read the following passage. Then answer the questions on the spaces provided.   ✓

You work as a computer programmer at Pacific Software Company. You have just been named the project leader of the team that will develop new spreadsheet software that will compete with the best-selling software packages on the market. The software must be completed eight months from now to be on the market before the competitors release the new versions of their software.

Your job duties are already quite extensive and you do not have much time to devote to this project. In order to develop this software, you and your team will have to do quite a bit of research on the competitors' software and on consumers' likes and dislikes.

1. What note taking strategies should you and your team members use to make your research more effective?

_____
_____
_____
_____

2. Since not all of the information you review will be relevant to spreadsheet packages, what steps should you and your team members follow to preview the material?

_____
_____
_____

SECTION 6.1

BASICS OF LISTENING

A **Active and Passive Listening**

Read each of the following situations. Then place a check mark in the appropriate column to indicate which kind of listening should be done.

	ACTIVE LISTENING	PASSIVE LISTENING	✓
1. voice-mail message from a coworker	1. _____	_____	_____
2. scuba diving instruction	2. _____	_____	_____
3. history class lecture	3. _____	_____	_____
4. special weather bulletin	4. _____	_____	_____
5. song on a CD while washing your car	5. _____	_____	_____
6. conversation with friends	6. _____	_____	_____
7. travel directions to a job interview	7. _____	_____	_____
8. explanation of a new job task	8. _____	_____	_____
9. tornado drill procedures	9. _____	_____	_____
10. medical instructions from your doctor	10. _____	_____	_____

B **External and Internal Noise in the Classroom**

List five sources of *external* noise that may interfere with listening while you are taking this class.

                                                                  ✓

1. _____ 1. _____

2. _____ 2. _____

3. _____ 3. _____

4. _____ 4. _____

5. _____ 5. _____

List five sources of *internal* noise that may interfere with listening while you are taking this class.

1. _____ 1. _____

2. _____ 2. _____

3. _____ 3. _____

4. _____ 4. _____

5. _____ 5. _____

C Dealing With External and Internal Noise in a Critical Situation

Reread the second paragraph in "Improving Your Listening Skills" on page 289 in your textbook. List any external and internal noises that could affect your listening to the flight attendant's safety speech. You may include those mentioned in the text and others that might possibly be present in such a situation.

EXTERNAL NOISE   ✓

1. _____   1. ____
2. _____   2. ____
3. _____   3. ____
4. _____   4. ____
5. _____   5. ____

INTERNAL NOISE

1. _____   1. ____
2. _____   2. ____
3. _____   3. ____
4. _____   4. ____
5. _____   5. ____

D Thinking Clearly

A good listener can weigh ideas to determine whether the ideas are facts or opinion or to determine whether more information is needed to make a decision. Below are ten statements heard in conversation or as part of television advertisements. In the space to the right of each, write the letter of one of the following choices to indicate:

F Fact. The statement is a fact that can be supported.
O Opinion. The statement is an opinion.
? Undecided. More information is needed to make a decision.   ✓

1. Don's Deli has the best cheesecake in town.   1. ____ ____

2. Admissions to the emergency room increased by 10 percent last month.   2. ____ ____

3. Becker Insurance offers a 10 percent reduction in insurance premiums if a person had no traffic tickets in the last four years.   3. ____ ____

4. You will enjoy reading Ms. Sutherland's latest novel.   4. ____ ____

5. The movie *Aliens From Beyond* will keep you in suspense from beginning to end.   5. ____ ____

6. Buying a minivan will be the best choice for you.   6. ____ ____

7. Professor Hartman teaches computer classes for junior high students during the summer.   7. ____ ____

8. Taking Vitapills twice a day will increase your energy level.   8. ____ ____

9. Twenty people completed applications for the marketing position.   9. ____ ____

10. I believe that Kristina Teng is the best candidate for the job, and you believe that Carmilita Mendosa is the best candidate.   10. ____ ____

E Distinguishing Sound Alikes

Choose the word from the pair in parentheses that correctly completes each sentence. Write the word in the space provided.   ✓

1. Completing his degree took longer than (than, then) Gregory expected because he was working full time.

   1. _____ ____

2. Campers should be aware of the wild (boar, bore) in the swamp area.

   2. _____ ____

3. Convincing the manager to increase the meal allowance was no easy (feat, feet).

   3. _____ ____

4. Mr. Hilderbrand's doctor warned him to be careful not to (overdo, overdue) during his first day back at work after his surgery.

   4. _____ ____

5. Jennifer was pleased to win (forth, fourth) place in the company-sponsored marathon.

   5. _____ ____

6. Both Mr. Nickolas and Ms. Mercer displayed (tact, tack) during their intense discussion.

   6. _____ ____

7. (Miners, Minors) flying alone must be met at the airport by parents or guardians or other responsible persons.

   7. _____ ____

8. Street vendors have been (band, banned) from a three-block area near the courthouse.

   8. _____ ____

9. Regina did a (grate, great) job with the Reynolds' account.

   9. _____ ____

10. Ms. Evans, we have hired a contractor to repair the (hole, whole) in the roof.

    10. _____ ____

F Recalling Key Points

To review what you learned about listening in Section 6.1 of your textbook, add appropriate terms to complete the following sentences.   ✓

1. Every day, business people spend more time _____ than they do speaking, reading, or writing.

   1. ____

2. Hearing is automatic, while _____ is an acquired skill.

   2. ____

3. _____ is appropriate when it is not important to remember what you hear.

   3. ____

4. _____ is appropriate when you need to remember the information that you hear.

   4. ____

5. Active listening requires _____ and mental preparation.

   5. ____

6. Usually a listener has only _____ to absorb and comprehend a speaker's words.

   6. ____

7. To _____ noise, a listener should identify what noise can be controlled and what noise cannot be controlled.

   7. ____

8. To avoid _____ toward a speaker, always assume that you can learn something from him or her.

8. _____

9. Listen with a _____ and an open mind even if you expect to disagree with the speaker.

9. _____

10. _____ involves putting the speaker's ideas into the simplest, clearest, and most direct words possible without changing the intended meaning.

10. _____

G Overcoming Listening Barriers

Read the following workplace situation. Then answer the questions about the situation.

Brad Scholes works as a designer at a small publishing company. His job duties include designing promotional pieces for new products. Allison Duarte, the marketing manager, is responsible for writing the advertising copy for the promotional pieces. Last week, Allison gave Brad the advertising copy for several new products and asked that he complete the designs in two weeks. However, Allison did not give Brad all the information he needs. Brad set up a meeting with Allison to discuss the promotional pieces. The meeting does not begin well. Brad is upset about the short time frame Allison has given him for completing the designs. Allison is working on the department budget for next year and is only half listening to what Brad is saying. When Allison does speak, she begins by commenting on how the design staff is always making mistakes and missing deadlines. Surprised by this comment, Brad is ready to interrupt Allison.

1. What internal noise is affecting Brad's listening? What internal noise is affecting Allison's listening?

_____

_____

_____

_____

_____

_____   **1.** _____

2. How could Brad manage his internal noise? How could Allison manage hers?

_____

_____

_____

_____

_____

_____   **2.** _____

3. How should Brad respond to Allison's comment about the design staff's missing their deadlines and making errors?

_____

_____

_____

_____

_____

_____   **3.** _____

 **SECTION 6.2**

LISTENING IN CASUAL CONVERSATIONS AND SMALL-GROUP AND CONFERENCE SETTINGS

A Identifying Good Listening Habits

Read the following sentences. If good listening habits are indicated, place a check mark in the *Yes* column. If good listening habits are *not* indicated, place a check mark in the *No* column.

	YES	NO	✓
1. An active listener interrupts a speaker who talks too slowly in order to give the speaker feedback. **1.**			
2. One way to screen out distractions is to close your eyes. **2.**			
3. Concentrate on what the speaker is saying by listening for ideas and feelings as well as listening for factual information. **3.**			
4. Try to identify the major points of a speech and determine whether each point has been supported. **4.**			
5. Pay attention to such nonverbal signals as gestures, posture, and facial expressions. **5.**			
6. Try to decide in advance whether it is worthwhile to listen to the speaker. **6.**			
7. Keep your eyes on the speaker as much as possible. **7.**			
8. Avoid doing another activity—such as reading a newspaper—while trying to listen. **8.**			
9. Stop listening if you do not agree with what the speaker is saying. **9.**			
10. Wait until a speaker has finished before asking for clarification of a point you missed, unless the speaker specifies otherwise. **10.**			
11. Be prepared to respond by thinking about what you will say next while the speaker talking. **11.**			
12. Listen carefully even if you dislike the speaker's appearance or mannerisms. **12.**			
13. If the speaker is uninteresting, let your mind wander to subjects that interest you. **13.**			
14. Continue to listen even if a great deal of effort is required to understand what the speaker is saying. **14.**			
15. Avoid eye contact with the speaker if you think the speaker is shy. **15.**			

B **Keep a Listening Journal**

During the next two days, keep a journal of listening situations in which you are a conversation participant or a listener. Include a variety of listening situations such as casual conversations, committee meetings, class lectures, telephone calls, and so on. Write your descriptions on the lines provided.

Listening Situation 1: _____

_____

_____

Active or Passive Listening Situation: _____

_____

_____

External Noise Present: _____

_____

_____

Internal Noise Present: _____

_____

_____

Effectiveness as a Listener: (Circle one)   Poor   Good   Excellent

Reasons for the Rating: _____

_____

_____

Ways to Improve as a Listener in the Above Situation:
(Complete this item if the rating was poor or good.)

_____

_____

Listening Situation 2: _____

_____

_____

Active or Passive Listening Situation: _____

_____

_____

External Noise Present: _____

_____

_____

Internal Noise Present: _____

_____

_____

Effectiveness as a Listener: (Circle one)   Poor   Good   Excellent

Reasons for the Rating: _____

_____

_____

Ways to Improve as a Listener in the Above Situation:
(Complete this item if the rating was poor or good.)

_____

_____

Team Listening

For this activity the class will be divided into teams of four students. You and your team members should agree to watch the same specific evening newscast and take notes on the items covered in the newscast. Type your notes and give copies of the notes to all team members. Meet with team members to compare notes. Using the best set of notes, merge additional notes from the other team members to form one final copy. Submit this final copy to your instructor.

Answer the following questions. Explain your answers as needed.   ✓

1. Were the notes you took adequate? Why or why not?

_____

_____

_____

_____   1. _____

2. What important points did you overlook that your team members included? What important points did you include that your team members overlooked?

_____

_____

_____

_____   2. _____

3. How did typing the notes help you remember the content of the newscast?

_____

_____

_____

_____   3. _____

4. How did discussing the notes with your team members help you remember the content of the newscast?

_____

_____

_____

_____   4. _____

5. What will you do differently the next time that you take notes?

_____

_____

_____

_____   5. _____

D Recalling Key Points

To review what you learned about listening in Section 6.2 of your textbook, add appropriate terms to complete the following sentences.

✓

1. Being _____ and showing _____ are two attributes of good listeners.

          1. ____

2. Use _____ to convey your interest in what a speaker is saying.

          2. ____

3. One way to determine your listening objectives is to find out the expected _____.

          3. ____

4. Note taking is not a substitute for _____ listening.

          4. ____

5. To improve your listening retention, read your notes within _____ hours.

          5. ____

6. Highlight only _____ points in your notes.

          6. ____

E Synonyms

Circle the letter of the word that is closest in meaning to the first word in each set.

✓

1. incriminate
   a. vindicate   b. implicate   c. resolve   d. prejudge

     1. ____

2. propitious
   a. predictive   b. steep   c. wicked   d. favorable

     2. ____

3. obtuse
   a. sharp   b. discerning   c. clever   d. dull-witted

     3. ____

4. constrain
   a. stress   b. compel   c. contract   d. forgive

     4. ____

5. aperture
   a. summit   b. overture   c. flame   d. gap

     5. ____

6. mitigate
   a. moderate   b. magnify   c. aggravate   d. confuse

     6. ____

F Antonyms

Circle the letters of the two words in each group that are antonyms (opposite in meaning).

✓

1. a. learned   b. transitory   c. momentary   d. illiterate

     1. ____

2. a. temerity   b. caucus   c. density   d. caution

     2. ____

3. a. adequate   b. mundane   c. spiritual   d. eventual

     3. ____

4. a. revoke   b. invoke   c. approve   d. take

     4. ____

5. a. responsive   b. avid   c. radical   d. conservative

     5. ____

 **SECTION 7.1**   USING WORDS EFFECTIVELY

A   **Defining Words by Forming Sentences**

Use each of the following words in a sentence that demonstrates your understanding of
the meaning of the word.   ✓

1. accommodate   _____

     _____   1. _____

2. equity   _____

     _____   2. _____

3. remittance   _____

     _____   3. _____

4. volume   _____

     _____   4. _____

5. consultant   _____

     _____   5. _____

6. synopsis   _____

     _____   6. _____

7. recommendation   _____

     _____   7. _____

8. negotiable   _____

     _____   8. _____

9. compensation   _____

     _____   9. _____

10. minimal   _____

     _____   10. _____

B   **Pronunciation Practice**

On the line provided, write the preferred pronunciation for each of the following
words, as indicated in the dictionary.   ✓

1. feasibility   _____   1. _____

2. addressee   _____   2. _____

3. maintenance   _____   3. _____

4. formalize   _____   4. _____

5. competitive   _____   5. _____

6. creditor _____ 6. ____ ✓

7. equitable _____ 7. ____

8. facility _____ 8. ____

9. implementation _____ 9. ____

10. statistics _____ 10. ____

11. fiscal _____ 11. ____

12. premise _____ 12. ____

13. implement _____ 13. ____

14. cooperation _____ 14. ____

15. adequate _____ 15. ____

C English Translations

In the space provided, write the meanings of the following foreign terms that have become familiar in English speech and writing.

✓

1. bona fide _____ 1. ____

2. per annum _____ 2. ____

3. de facto _____ 3. ____

4. vice versa _____ 4. ____

5. status quo _____ 5. ____

6. ad hoc (adjective) _____ 6. ____

7. modus operandi _____ 7. ____

8. quid pro quo _____ 8. ____

9. tour de force _____ 9. ____

10. pro tempore _____ 10. ____

D Hyphenation Practice

Use diagonals (/) to indicate where each of the following words may be divided into syllables. Example: in/di/ca/tion

✓

1. assistance 1. _____ ____

2. necessary 2. _____ ____

3. recommend 3. _____ ____

4. acknowledge 4. _____ ____

5. immediate 5. _____ ____

6. disinterested 6. _____ ____

7. requirement 7. _____ ____

8. certification 8. _____ ____

9. substantial 9. _____ ____

10. volume 10. _____ ____

11. occasion 11. _____ ____

✓

12. quarterly   12. _____ _____

13. permanent   13. _____ _____

14. ingenuity   14. _____ _____

15. electronic   15. _____ _____

E Using the Thesaurus

Next to each of the following sentences, list several words that may be substituted for the word in italics.

✓

1. One *clear* advantage to using this design is its flexibility. 1. _____

  _____ _____

2. Marsha is a *hardworking* employee who gets the job done right every time. 2. _____

  _____ _____

3. All the managers *backed* the proposal to allow workers to telecommute. 3. _____

  _____ _____

4. We need to *change* our customer service procedures to ensure that customers' needs are being met. 4. _____

  _____ _____

5. Joetta and Carl will *look over* the results of the survey. 5. _____

  _____ _____

6. Stockbrokers are accustomed to making *fast* decisions about which stocks to purchase. 6. _____

  _____ _____

7. Mr. Erikson said he would *concur* with our decision regarding the purchase of a videoconferencing system. 7. _____

  _____ _____

8. Our development team has created a *top-notch* software product. 8. _____

  _____ _____

9. Dwight Yeager suggested that we *implement* the change in hiring procedures immediately. 9. _____

  _____ _____

10. Ms. Ruscilli's testimony on behalf of the defendant was very *effective*. 10. _____

  _____

F Using the Right Word

Fill in each blank with an appropriate word from the following list. On the line at the right, write the letter that identifies the word selected.

✓

a. appraise	**f.** definitive	**k.** precede
b. apprise	**g.** formally	**l.** proceed
c. comprise	**h.** formerly	**m.** statue
d. constitute	**i.** personal	**n.** stature
e. definite	**j.** personnel	**o.** statute

1. Each employee must complete a _____ information form to be filed in the Human Resources Department. 1. _____ _____

2. Before we _____ with the testing, you must get approval from your insurance company. 2. _____ _____

3. Mr. Gallagher was _____ sworn in as mayor on January 5. 3. _____ _____

4. He was _____ about the description of the suspect he gave the police. 4. _____ _____

5. A lawyer must _____ clients of their rights. 5. _____ _____

6. Sheila's presentation will _____ the keynote speech. 6. _____ _____

7. Rosalie Pedrosa gave the _____ answer to the question. 7. _____ _____

8. Each subdivision in the housing development will _____ 30 lots. 8. _____ _____

9. The legislature approved a tougher _____ against industrial pollution. 9. _____ _____

10. Satish Patel was _____ with the accounting firm of Parkhurst and Owen. 10. _____ _____

G Sound-Alikes

Choose the word in parentheses that correctly completes each sentence, and write the word in the space provided. ✓

1. Michael's (principal, principle) reason for accepting the job offer was the opportunity for advancement. 1. _____ _____

2. To complete the warranty card, include the (cereal, serial) number of the item that you purchased. 2. _____ _____

3. I would appreciate your (assistance, assistants) with this lab procedure. 3. _____ _____

4. You must exercise (patience, patients) in dealing with customers who have a complaint. 4. _____ _____

5. One-third of the (residence, residents) in the apartment complex are eligible for a two-year lease. 5. _____ _____

6. We made a (miner, minor) adjustment to the blueprints for the Steele project. 6. _____ _____

7. If you are an employee of Meyer Memorial Hospital, we will (waive, wave) the membership fee for the health club. 7. _____ _____

8. The student advisory (council, counsel) will meet with school officials next week to discuss the topic. 8. _____ _____

9. Do you know (weather, whether) the new contract with the technicians' union has been approved? 9. _____ _____

10. We are working to (lessen, lesson) the number of backorders we have for our products. 10. _____ _____

H Replacing Negative Words

In each of the following sentences, replace the negative word or words with more positive wording. Write your answers in the space provided. ✓

1. Your delay in processing the order caused us to miss the shipping deadline.

_____

_____ 1. _____

2. Your mistake in entering the information caused the money to be credited to the wrong account.

_____

_____ 2. _____

3. Due to your inability to remain on schedule, we will need to postpone the release date for the product.

_____
_____   **3.** _____

4. You failed to indicate which version of the software you want. As soon as you give us this information, we can complete your order.

_____
_____   **4.** _____

5. Your trouble with the telephone line is due to faulty wiring.

_____
_____   **5.** _____

I Antonyms

For each italicized word at the left, select the letter of the word that is most nearly opposite in meaning. Write your answers on the lines provided.   ✓

1. *coincide*	(a) correspond	(b) agree	(c) concur	(d) dissent	**1.** ____ ____
2. *reinforce*	(a) strengthen	(b) abandon	(c) bolster	(d) support	**2.** ____ ____
3. *impose*	(a) offer	(b) oblige	(c) demand	(d) intrude	**3.** ____ ____
4. *expend*	(a) consume	(b) spend	(c) conserve	(d) waste	**4.** ____ ____
5. *specify*	(a) designate	(b) suggest	(c) distinguish	(d) itemize	**5.** ____ ____

J Spelling and Vocabulary

Underline any spelling and vocabulary errors in the following sentences, and write your corrections on the lines provided. Write *OK* for any sentence that has no error.   ✓

1. We requested bids from three studios for the production of updated versions of our training videoes.

1. _____ ____

2. Miriam Knowles is an imminent financial analyst.

2. _____ ____

3. Craig will need to appraise both Mr. Brock and Ms. Mershon of the change in the itinerary.

3. _____ ____

4. Currently, there are many more job openings then there are job applicants.

4. _____ ____

5. Only employees who have three or more years of service are illegible for two weeks of vacation.

5. _____ ____

6. Advertising our products on the Internet has had a positive effect on sales.

6. _____ ____

7. If you would like to receive a more detailed discription of our training seminars, please call our toll-free number.

7. _____ ____

8. Our insurance agency was formally located on Cross Creek Boulevard.

8. _____ ____

9. Be sure to check all colums of figures in the appendices for the report.

9. _____ ____

10. Do you have a copy of the latest modifikations for the software templates?

10. _____ ____

K Improving Sentences

In each of the following sentences, delete any unnecessary words or replace any overused words with more exact expressions. Write your answers in the space provided. ✓

1. These sales figures are adequate enough for our purposes.

1. _____ ____

2. We would like to acknowledge the good job you did in coordinating the sales meeting.

2. _____ ____

3. Mr. Summerson gave an interesting presentation on the pitfalls of using e-mail.

3. _____ ____

4. He gave several good examples of what not to do when writing e-mail messages.

4. _____ ____

5. Jeanette Taggart had a hard time hearing the speaker in the crowded conference room.

5. _____ ____

6. For help in using the new e-mail system, refer back to the handouts from Mr. Summerson's presentation.

6. _____ ____

7. Both of us were impressed with the fine report you compiled on the options for short-term investments.

7. _____ ____

8. We rarely ever see Monica since she moved to Tempe last year.

8. _____ ____

9. From past experience, we know that Neil Weber is a capable engineer.

9. _____ ____

10. The advertisements that Gene created have been good in generating interest in our products.

10. _____ ____

L Eliminating Clichés

For each cliché you find in the following sentences, substitute more effective wording. Write your answers on the lines provided. ✓

1. Thank you for your recent communication regarding our fitness programs.

1. _____ ____

2. Inasmuch as we wrote the questionnaire sent to all hospital patients, we are the logical ones to analyze the responses.

2. _____ ____

3. Each and every travel agent will need to be trained to use the new reservation software.

3. _____ ____

4. Trevor Onofrio handled the licensing deal with Giamatti Foods.

4. _____ ____

5. We must face up to the criticism we received for the decision we made.

5. _____ ____

SECTION 7.2   MASTERING SPELLING TECHNIQUES

A Proofreading for Spelling Errors

In the sentences below, underline the incorrectly spelled words, and write their correct spellings in the answer column. Indicate correct sentences by writing *OK*.   ✓

1. Chris works as a computer technision in the Business Systems Department.

    1. _____ _____

2. Were you able to pursuade Masaki to assist us in completing the telephone survays?

    2. _____ _____

3. Two court-appointed attornies met with the defendant to discuss a possible plea bargain.

    3. _____ _____

4. The banquet room can accomodate up to 300 people.

    4. _____ _____

5. Financialy, we are in an ideal position to expand our business.

    5. _____ _____

6. Our sales representatives are commited to providing excellent service to all customers.

    6. _____ _____

7. Do you know if this pen contains permanant ink?

    7. _____ _____

8. We will need to overcome several obstacals in order to achieve our sales goal.

    8. _____ _____

9. You will be eligible for a promotion in one year.

    9. _____ _____

10. A good administrator is energetic, recourcefull, and decisive.

    10. _____ _____

11. Over one-half of our internal documents are transmited by electronic mail.

    11. _____ _____

12. Order the miscellaneus computer supplies from Office Clearinghouse.

    12. _____ _____

13. When interest rates are high, few people can get morgages.

    13. _____ _____

14. Customer demand for our new keyboarding software has exceded our expectations.

    14. _____ _____

15. We will basicaly start from scratch in designing our new line of active wear.

    15. _____ _____

16. Did you percieve anything unusual about Joel's request?

    16. _____ _____

17. Our company offers extended warrantys on every washer and dryer we manufacture.

    17. _____ _____

18. The weather service issued a travel advisery due to the heavy snowfall.

    18. _____ _____

19. An independant auditor was brought in by the stockholders to review the company's pension plan.

    19. _____ _____

20. Check with your insurance agent about the deductable on your automobile insurance.

    20. _____ _____

B Spelling Practice

On the lines provided, spell the phonetically written words that are enclosed in parentheses in the following sentences. ✓

1. The owners of the factory received a fine because they did not (dispoz) of the hazardous waste correctly.

    1. _____ _____

2. Whitney was very (prampt) in handling the request.

    2. _____ _____

3. The board of directors (konkurd) with the president's decision.

    3. _____ _____

4. Each (vender) may establish the markup on these products.

    4. _____ _____

5. Business writers should avoid needless (repetishun) of words in all correspondence.

    5. _____ _____

6. We have decided to (advertize) on the World Wide Web.

    6. _____ _____

7. (Okazunully), we contract with consultants to handle our market research.

    7. _____ _____

8. Due to an (inkres) in sales the past two years, we will need to expand our offices.

    8. _____ _____

9. After a thorough investigation, the safety board found the company to be in (komplyuns) with the law.

    9. _____ _____

10. Please (skejul) the surgery for Ms. Brady for next Thursday.

    10. _____ _____

11. Nicole will contact the (klient) regarding the change in the court date.

    11. _____ _____

12. When you return your payment, please list the (amaunt) on the payment stub.

    12. _____ _____

13. Ms. Nunez is not (konshus) of her annoying mannerisms, such as constantly tapping her foot.

    13. _____ _____

14. The (perpus) of the meeting was to review the changes in the medical plan.

    14. _____ _____

15. A (substanshul) raise in pay came with the promotion.

    15. _____ _____

16. You should base your (disizhen) on the evidence that has been presented.

    16. _____ _____

17. I advise you to (proseed) cautiously.

    17. _____ _____

18. Have you submitted the (inishel) bid for the project?

    18. _____ _____

19. We will begin the first (faz) of the construction in April.

    19. _____ _____

20. The company hired (teknikul) writers to produce its software manuals.

    20. _____ _____

C Spelling Checkup

On the line provided, write the letter that represents the correctly spelled word in each group. If none of the words is spelled correctly, select *d*. ✓

1. (a) responsibilety   (b) responsibilaty   (c) responsibility   (d) none

    1. _____ _____

2. (a) consciensious   (b) conscientious   (c) consientious   (d) none

    2. _____ _____

3. (a) assistant   (b) asistant   (c) assistent   (d) none

    3. _____ _____

✓

4. (a) preceed	(b) presede	(c) preseed	(d) none	4. _____ ___
5. (a) comittee	(b) committee	(c) committe	(d) none	5. _____ ___
6. (a) incidentally	(b) incidentlly	(c) incidentaly	(d) none	6. _____ ___
7. (a) forgetable	(b) forgetible	(c) forgettable	(d) none	7. _____ ___
8. (a) sincerly	(b) sincerely	(c) sinserely	(d) none	8. _____ ___
9. (a) ocasional	(b) occassional	(c) occasional	(d) none	9. _____ ___
10. (a) warranties	(b) warrantees	(c) waranties	(d) none	10. _____ ___

D Selecting the Right Word

From the words in parentheses, select the one that correctly completes the meaning of
the sentence, and write it on the line provided.   ✓

1. The new personnel director was (formerly, formally)
   introduced at the staff meeting.   1. _____ ___

2. We (least, leased) the office space for two years.   2. _____ ___

3. Ms. Rizzo gave me some good (advise, advice).   3. _____ ___

4. We were (quiet, quite) surprised to hear that Shannon
   had left the company.   4. _____ ___

5. To succeed in today's job market, job seekers must be
   (assertive, asertive).   5. _____ ___

6. Bonita was so (intense, intent) on completing the report
   that she did not take a (brake, break).   6. _____ ___

7. Employees are allowed to wear (casual, causal) business
   attire on Fridays.   7. _____ ___

8. Steve is (illegible, ineligible) for the pension plan because
   he has only been with the company for eight months.   8. _____ ___

9. Who were the (defendants, defendents) in this case?   9. _____ ___

10. Have all the (patients, patience) completed their
    insurance forms?   10. _____ ___

E The Correct Form of Words

For each word enclosed in parentheses, spell the form that the meaning of the sentence
implies.   ✓

1. We received (confirm) of our flight reservations two
   weeks before our trip to Japan.   1. _____ ___

2. Maureen is the (healthy) member of our family.   2. _____ ___

3. Greg (modify) the computer workstation for the new
   employee.   3. _____ ___

4. The doctor said that Ahmed's blood pressure was
   (abnormal) high.   4. _____ ___

5. Due to a promotion, we will have to hire a new
   (administrate) assistant.   5. _____ ___

6. Her (perform) on the sales staff has been excellent.

6. _____ ___

7. We decided to accept the bid that was (submit) by Kendall Consulting.

7. _____ ___

8. Based on your (recommend), we have decided to install a voice-mail system in the office.

8. _____ ___

9. This (enhance) will increase the memory capacity of your computer.

9. _____ ___

10. An (account) must be skilled in mathematics.

10. _____ ___

11. Our company has been in (exist) for 15 years.

11. _____ ___

12. The executive committee discussed the (possible) of opening several branch offices in the next two years.

12. _____ ___

13. All of our buildings are (access) by people in wheelchairs.

13. _____ ___

14. The (install) of the upgraded computer system will take place this weekend.

14. _____ ___

15. Kenneth has been promoted to a (supervise) position.

15. _____ ___

16. Your (participate) in the company's charity golf tournament is greatly appreciated.

16. _____ ___

17. We have (temporary) suspended our shipping operations.

17. _____ ___

18. Dorothy is very (knowledge) about the new desktop publishing software.

18. _____ ___

19. Police officers are (commit) to protecting the public.

19. _____ ___

20. The fire department ordered an (evacuate) of the town due to the hurricane.

20. _____ ___

F Words in Context

Underline any word that is out of context. On the line at the right, write a correct substitute for each word. Write *OK* for any sentence that has no error.

1. Beth's report contained too many irreverent details.

1. _____ ___

2. The company hired a surveyor to mark the property line between the adjoining properties.

2. _____ ___

3. The notice of Norman Colley's recent promotion stated that Mr. Colley was superseded in the position by Robin Davis, who was promoted to vice president.

3. _____ ___

4. Ms. Elias is one of the company's perspective clients.

4. _____ ___

5. The precedings of the symposium are to be published next November.

5. _____ ___

6. Harvey's ingenuous invention saved the company millions of dollars.

6. _____ ___

7. The first- and second-place winners were Lisa and Ben, respectfully.

7. _____ ___

8. Her accountant deprecated the cost of Ann's computer system over a three-year period.

8. _____ ___

STRUCTURING PHRASES AND CLAUSES

A Sentences With Unclear Thought Units

The following sentences contain misplaced words, phrases, or clauses or confusing
thought units. Rewrite each sentence so that its meaning is clear and reasonable.   ✓

1. When you mail your completed order form on the self-addressed envelope, please
   place a stamp.

   _____

   _____   1. _____

2. Anyone who has studied the user's guide in fifteen minutes can prepare a slide
   using the presentation software.

   _____

   _____   2. _____

3. Mr. Rodriguez was only willing to sell a part of the property.

   _____

   _____   3. _____

4. Yesterday Ms. Kozell chaired a meeting on conflict resolution while in New York.

   _____

   _____   4. _____

5. Carla and Patrice agreed that her proposal for expanding the sales territory would
   be reviewed at the next managers' meeting.

   _____

   _____   5. _____

6. Stuart used the new presentation software to prepare his slides, but he was not
   pleased with it.

   _____

   _____   6. _____

7. Before you file the brief for the DeMoyne case, please make a copy of it.

   _____

   _____   7. _____

8. These contracts should be filed near the door in the lateral file.

   _____

   _____   8. _____

9. Refer to my memorandum to all lab technicians about new lab codes dated August 14.

   _____

   _____   9. _____

10. The consultant's evaluation of the new procedure included suggestions for further increasing productivity, which the committee will review on Wednesday.

_____

_____   **10.** _____

11. Sales representatives can't access our inventory system. This has caused delays in processing orders.

_____

_____   **11.** _____

12. Answering the telephone, the patient's request was handled by Aldrina.

_____

_____   **12.** _____

13. Here are some guidelines for saving your computer files from the computer systems staff.

_____

_____   **13.** _____

14. Ross Westerfield successfully renegotiated the contract with Jarrel, Inc., thus proving he is a capable attorney.

_____

_____   **14.** _____

15. In the status report from you, it says the Griffey project is behind schedule.

_____

_____   **15.** _____

16. Robert Clemente sent the e-mail message to Melissa Sidun sitting at his computer.

_____

_____   **16.** _____

17. Being a diligent worker, the promotion was easy to get.

_____

_____   **17.** _____

18. The job openings for all departments are posted outside the Human Resources office on the bulletin board.

_____

_____   **18.** _____

19. We offer a wide range of productivity audiotapes for all employees, which you can purchase at a special discount rate.

_____

_____   **19.** _____

20. Do you know where they sell computer supplies at wholesale prices?

_____

_____   **20.** _____

B Because Clauses

Thought-unit errors with *because clauses* often misstate people's reasons for acting. Correct any such errors in the following sentences.   ✓

1. Mr. Rosenthal did not review the report that Barbara completed because he was detained at a meeting.

   _____

   _____   1. ____

2. Ms. Barnett will be unable to attend the groundbreaking ceremony scheduled for Friday because she is traveling on business.

   _____

   _____   2. ____

3. Alonzo did not approve the request for reimbursement you submitted because the paperwork was incomplete.

   _____

   _____   3. ____

4. Maureen did not finish the research you requested because she was sick.

   _____

   _____   4. ____

5. Judina barely listened to the speech the mayor made because she was distracted by problems at home.

   _____

   _____   5. ____

C Recognizing Unclear Thought Units

On the line provided, write the letter of the answer that best completes the sentence. Choose *e* if none of the answers is correct.   ✓

1. The sentence "After working overtime for several weeks, our annual report was finally completed" contains ____.
   a. a misplaced word
   b. a misplaced phrase
   c. a misplaced clause
   d. a confusing pronoun reference
   e. none of these   1. ____   ____

2. The sentence "Mr. Tanaka asked Mr. Hideo to assume management of the restaurant as soon as he returns from his vacation" contains ____.
   a. a misplaced word
   b. a misplaced phrase
   c. a misplaced clause
   d. a confusing pronoun reference
   e. none of these   2. ____   ____

3. The sentence "Kenneth only compiled the statistics for the report" contains _____.
   a. a misplaced word
   b. a misplaced phrase
   c. a misplaced clause
   d. a confusing pronoun reference
   e. none of these

3. _____ _____

4. The sentence "As we left the meeting, Ms. Kaplan complimented us on our presentation" contains _____.
   a. a misplaced word
   b. a misplaced phrase
   c. a misplaced clause
   d. a confusing pronoun reference
   e. none of these

4. _____ _____

5. The sentence "You can protect your home by using our new security system from thieves" contains _____.
   a. a misplaced word
   b. a misplaced phrase
   c. a misplaced clause
   d. a confusing pronoun reference
   e. none of these

5. _____ _____

6. The sentence "Ms. Soong agreed on the next day to interview the job candidates" contains _____.
   a. a misplaced word
   b. a misplaced phrase
   c. a misplaced clause
   d. a confusing pronoun reference
   e. none of these

6. _____ _____

D **Correcting a Memo**

Proofread the following memo and underline any errors. Write your corrections on the lines provided.

✓

MEMO TO:	All Employees
FROM:	Louisa Furman, Human Resources Director
DATE:	May 7, ‹YEAR›
SUBJECT:	Credit Union

Employees of Atco Chemicals are eligible to become
members of the Global Credit Union. This credit union
offer a complete range of services. Employeees can arrange
to have monies deposited thorough payroll deductions
to their checking or savings accounts. In addition to
direct deposits to interest-bearing accounts the credit union
offers the following services:

- Certificates of deposit ranging from $1,000 to $50,000
  for periods of six months to 36 months.

✓

- Loans for vacation, tuition, home remodeling, and new or used cars.

  _____ ____
  _____ ____

- Home morgages at both adjustable and fixed rates ranging from 3 to 30 years in length.

  _____ ____
  _____ ____

If your interested in becoming a member of the Global Credit Union, information concerning the companys' services as well as applications for membership is available from the Human Resources Department.

  _____ ____
  _____ ____
  _____ ____
  _____ ____

E Proofreading Practice

Underline any errors in the following sentences, and write your corrections on the lines provided. Write *OK* for any sentence that has no error.

✓

1. When the Marshs return from vacation, they will need to call their insurance agent regarding the damage from the tornado.

1. _____ ____

2. In your opinion, do you think its necessary to request more than three competitive bids for this project?

2. _____ ____

3. Call the Walshs with information about the upcoming computer applications seminar.

3. _____ ____

4. Should us sales representatives review these marketing plans for new products more carefully?

4. _____ ____

5. Yes, Troy Acuff is the person who you met at the annual convention in New Orleans.

5. _____ ____

6. Are you sure that the refreshments has been ordered for our grand opening celebration?

6. _____ ____

7. The attorney generals in several states are prosecuting fraudulent credit companies.

7. _____ ____

8. Every executive in the company should order a copy of the new book *Networking for Success* for each member of their staff.

8. _____ ____

9. All the kitchen knifes that we manufacture have stainless steel blades.

9. _____ ____

10. Jeanette and myself have been working on the Fostoria account for the past six months.

10. _____ ____

11. Fortunately, the testing indicated that the bacteria in the water are not harmful.

11. _____ ____

12. Did you explain the new procedures to the Santos's?

12. _____ ____

13. Any surgical technician who wishes to attend the two-day training seminar should sign up in the Human Resources Department.

13. _____ ____

14. All electronic résumés that is submitted to our Web site should be forwarded to Diane McDougal in Human Resources.

14. _____ ____

15. The board of directors does not expect many vetos at the next stockholders' meeting.

15. _____ ____

16. Several islands in the Pacific Rim are dotted with volcanos.

16. _____ ____

17. The newspaper article in the *Columbus Courier* stated where the tax levy for the city schools has been placed on the ballot.

17. _____ ____

18. Ms. Watson could not help from asking Mr. Carpenter about the latest change to the contract.

18. _____ ____

19. No one from the Trauma Services Department beside Elaine Haskell attended the in-service training last week.

19. _____ ____

20. Nearly two-thirds of the staff have agreed to assist with the food drive and adopt-a-family program during the holiday season.

20. _____ ____

21. Danville Advertising was real fortunate to find such a talented design director as Ben Grissom.

21. _____ ____

22. Being that the estimated unit cost is over $12 a unit, we decided to increase the sales price.

22. _____ ____

23. Neither the supervisor nor the associates was aware of the change in the delivery date for the shipment.

23. _____ ____

24. One floor of the building on West 57th Street have been allocated for our regional sales staff.

24. _____ ____

25. Most of the delays in shipping the computer monitors were due to incorrect addresses.

25. _____ ____

SECTION 7.4   WRITING EFFECTIVE SENTENCES

   Improving Sentences

In the space provided, rewrite each sentence to improve it.   ✓

1. Lorraine did not fail to complete all her projects on time last year.

_____

_____   1. ____

2. He is qualified, if not better qualified, than the other accountant.

_____

_____   2. ____

3. The job is demanding, challenges are stimulating.

_____

_____   3. ____

4. I was preparing PowerPoint slides when the new vice president toured the office.

_____

_____   4. ____

5. The company wanted to become involved in the community, and so I suggested we participate in the Big Brothers/Big Sisters program.

_____

_____

_____   5. ____

6. Linda wanted to learn more about Web browsers, so she signed up for a seminar on using the Internet.

_____

_____

_____   6. ____

7. Only reports dealing with a reported rise in costs will be reported on at the division meeting on Wednesday.

_____

_____

_____   7. ____

8. Attached are the sales figures requested in your June 16 e-mail message.

_____

_____   8. ____

9. The advertising project requires a copywriter and graphic artist.

_____

_____   9. ____

10. Francine is, given the delicate nature of the negotiations, the best mediator for the situation.

_____

_____ **10.** _____

11. Colleen likes using the voice-mail system more than Dwayne.

_____

_____ **11.** _____

12. To promote teamwork, cubicles were replaced with open work areas and the desks moved closer together.

_____

_____

_____ **12.** _____

13. Rafael convinced the product engineers to test his design, and they had rejected it originally.

_____

_____

_____ **13.** _____

14. To avoid confusion about how to complete the procedure, you should revise the instruction manual.

_____

_____ **14.** _____

15. Three of the seven responses were incorrect.

_____

_____ **15.** _____

16. Mr. Nouri stated that the product testing had been successful and manufacturing would begin in January.

_____

_____ **16.** _____

17. It wasn't hard to understand why Natalie Ramos was named the director of nursing.

_____

_____ **17.** _____

18. Timothy is logical, detailed, and likes to troubleshoot problems.

_____

_____ **18.** _____

19. The report was time-consuming to read, not because it was long but it was poorly written.

_____

_____ **19.** _____

20. Apryl is interested, as you mentioned yesterday, in working on the editorial staff.

_____

_____ **20.** _____

B Identifying Positive and Negative Words

Classify each word in the following list as positive or negative, and write your answers in the space provided. Be prepared to explain your decisions.

commend	exemplary	deception	facilitate	impasse
inhibit	solvent	accredit	discrepancy	fidelity
liability	objection	invaluable	advocate	default
bankruptcy	incentive	provoke	compensation	compulsory

Positive   **Negative**

_____ _____   _____ _____

_____ _____   _____ _____

_____ _____   _____ _____

_____ _____   _____ _____

_____ _____   _____ _____

C Joining Sentences

In the space provided, rewrite each pair of sentences as one sentence. Use a subordinating conjunction to join the sentences.

✓

1. Mr. Ferguson was traveling on business in India. His department was reorganized.

   _____

   _____   1. ____

2. Kendra will distribute the flyers. Marlon will make the telephone calls.

   _____

   _____   2. ____

3. We preregistered for the conference. We were unable to get hotel accommodations.

   _____

   _____   3. ____

4. The customer service representatives attended the training session. The marketing manager rescheduled the staff meeting.

   _____

   _____   4. ____

5. We start our carpool at six in the morning. The traffic on the expressway gets congested.

   _____

   _____   5. ____

6. Selena was given the option of working a flexible schedule. She has two preschool children at home.

_____

_____ 6. _____

7. Other sites were considered for the headquarters, but this site was nearest the airport.

_____

_____ 7. _____

8. The stock of copier paper was getting low. Christian ordered 50 reams from the warehouse.

_____

_____ 8. _____

9. Ms. Latham delayed the start of the status meeting. Mr. Panico, the manufacturing coordinator, had arrived.

_____

_____ 9. _____

10. All the group members worked hard. They had never worked harder before.

_____

_____ 10. _____

D The You-Attitude

Rewrite each of the following sentences to use the you-attitude and positive wording.

✓

1. Gemma is anxious to hear your reaction to the proposal.

_____

_____

_____ 1. _____

2. We have reviewed your complaints regarding our Dynamo computerized day planner.

_____

_____

_____ 2. _____

3. Do you know who is to blame for the error in placing the order?

_____

_____

_____ 3. _____

4. We are sorry but we will have to delay shipment of your order until we receive all items from the manufacturer.

_____

_____

_____ 4. _____

5. You need to give me the completed report by Thursday, November 18.

_____

_____

_____ 5. _____

E **Active and Passive Voice**

Make the following sentences more positive by changing them from passive voice to
active voice. Write your answers in the space provided.

✓

1. New procedures for tracking customers' orders have been adopted by the inventory
   department.

   _____

   _____   1. _____

2. The software was tested by a team of quality-control inspectors.

   _____

   _____   2. _____

3. A copy of the company's code of ethics was received by all employees.

   _____

   _____   3. _____

4. Carmella has received some helpful feedback from her supervisor.

   _____

   _____   4. _____

5. Bruce has been recommended for promotion by the plant manager.

   _____

   _____   5. _____

6. Updates to the medical insurance coverage were discussed by Margarita Duran.

   _____

   _____   6. _____

7. Instructions for participating in the recycling program were included on the flyers.

   _____

   _____   7. _____

8. The hospital staff was surprised by the news of the proposed merger with
   Metropolitan Health Care.

   _____

   _____   8. _____

9. Kimberly was congratulated by Ms. Dalton for achieving the highest sales for the
   year.

   _____

   _____   9. _____

10. Lawrence was often discouraged by temporary setbacks in his progress, but his
    goals were never lost sight of.

    _____

    _____   10. _____

F Balancing Sentences

Rewrite each of the following sentences to balance the elements. Write your answers in the space provided. ✓

1. Adrian was the logical choice for the Web site coordinator because he is knowledgeable, detail-oriented, and has much creativity.

_____

_____   1. _____

2. We reviewed the preliminary budget figures this morning and copies distributed to the production managers for their review.

_____

_____   2. _____

3. To staff our new office, we will need to hire a claims specialist and administrative assistant.

_____

_____   3. _____

4. Roselle can prepare the advertising copy just as well, if not better, than Darryl.

_____

_____   4. _____

5. A competent trial attorney must speak to and confer clients on a regular basis.

_____

_____   5. _____

6. Judy spends more time at work than home.

_____

_____   6. _____

7. Has Lester completed the design for the brochure or his assistant?

_____

_____   7. _____

8. The Webnet Internet browser provides as much flexibility as, if not more flexibility, than the Linknet Internet browser.

_____

_____   8. _____

9. Our survey indicates that teenagers know more about computers than adults.

_____

_____   9. _____

10. The one-day seminar on customer service relations was practical and gave much information.

_____

_____   10. _____

✓

11. Before this agreement can be considered binding, both parties must agree to and abide the terms specified in the letter of intent.

_____

_____   **11.** _____

12. Hull and Associates has offices both in San Antonio and Toledo.

_____

_____   **12.** _____

13. The specialists who staff our software hotline are skilled in troubleshooting problems and have the ability to answer questions.

_____

_____   **13.** _____

14. Airline passengers traveling with pets are as demanding as passengers with children.

_____

_____   **14.** _____

15. This latest laptop computer is lightweight and small in size.

_____

_____   **15.** _____

16. Any incidents of harassment should be reported to the supervisor and personnel director.

_____

_____   **16.** _____

17. Please verify that the electrical engineer is aware of and agreeable the changes in the blueprints.

_____

_____   **17.** _____

18. Grace Schmidt would neither drop the charges nor would she accept a plea bargain.

_____

_____   **18.** _____

19. Mr. Shimomura discussed the trip he met with the minister of trade.

_____

_____   **19.** _____

20. Do you know if Courtney vacationed in Florida or her sister?

_____

_____   **20.** _____

G Correcting Errors

Proofread the following memo and correct any errors. Write your corrections on the lines provided. ✓

MEMO TO: All Employees

FROM: Constance Palmeri

DATE: September 25, ‹YEAR›

SUBJECT: Red Cross Blood Drive

Our annual Red Cross Blood Drive have been scheduled for Wenesday, November 19, from 9:00 a.m. to 2:30 p.m. in the main conference room. Last year's drive was extremely sucessful, and we expect to do even better this year.

Please stop by the reception desk in Human Resources between now an November 15 to sign up for you're appointment time. If you prefer, you may call me at extension 5697 to schedule an appointment. Once all appointments have been set I will send each participant a confirmation card.

We encourage you to take advantage of this opportunity to make a difference in your community by helping with a very worthwhile cause. Remember; the more blood we donate, the more lifes we save.

_____ ____
_____ ____
_____ ____
_____ ____
_____ ____
_____ ____
_____ ____
_____ ____
_____ ____
_____ ____
_____ ____
_____ ____

BUILDING EFFECTIVE PARAGRAPHS

 Sentences, Paragraphs, and Messages

From the following list, select the word or words that *best* complete the sentences.
Write your answers in the blanks.

bury	main idea
choppy	one
connections	readability
eight	sentence length
first	sentence structure
five	six
length	structure
odd	topic sentence
10	20
transitional	unity
two	vary

✓

1. A written message should have _____ purpose, and each paragraph
   in that message should have one _____.   1. _____

2. _____ refers to the ease with which a message can be read.
   _____ and _____ both affect readability.   2. _____

3. As a business writer, your goal should be to _____ the
   _____ and _____ of sentences.   3. _____

4. The main idea of a paragraph is usually stated in a _____ that
   is often the first sentence in the paragraph.   4. _____

5. _____ words and phrases provide _____
   between sentences and between paragraphs.   5. _____

6. Combining several short paragraphs into one paragraph helps avoid a
   _____ appearance.   6. _____

7. Most sentences in a message should range in length from _____
   to _____ words.   7. _____

8. Keep the first and last paragraphs of a message short, usually _____
   to _____ lines.   8. _____

9. Extremely long sentences seem to _____ the main thought.   9. _____

10. In general, a paragraph should have no more than _____ to
    _____ lines.   10. _____

11. When all sentences of a paragraph support the main idea, the paragraph has
    _____.   11. _____

12. In general, use an _____ number of paragraphs in a
    message for a better appearance.   12. _____

B One Main Idea

Read each of the following paragraphs. Underline any sentences that do not develop the main idea of each paragraph.

1.   As of September 2, all personal computers in our Columbus and Peoria offices have been connected to the company-wide computer network. Effective immediately, all employees may use their computers to access data from the network directory. Passwords for each employee have been assigned, and a list of available programs has been distributed to all employees. We are currently investigating the cost of providing Internet access. Any employee who needs more information concerning the computer network should contact Antonia Tomlinson in the Business Systems Group.

1. _____

2.   Nora Wylie has been promoted to vice president of public affairs for Universal Network Services (UNS). In the past few months, UNS has been making noticeable progress in controlling expenses and in reducing overhead costs. Ms. Wylie has been the manager of the UNS communications department for three years. She replaces Donald Suto, who recently left the company to take a position with DataCom Systems in Georgia.

2. _____

C Making Smooth Transitions

From the following list, select the transitional word or phrase that best links each of the following pairs of sentences, and write your answer in the blank. Do not use the same word or phrase more than once.

at present	for example	nevertheless	such as
consequently	in addition	on the other hand	that is
especially	in fact	second	then
finally	moreover	specifically	therefore

1. Security at the hospital has been upgraded. _____, surveillance cameras have been posted in all parking lots and inside the parking garage.

1. _____

2. We are, _____, planning to expand our product line in interactive computer games.

2. _____

3. Janice has proven to be a gifted legal researcher. _____, she is skilled in preparing legal briefs.

3. _____

4. Employees are encouraged to take continuing education classes. _____, the company offers tuition reimbursement for completing work-related classes.

4. _____

5. Several members of the nursing staff are interested in attending the in-service training. They are _____ interested in learning the latest infection-control techniques.

5. _____

6. Productivity has increased in all our divisions. _____, our profit margin has increased.

6. _____

7. Our travel agency is now taking reservations for vacation packages for winter holidays. _____, we are accepting reservations for spring getaways.

7. _____

8. First, Naomi will outline the sales history. Second, Maurice will present the slide show. _____, John and Deanna will answer any questions.

8. _____

✓

9. On the one hand, our business has increased by 8 percent. _____,
our expenses have increased by 15 percent.

9. _____

10. Gabriel Cohen has been with the firm for only four years. _____,
he has been named a full partner.

10. _____

11. The company is offering more options for health care coverage this year.
_____, the company is offering coverage with Blue Cross/Blue
Shield and Central Western HMO.

11. _____

12. Most of the residents of the elder care facility will be spending the holidays with
their families. _____, we have decided to close one wing of
the facility during that time.

12. _____

13. Any change in plans, _____ a layover at the airport, should be
allowed for in your travel itinerary.

13. _____

14. You should make arrangements with your insurance agent to increase your
automobile coverage. _____ you should plan to update your
life insurance.

14. _____

15. Most automobile accidents are avoidable; _____, they should
never happen so long as drivers are careful.

15. _____

D Varying Sentence Length

Rewrite the following long sentences, making each one into two or more sentences.
Insert transitional words or phrases as needed.

✓

1. In an effort to reduce our operating expenses for the remainder of the year, our
vice president of operations, Allen Strauss, has requested that all managers review
their budgets for the period of July to December and cut the personnel and training segment from $50,000 to a total of $35,000 and to accomplish this we would
like each manager to suggest expenses that can be canceled or postponed.

_____

_____

_____

_____

_____

1. _____

2. As part of the next Professional Women's Forum meeting on November 5 at the
Stauffer Inn, a panel of women who are in management positions will discuss their
career tracks.

_____

_____

_____

_____

_____

2. _____

3. The company's tuition-reimbursement plan is designed to encourage employees to continue their education and it does so by paying for the complete cost of tuition for approved courses and naturally we encourage all interested employees to take advantage of this opportunity.

_____

_____

_____

_____   **3.** _____

Rewrite the following short sentences to combine them into one longer sentence.

4. Effective March 1, all employees are required to use the new Travel and Entertainment form. This form is to be used to report all company-related travel expenses.

_____

_____

_____   **4.** _____

5. William and I are coordinating the production team. Cynthia will obtain the bids. James will set the schedule. Yolanda will oversee the quality control.

_____

_____

_____

_____   **5.** _____

E Smooth Communication

Rewrite the following paragraph from a company newsletter so that the message is communicated more smoothly.

Coleman Telecommunications took part in National Health Awareness Week. National Health Awareness Week was April 21-25. Health information sessions were held in the company cafeteria. They were held Monday through Friday. Tara Vernon was on hand to answer questions. She is a registered nurse. She answered questions about health-related issues. Ms. Vernon shared information and literature about preventive health care. She also shared information and literature about health maintenance.

_____

_____

_____

_____

_____

_____

_____

_____

_____

F Making Paragraphing Decisions

Break the following excerpt from a message into four effective paragraphs. At the points marked (T), insert an appropriate transitional word or phrase. ✓

In August, one of our supervisors, Troy Simmons, suggested that we investigate ways to reduce the paperwork overload in our division. (T) we asked Troy and his two assistants to analyze the procedures in their department and to submit some recommendations for reducing unnecessary paperwork. Not surprisingly, they found that we now make and distribute far too many copies of routine forms. (T) we now distribute 23 copies of purchase orders throughout the company. (T) they found that 16 of the employees who received these purchase orders simply file the copies for future use. (T) Troy and his coworkers found that other routine forms are copies that are distributed unnecessarily. (T) copies of budget estimates for each project are sent to every manager in the division. (T) copies should be sent only to members of the project team, their supervisors, and the division vice president. When Troy and his two assistants complete their report, we will share their findings with you. (T) if you should have any suggestions for reducing our paper overload, please let us know.

_____
_____
_____
_____
_____
_____
_____
_____
_____
_____
_____
_____
_____
_____
_____
_____
_____
_____
_____
_____
_____
_____
_____

G Editing for Accuracy

Underline any errors in the following sentences, and write your corrections on the lines provided. Write *OK* for any sentence that has no error. ✓

1. Gary said, "I hope that Marie working so hard will pay off for her in the long run."

   1. _____ ____

2. Are you sure that the flight has been delayed until tomorrow?

   2. _____ ____

3. Our CEO thinks that the proposal with the most merit is your's.

   3. _____ ____

4. Has you ordered the latest version of the tax software for all our accountants?

   4. _____ ____

5. Obviously, its in our best interest to offer exceptional customer service.

   5. _____ ____

6. For every message you send using electronic mail, you save the company time and money.

   6. _____ ____

7. Of all our competitors, Allegre Industries is most highly regarded for their fair prices and excellent service.

   7. _____ ____

8. In my opinion, Stephanie's sales record is superior to Luke.

   8. _____ ____

9. At Mr. Moore's, our vice presidents' suggestion, we purchased the computer system.

   9. _____ ____

10. Did you find out if Ben's and Jerry's class meets tonight?

    10. _____ ____

H Proofreading Practice

Underline any errors in the following memo, and write your corrections in the spaces provided. ✓

MEMO TO: Fernando Lawrence   _____ ____

FROM: Katharine Leffler   _____ ____

DATE: Septembr 23, ‹YEAR›   _____ ____

SUBJECT: Borden Project   _____ ____

As you know, we had began the design work for the Borden   _____ ____

headquarters building several weeks ago, but the project was   _____ ____

sit aside in order to complete the O'Neil project. As a result,   _____ ____

we are behind schedule on the Borden project.   _____ ____

In order to kept the Borden project on schedule, we will   _____ ____

need to paid overtime for several staff members the next three   _____ ____

weeks'. I would like your permission to authorize overtime work   _____ ____

for three architects and two engineers.   _____ ____

 **SECTION 7.6**

REVISING, EDITING, AND PROOFREADING

A **Using Proofreaders' Marks**

Using the proofreaders' marks introduced in Section 7.6 of your text, make corrections in the following sentences.

✓

1. Three of our Company representatives attended the conference in Landover Maryland.   1. _____

2. Our store ofers a three year warranty on all electronic appliances we sell.   2. _____

3. You may place orders four our latest software programs with your regional sales person.   3. _____

4. In August we must send copys of our anual report to stockholders.   4. _____

5. When may we expect to recieve your reply to our offer.   5. _____

6. You may at any time, elect to withdraw the funds from your certificate of deposit account and within 30 days.   6. _____

7. Our Internet site provides up to date stock market quotations 24 hours a day.   7. _____

8. Please send the contracts to the New york office.   8. _____

9. Be sure that you sign the authorization form to.   9. _____

10. Unless we obtain a written release from form the patient we cannot release the information to the insurer.   10. _____

11. Has the Doctor received the results of my tests?   11. _____

12. Febuary 20 will mark our 15 year in busniess.   12. _____

13. Will you be able to complete the report by 4:00 P.M.?   13. _____

14. The contract for the Petrofsky project has been aproved.   14. _____

15. Which para legal is conducting the research for the Kramer vs. Hawley case?   15. _____

16. Most of the slides for our salespresentation has been completed.   16. _____

17. Will you be able to respond to the e-mail mesage by 5p.m?   17. _____

18. Ms. Mendez wil travel to our offices in Albuquerque New Mexico; San Antonio Texas; and Salem Oregon.   18. _____

19. Occassionally our computer net work has to be shut down in order to instal upgraded programs.   19. _____

20. Our new offices will be located in the Easton business complex on Morse Rd.   20. _____

B Improving Tone and Organization

In the space provided, revise the following memo to improve the tone and to make the organization more logical.

✓

MEMO TO: All Employees

FROM: Security Department

DATE: May 16, ‹YEAR›

SUBJECT: Facility Security

Employees who violate this procedure will be subject to company discipline.

Employees are hereby warned not to take company property from the facility unless it is essential to their work and is approved by the appropriate supervisor. Employees must get a property pass from a security guard, and they must get the guard to sign the pass. But first they must obtain approval from their supervisor to take company property from the premises. The property must be fully described on the pass.

_____

_____

_____

_____

_____

_____

_____

_____

_____

_____

_____

_____

C Revising Tone

Revise the following sentences so that they reflect a positive tone.

✓

1. Unfortunately, a backlog of orders for our Pocket Pal Computer makes it impossible for us to ship your order until two weeks from today.

_____

_____

_____

1. _____

2. Don't you realize that we cannot pay your invoice sooner than 30 days from now?

_____

_____

_____

2. _____

3. You carelessly forgot to include your social security number on your application form.

_____

_____

_____

3. _____

4. We are in receipt of your letter of October 8 in which you complain about our service.   ✓

_____

_____

_____   **4.** _____

5. How can you be so silly to think that we will refund your money?

_____

_____

_____   **5.** _____

D More Effective Sentences

Revise each sentence according to the directions in italics. Write the revised sentence in
the space provided.   ✓

1. New spreadsheet software for the accounting department has been ordered by us.
Change to active voice.

_____

_____   **1.** _____

2. Each day our customer service representatives work to provide courteous, helpful
service to our customers.
Substitute a more colorful verb.

_____

_____   **2.** _____

3. The cultural-awareness program has been so successful over the past two years that
our European affiliates have adopted it.
Begin the sentence with a prepositional phrase.

_____

_____   **3.** _____

4. Bawden & Company regretfully must close its manufacturing plant in Savannah,
Georgia.
Begin the sentence with an adverb.

_____

_____   **4.** _____

5. The reason why we are flying to our destination on Saturday is to take advantage
of reduced weekend airfare offered by the airline.
Eliminate unnecessary words.

_____

_____   **5.** _____

6. Because she is employed by the company sponsoring the design contest, Deanna is
illegible to enter the competition.
Use the correct word.

_____

_____   **6.** _____

7. To apply for a position with Cardinal Credit Services, prospective employees must complete an application that outlines their qualifications for employment with Cardinal Credit Services.
Eliminate unnecessary repetition.

_____

_____   **7.** _____

8. You are cordially invited to our best sale ever to take advantage of the best prices on computer equipment.
Use more specific, colorful words.

_____

_____   **8.** _____

9. The letter from the insurance agent said, "Notification to discontinue automobile insurance has not been received by our office."
Change to active voice.

_____

_____   **9.** _____

10. Ms. Yates told all sales associates that sales goals for the next year would be based on the sales from the previous two years.
Substitute a more colorful verb.

_____

_____   **10.** _____

E More Effective Language

In the space provided, revise the following paragraph from a memo to improve the language and the sentence structure.

Our company employs a relocation specialist. This specialist, Dawn Roberts, works in the Personnel Department. Her job is to assist employees in relocating to another city. She handles details such as selling a home, moving to another location, and buying a new home in that location. She has prepared a booklet titled "Tips for Moving" that answers questions that are frequently asked about relocating. She also has information on the policy of the company on the company's buying your existing home so that you can purchase a new home in the city to which you are moving.

_____

_____

_____

_____

_____

_____

_____

_____

_____

_____

_____   _____

F   Being More Specific

In the space provided, list adjectives that would make each noun more specific.

1. calendar   ✓   **2.** meeting   ✓

_____ ___   _____ ___

_____ ___   _____ ___

_____ ___   _____ ___

3. envelope   **4.** folders

_____ ___   _____ ___

_____ ___   _____ ___

_____ ___   _____ ___

In the space provided, list more specific and colorful verbs that could be substituted for the verb in each phrase.

5. went to Indianapolis   **6.** wrote a report

_____ ___   _____ ___

_____ ___   _____ ___

_____ ___   _____ ___

7. suggested a change   **8.** do a task

_____ ___   _____ ___

_____ ___   _____ ___

_____ ___   _____ ___

In the space provided, list more specific and colorful nouns that could be substituted for each noun.

9. book   **10.** machine

_____ ___   _____ ___

_____ ___   _____ ___

_____ ___   _____ ___

G   Identifying Questionable Content

Block and query questionable content in the following sentences. Use a different letter of the alphabet to label each block. Write the reason for your query in the space provided.   ✓

1. You are booked on Fight 6257 which leaves Minneapolis at 6:71 p.m.

_____ **1.** ____

2. All our checks were listed on the bank statement except the three written yesterday: 3197, 3198, and 199.

_____ **2.** ____

3. The conference will be held from September 31 to October 5.

_____ **3.** ____

4. For only $19.95, you will receive 21 issues—one each month for a whole year.

_____   4. _____

5. Our storewide Fourth of July sale will begin at 8 p.m.

_____   5. _____

H Editing for Conciseness

Without changing the meaning, rewrite the following items, omitting any overused words. Underline any words that are overused and should be omitted.

1. The copier room contains some very extremely sensitive equipment, which is easily damaged by extremely hot or humid weather. You must be extremely careful when you use these machines. Monitor the temperature controls extremely carefully.

_____

_____

_____

_____   1. _____

2. Yorktown Realty, Inc., has four company cars and three company vans. The company cars are two years old, and the company vans are four years old. As your company accountant, I recommend selling your current company vehicles and leasing new ones.

_____

_____

_____

_____   2. _____

I Editing for Consistent Sequence

In the space provided, rewrite each item to make it consistent in sequence.

1. We will hold regional sales meetings on July 16, September 4, and August 8.

_____

_____

_____   1. _____

2. Norinda Enterprises plans to open a plant in Mexico, Taiwan, or Puerto Rico.

_____

_____

_____   2. _____

3. Training sessions for new employees are scheduled for 9:30 a.m., 10:45 a.m., 2:30 p.m., and 1:15 p.m.

_____

_____

_____   3. _____

✓

4. You may purchase gift certificates for $25, $50, $100, and $75.

_____

_____

_____   4. _____

5. Do you think that Megan, Karin, or Steve should get the assignment?

_____

_____

_____   5. _____

6. New representatives on the board of directors include Breyer, Trueman, Marshall, and Thurgood.

_____

_____

_____   6. _____

7. Interviews with the job candidates are scheduled for 8:30 a.m., 9:45 a.m., 1:30 p.m., and 11 a.m.

_____

_____

_____   7. _____

8. Should we hold the seminar in April, June, or May?

_____

_____

_____   8. _____

9. Three purchase orders have not been filled: M1639, M1643, and M1640.

_____

_____

_____   9. _____

10. Send copies of the contract to Kim Millwater, Nancy Harvey, and Darlene Shores.

_____

_____

_____   10. _____

J More Proofreaders' Marks

Make the changes indicated by the proofreaders' marks. Write the corrected items in the space provided.

✓

1. Ms. Cascade's assistant advised me to schedule an appointment to discuss the programing changes.

_____

_____

_____   1. _____

2. Our ③ computer programmers are knowledgeable about <u>Fortran</u> and <u>Cobol</u>. ✓

_____

_____

2. ____

3.]CONSUMER TRENDS [
Many personal computer users sign up with a commercial on-line service to gain access to the INTERNET. In addition to helpful customer support, such services provide access to e-mail, bulletin board services, and news groups.

_____

_____

_____

3. ____

4. Ms. Phylis Parsons
5305 N. Main St.
Columbus, OK 43235

_____

_____

4. ____

K Editing for Courtesy

In the space provided, rewrite the following message to improve the tone. Add transitions as needed, and break the message into paragraphs. Also, include any details necessary to make the message complete. Barry Hines, who purchased his car from Schaefer Motors, received this message.

> We at Schaefer Motors would like to remind you that you're due for an oil change. If you're smart, you'll bring your car in for service now. Otherwise, you'll probably have serious problems later. At Schaefer Motors we use only quality parts and have excellent, factory-trained mechanics. You have to do your part. If you don't have your car serviced regularly, we can't be responsible if something goes wrong. So come in now. For a short time, we are providing a special service to customers. We'll give you a ride to and from work on the day of your service appointment as long as it isn't too far. We're proud of this extra service. Call our Service Department for an appointment.

_____

_____

_____

_____

_____

_____

_____

_____

_____

_____

_____

_____

L Detecting Embarrassing Mistakes

Spelling checkers would not find the correctly spelled but incorrectly used words in the following sentences. Underline each incorrectly used word, and write the correct word in the space provided.   ✓

1. Angela requested a new keyboard fore her computer.   1. _____ ____

2. The local community college is offering a coarse on using the Internet to start a business.   2. _____ ____

3. If you have any questions, please contact the personal director.   3. _____ ____

4. Dr. Sykes has a lot of patients when working with children.   4. _____ ____

5. The new sight for our company headquarters has yet to be determined.   5. _____ ____

6. All the employees accept eight have signed up for the company picnic at the zoo.   6. _____ ____

7. We will be prepared when the case comes to trail.   7. _____ ____

8. My sister received a job offer from a perspective employer.   8. _____ ____

9. They have no evidence to support there claims.   9. _____ ____

10. Our principle concern with the benefits package is the pension option.   10. _____ ____

M Proofreading for Content Errors

Use proofreaders' marks to insert omitted words and to delete repeated words in the following sentences.   ✓

1. Ms. Anderson will oversee all overseas operations, including those Japan.   1. ____

2. Do you prefer to schedule a morning or an appointment with the doctor?   2. ____

3. The merchandise arrived on Thursday, and and the invoice arrived.   3. ____

4. When placing your order by telephone, please provide your name, telephone number, telephone number, and credit card account number.   4. ____

5. Colleen ordered three keyboard trays, two sets of bookends, one dozen highlighter pens, one dozen highlighter pens, and three mouse pads.   5. ____

N Proofreading for Punctuation Errors

Use proofreaders' marks to insert, delete, or change punctuation as needed in the following sentences.   ✓

1. Plan to register by Monday October 6 to reserve your hotel accommodations for the conference.   1. ____

2. Joe Morgan has worked for the Tennessee based company for 15 years.   2. ____

3. Michelle's exact words were "Correct the error immediately!   3. ____

4. Oliver typed the memo then he proofread it.

4. ____

5. Cheryl Ianelli M.D. will be the keynote speaker at the American Medical Association conference next spring.

5. ____

O   Proofreading for Number Usage Errors

Use proofreaders' marks to make corrections in number usage in the following sentences.

1. The two-day seminar on desktop publishing costs only $199.00 and covers 6 different applications.

1. ____

2. 300 customers were surveyed, and only eight percent expressed dissatisfaction with the company's service.

2. ____

3. Our restaurant will open at 6:00 a.m. each day, 7 days a week.

3. ____

4. To receive the full discount, mail your rebate form by June first.

4. ____

5. The family room in the house measures fourteen feet by sixteen feet.

5. ____

P   Proofreading on the Computer

Yesterday you typed the following portion of a message and saved it on your computer before you proofread it. Proofread the paragraphs now, correcting any errors as you do so. Write your corrections on the lines provided.

More and more businesses are contracting with independant firms that provide alternative dispute resolution services. Such firms provides mediation and arbitration services to clients as constructive ways too resolve employment-related disputes.

The majority of alternative dispute resolution firms employ former judges and experienced attornies to serve as mediators and arbitrators. These neutral parties has diverse background and include women and men of different ages, races, and religions.

SECTION 8.1 BASICS OF ORAL COMMUNICATION

A Planning Telephone Calls

Listing a brief outline of topics to be covered during a telephone call makes efficient use of your time and the time of the person you call. It also reduces the number of times that you have to call again to say, "I forgot to ask" or "I forgot to tell you about...."

Read each of the following situations. Using complete sentences, finish the printed outline. Create any details that you need.   ✓

SITUATION 1

You need to make a follow-up telephone call to a patient who visited the doctor's office where you work. Three days ago the patient saw the doctor about an acute sinus infection. The purpose of your call is to check the patient's progress and to see if additional medication is needed. Supply any necessary details.

Identification: _____

_____

_____

_____

Message: _____

_____

_____

_____

_____

_____

_____

_____

_____

_____

Closing: _____

_____

_____

SITUATION 2

You are planning to transfer to a senior college after you graduate from the community college in June. You plan to call the toll-free number of several senior colleges to request information needed to apply for the upcoming fall semester. Be specific in requesting the information you need.

✓

Identification: _____

_____

_____

Message: _____

_____

_____

_____

_____

_____

_____

_____

_____

Closing: _____

_____

SITUATION 3

As part of a class project, you are to call Ms. Stephanie Wheeler and invite her to speak to your business communication class on the use of visual aids in presentations. She comes highly recommended as a knowledgeable speaker on the proposed subject. Supply all the details Ms. Wheeler would need to know to make her decision to speak to your class. Assume that she will accept your invitation.

Identification: _____

_____

_____

Message: _____

_____

_____

_____

_____

_____

_____

_____

_____

Closing: _____

_____

B **Outgoing Voice-Mail Messages**

For each of the following situations, write an appropriate message to be recorded as your outgoing voice-mail message for incoming calls. A word of caution: Avoid informing callers that your business will be closed for an extended period of time or that you will be out of town.   ✓

SITUATION 1

You are the administrative assistant for a medical practice. One of your duties is to record a voice-mail greeting that will be used for calls received. Identify the business. Suggest that the caller telephone during regular business hours and include the specific business hours that the office will be open. Include an after-hours number (for medical emergencies) that will be answered whenever the office is not open.

_____

_____

_____

_____

SITUATION 2

You and your spouse own Murphy's Upholstery Shop. You use your voice mail any time you are away from the shop for any reason, such as picking up furniture, delivering furniture, or giving estimates. This week, you and your family are away on vacation. Even though you are on vacation, you plan to return your telephone calls by using the remote feature of your voice mail. You would like callers to leave their names and telephone numbers so that their calls can be returned.

_____

_____

_____

_____

SITUATION 3

You are the owner and the only employee of Zappers Pest Control, a business you started three months ago. You use your voice mail both after hours and during the business day when you are out on calls. You run the pest control business from your home and gladly return calls 24 hours a day. Tell the caller that you will return calls within two hours.

_____

_____

_____

_____

C Answering the Telephone

Assume that you are the person answering the telephone in each of the following situations. In the space provided, write the response you would say when you answer the telephone.

✓

1. You are an accountant at Lindy and Associates, Inc., a small public accounting firm. Your receptionist is on vacation, and the accountants are taking turns answering the telephone.

_____

_____

_____   1. _____

2. You indicate to a caller that he/she has reached the Human Resources Department. The caller says, "I'm sorry. I wanted the Accounts Payable Department."

_____

_____

_____   2. _____

3. You are Hannah Pearson's administrative assistant. A caller wants to speak with Ms. Pearson, who will be out of the office until tomorrow at 8 a.m.

_____

_____

_____   3. _____

4. You are the sales coordinator for a regional sales office. Amanda Selby has left three messages for Mr. Harris, the office manager, to call her. Mr. Harris has not returned the calls because he has told Ms. Selby twice that he has no interest in her product. Mr. Harris has told you to handle the situation if Ms. Selby calls again. Ms. Selby calls again and wants to leave another message for Mr. Harris.

_____

_____

_____   4. _____

5. Patricia Wexler of the Shipping Department will return to her office at 3 p.m. She asked you to handle all her calls until that time. Her telephone rings.

_____

_____

_____   5. _____

D Word Wizard

Learning new words increases your ability to communicate. Below are some definitions and their corresponding words. Match the definition with its word by writing the appropriate letter beside each numbered item.

✓

1. incapable of error	a. defer	1. _____ _____
2. to arrange according to a definite scheme	b. exempt	2. _____ _____
3. to release from liability	c. infallible	3. _____ _____
4. negligent in the performance of duty	d. remiss	4. _____ _____
5. to put off until a later time	e. systematize	5. _____ _____
6. tiresome because of dullness	f. tedious	6. _____ _____

SECTION 8.2

NONVERBAL COMMUNICATION
AND SPEECH QUALITIES

A Factors Influencing Oral Communication

Read each question, then answer by placing a check mark in the appropriate column:
A for Always; *MT* for Most of the Time; *ST* for Sometimes; or *SN* for Seldom or Never.

Score yourself on these important factors as follows: Always, 5 points; Most of the
Time, 4 points; Sometimes, 3 points; Seldom or Never, 0.

	A	MT	ST	SN	✓
1. Do you convey to others that you are listening?	____	____	____	____	**1.** ____
2. Do you dress appropriately for various situations?	____	____	____	____	**2.** ____
3. Are you neatly dressed and well groomed?	____	____	____	____	**3.** ____
4. Do you sit up straight?	____	____	____	____	**4.** ____
5. Do you stand erect with shoulders back?	____	____	____	____	**5.** ____
6. Do you walk confidently, with poise and good posture?	____	____	____	____	**6.** ____
7. Do you refrain from fidgeting with items such as paper clips while conversing with others?	____	____	____	____	**7.** ____
8. Do you avoid extremes in clothing styles and accessories?	____	____	____	____	**8.** ____
9. Do you avoid wearing too much jewelry or jewelry that is not tasteful?	____	____	____	____	**9.** ____
10. Do you gesture naturally while speaking?	____	____	____	____	**10.** ____
11. Do you refrain from resting your elbows on a desk or table while speaking?	____	____	____	____	**11.** ____
12. Are your expressions appropriate for the subject matter?	____	____	____	____	**12.** ____
13. Do you maintain appropriate eye contact with others?	____	____	____	____	**13.** ____
14. Do you avoid extremes in cosmetics and/or fragrances?	____	____	____	____	**14.** ____
15. Do you listen while others are talking?	____	____	____	____	**15.** ____

16. Do you refrain from interrupting others while they are talking? ___ ___ ___ ___ **16.** ___

17. Do you speak distinctly? ___ ___ ___ ___ **17.** ___

18. Are you genuinely interested in what others are saying? ___ ___ ___ ___ **18.** ___

19. Do you try to pronounce each word correctly? ___ ___ ___ ___ **19.** ___

20. Do you look up the meanings of unfamiliar words? ___ ___ ___ ___ **20.** ___

Now, total your points and evaluate your score using the following chart.

Total Score: _____

90–100 points	Excellent
75–89 points	Good
60–74 points	Average
Below 60 points	Poor

Suggestions for improvement:

_____

_____

_____

_____

B Enunciation Practice

The following words often sound slurred when speakers do not articulate each word part distinctly. First, practice enunciating the word correctly; then, on the lines provided, write a sentence using that word. Be prepared to read your sentences aloud correctly in class.

1. adequate

_____

_____ **1.** ___

2. aluminum

_____

_____ **2.** ___

3. library

_____

_____ **3.** ___

4. interesting

_____

_____ **4.** ___

5. treasurer

_____

_____ **5.** ___

Pronunciation Practice

When speaking the following words, speakers often add letters or change the sound of the existing letters. Pronounce each word properly. On the short line provided, write the dictionary pronunciation for each word. Then write a sentence using the word. Be prepared to read the sentences aloud, using proper pronunciation.

✓

1. suggest _____

_____

_____   **1.** _____

2. per diem _____

_____

_____   **2.** _____

3. per capita _____

_____

_____   **3.** _____

4. actual _____

_____

_____   **4.** _____

5. corporation _____

_____

_____   **5.** _____

6. cooperation _____

_____

_____   **6.** _____

7. humble _____

_____

_____   **7.** _____

8. honorarium _____

_____

_____   **8.** _____

9. aesthetic _____

_____

_____   **9.** _____

10. recognize _____

_____

_____   **10.** _____

D Selecting the Best Sentence

In each of the following groups, one sentence is best in terms of spelling, grammar, and punctuation. Select the sentence and write its identifying letter on the line provided.   ✓

1. a. Most of our employees have excellent attendance records.

   b. Congradulations on your promotion to senior administrative assistant.

   c. Tom asked if we had plans to expand our operations in Mexico?

   d. Joseph is a talented intelligent high school senior and should win the scholarship.

1. _____ _____

2. a. Marianna and Bill, of Springs Realty Company, is involved with developing the property.

   b. He bought paint, brushes and wall paper for the remodeling project.

   c. Mr. O'Leary mowed your lawn while you was recuperating in the hospital.

   d. Our company has a softball team participating in the industrial league.

2. _____ _____

3. a. Ms. Valdez is moving to Seattle early next Spring.

   b. Every one of our clerks completes his or her assignments on time.

   c. Please reserve a suit of rooms for Mrs. O'Dell.

   d. After pointing out some false conclusions Mr. Davidson recommended that the plan be revised.

3. _____ _____

4. a. Without question, Dr. Reynolds is qualified to perform that surgery.

   b. We bought 3 desks and 3 chairs that match our other furniture.

   c. Either the chair or the cushions is to be replaced.

   d. We shall be glad to take them reconditioned computers and donate them to the city schools.

4. _____ _____

5. a. Harry's speech is just as polished as Susan's.

   b. At the conference you will speak, on international accounting procedures.

   c. Yours seems to be the only descenting opinion.

   d. Do not use "different than", but do use "different from".

5. _____ _____

6. a. Consumer confidence in the economy should raise soon.

   b. He has a well earned reputation as a troubleshooter.

   c. Everybody is to list his or her choice on a separate sheet.

   d. A managers' duties are varied and numerous.

6. _____ _____

7. a. Nobody but Emily and I knew about the merger talks.

   b. The number of experts in this industry is surprisingly few.

   c. Leonard is the more industrious of any of our managers.

   d. Simon is the one whom we think merits promotion.

7. _____ _____

8. a. Be courteous to whoever telephones our office.

   b. Have the travel agents sent in there reservations?

   c. Her ideas always sound well.

   d. Was the confidential folder lain in the bottom drawer?

8. _____ _____

States and Capitals

Underline each incorrectly spelled state or state capital. Write the correction in the space provided. Write *OK* in the space if all five items in the group are spelled correctly.   ✓

1. Bismarck, North Dakota   1. _____ ____

    Carson City, Nevada

    Atlanta, Georgia

    Denver, Colorado

    Piere, South Dakota

2. Raleigh, North Carolina   2. _____ ____

    Austen, Texas

    Boise, Idaho

    Jackson, Mississippi

    Nashville, Tennessee

3. Indianapolis, Indiana   3. _____ ____

    Lansing, Michigan

    Columbia, South Carolina

    Jefferson City, Missouri

    Mountpelier, Vermont

4. Baton Roudge, Louisiana   4. _____ ____

    St. Paul, Minnesota

    Boston, Massachusetts

    Richmond, Virginia

    Charleston, West Virginia

5. Phenix, Arizona   5. _____ ____

    Montgomery, Alabama

    Salem, Oregon

    Helena, Montana

    Madison, Wisconsin

6. Lincoln, Nebraska   6. _____ ____

    Harrisburg, Pennsylvania

    Oklahoma City, Oklahoma

    Concord, New Hamshire

    Cheyenne, Wyoming

7. Columbus, Ohio

Augusta, Maine

Montgumery, Alabama

Annapolis, Maryland

Trenton, New Jersey

7. _____ ____

8. Little Rock, Arkansaw

Des Moines, Iowa

Juneau, Alaska

Albany, New York

Olympia, Washington

8. _____ ____

9. Springfield, Illinois

Salt Lake City, Utah

Sacramento, California

Providence, Rhode Island

Tallahassee, Florida

9. _____ ____

10. Honolulu, Hawaii

Topeka, Kansas

Frankfort, Kentucky

Hartford, Connectticut

Dover, Delaware

10. _____ ____

SECTION 8.3 — CONDUCTING MEETINGS AND COMMUNICATING IN GROUPS

A Role Playing a Meeting

This is a fun exercise that can teach you much from using negative examples. The class will be divided into committees of three to six members each. Choose a job-related or campus-related issue as a topic for your committee meeting. Select a committee member to chair the meeting. The committee chair is responsible for keeping the meeting on track.

The committee chair will ask each of the other committee members to play one or more of the following obnoxious characters. Use as many of the characters as feasible for your chosen committee meeting. Write enough of the role-play skit to enable each member to grasp the general direction of the committee meeting and his or her contribution to the meeting. *Remember:* This exercise demonstrates behaviors that you should *not* use in the real world.

Information Hog:	The Information Hog knows all the details but will not tell the group. "The boss told me the answer to that question, but I cannot release that information."
Time/Date Bug:	The Time/Date Bug keeps interrupting with insignificant details related to times or dates. "Did you talk with Mr. Starns at 9 a.m. or 10 a.m.? What time will the meeting be over?"
Fidget Master:	The Fidget Master has annoying habits such as playing with keys or coins, tapping fingers, sitting restlessly, shaking his or her watch to make sure it is still running, and so on.
Topic Changer:	The Topic Changer asks questions or makes comments that have little or no relevance to the topic being discussed. "Did you see the movie on channel 18 last night?"
Mr. (or Ms.) Negative:	Mr. (or Ms.) Negative is critical of every suggestion made. "That will never work; it will cost too much; management will never approve it; we tried it two years ago and it didn't work then."
Millie (or Willie) Giggler:	This character thinks that everything is funny.
Repeat Pete (or Rita):	Repeat Pete (or Rita) doesn't have an original idea but repeats what he (she) has heard from others.
Thunder Boomer:	Thunder Boomer always talks too loud.
Whisper Wallflower:	Whisper Wallflower speaks only when asked a question. This character's voice is barely audible, and another committee member always has to ask that his or her comments be repeated.

STUDENT NAME   **CHARACTER/S**

_____   _____

_____   _____

_____   _____

_____   _____

_____   _____

COMMITTEE MEETING TOPIC

_____

_____

GENERAL DIRECTION OF SKIT

_____

_____

_____

_____

_____

_____

_____

_____

_____

_____

_____

_____

_____

_____

_____

_____

SUGGESTIONS FOR IMPROVING THE MEETING

_____

_____

_____

_____

_____

_____

_____

_____

B Preparing Agendas

An agenda is a list of topics that will be discussed in a specific meeting. Prepare a five-item agenda for each of the committee meetings in the following list. Make up details as needed. Use the illustration of an agenda on page 401 of your textbook as a guide.

Agenda
Committee for Parking Lot Security
Monday, February 18, <YEAR>
Conference Room 308

_____

_____
_____
_____
_____
_____
_____
_____
_____
_____
_____
_____
_____

Agenda
Annual Picnic Committee
Wednesday, March 18, <YEAR>
Board Room

_____
_____
_____
_____
_____
_____
_____
_____
_____
_____
_____
_____
_____

Agenda
Advisory Committee
Proposed Company-Sponsored Day Care Center
Thursday, October 4, <YEAR>
President's Office

_____

_____

_____

_____

_____

_____

_____

_____

_____

_____

_____

_____

_____

_____

_____

_____

_____

_____

_____

_____

C Diplomacy for Group Progress

From each of the following pairs of statements, select the statement that better contributes to group progress. Write the letter identifying that statement in the space provided.   ✓

1. a. Your recommendation is ridiculous.

   b. Your recommendation sounds interesting. Can you explain how it will work in our situation?   1. _____   _____

2. a. Your idea has merit! Let's talk a little more about the cost of implementation.

   b. Your idea will never work here. And, it is too expensive.   2. _____   _____

3. a. Put me on the team where I can be most helpful.

   b. I really should be in charge of the team, not just a member.   3. _____   _____

4. a. May I answer any questions that you have about the new procedures?

   b. Don't ask for reasons; just do it.   4. _____   _____

5. a. Our division managers might make some embarrassing mistakes if we send them to Japan without teaching them about Japanese culture.

   b. Should we provide instruction on Japanese culture before sending our division managers to Japan?   5. _____   _____

D **Enhancing Group Discussion**

The following statements were made during a committee meeting of the Gilreath Corporation. Rewrite each statement so that it will enhance group discussion rather than detract from it.

✓

1. The executive committee will never endorse such a proposal.

   _____

   _____   1. _____

2. I'm going to make sure no one monopolizes the discussion at this meeting. I get tired of listening to the same people do all the talking.

   _____

   _____   2. _____

3. As chairperson, I can make the final decision when there is a tie in the voting.

   _____

   _____   3. _____

4. Your ideas are upsetting many of the group members. The ideas are so radical that no one can agree with them.

   _____

   _____   4. _____

5. I really don't care what the rest of you think; I want to see this motion passed.

   _____

   _____   5. _____

6. I don't understand the difference between the two computer operating systems, so let's toss out the idea of installing a new one.

   _____

   _____   6. _____

7. (Chairperson speaking): What was on the agenda for today's discussion? I've forgotten what we had planned.

   _____

   _____   7. _____

8. Since everyone voted against my suggestion, I don't care what you do.

   _____

   _____   8. _____

9. I strongly disagree.

   _____

   _____   9. _____

10. I know this plan won't work because I tried it in another situation.

   _____

   _____   10. _____

E Understanding Meanings of Words

In order to be a good listener, you must be able to understand the meanings of common words. In the space provided, write the meaning of each underlined word. ✓

1. We will use a computer to analyze the <u>data</u> obtained.

   _____   1. ____

2. The <u>recession</u> will continue unless we develop an inexpensive source of energy.

   _____   2. ____

3. Are you <u>vulnerable</u> to every criticism, no matter how unjust?

   _____   3. ____

4. The computer was <u>programmed</u> to perform that operation.

   _____   4. ____

5. Representatives from many consumer groups <u>clamored</u> for stronger action against inflation.

   _____   5. ____

FORMAL AND INFORMAL PRESENTATIONS

A Speech Topics and Purposes

List five topics that would be appropriate for an impromptu speech to be presented to your classmates. For each topic you list, write the purpose of the speech in the space provided. ✓

TOPIC	PURPOSE
1. _____	1. _____
2. _____	2. _____
3. _____	3. _____
4. _____	4. _____
5. _____	5. _____

B Impromptu Speaking Exercise

Take the five speech topics you listed in exercise A and write each topic on a separate index card. Place your cards in a pile along with the cards of your classmates. Select three cards from the pile. From the three cards, select one topic on which you would like to speak. In the space provided, write five sentences about the topic that you would use in giving a one-minute impromptu speech on the topic. ✓

_____
_____
_____
_____
_____
_____
_____
_____
_____
_____
_____
_____
_____
_____
_____

C Analyzing Your Audience

Select another topic from the list you developed in exercise A. For a five-minute speech you will give to your classmates, list some steps you would take to analyze your audience.

✓

_____

_____

_____

_____

_____

_____

_____

___

D Developing Your Speech

For the topic you selected in exercise C, describe the information you would use to develop your speech in terms of the content, clarity, treatment, and humor.

✓

CONTENT

_____

_____

_____

_____

___

CLARITY

_____

_____

_____

_____

___

TREATMENT

_____

_____

_____

_____

___

HUMOR

_____

_____

_____

_____

___

Rating Sheet for Speakers

The following chart is to be used either with preceding exercise D or with Practical Application C at the end of Section 8.4 in the textbook. Prepare a short speech on one of the topics in those exercises. Before making your presentation, give this chart to your instructor. Your instructor will give the chart to one of your classmates. Your classmate will rate your speech anonymously. Then your instructor will return the chart to you.

PRESENTATION EVALUATION

NAME: _____ GRADE: _____

TOPIC: _____ CLASS: _____

CONTENT (SCALE OF 1–35 POINTS) _____
Related to Topic
Clearly Expressed
Organized Logically
Adequate Coverage
Preparation/Research Evident
Language Usage

DELIVERY (SCALE OF 1–35 POINTS) _____
Professional Appearance
Eye Contact
Attire
Gestures
Grooming
Posture

PRESENTATION DYNAMICS _____
Composure
Pace
Pronunciation/Enunciation
Demeanor
Timing
Volume
Expression
Audience Rapport
Audience Attentiveness

VISUAL AIDS (SCALE OF 1–20 POINTS) _____
Appropriate Type (slides, overheads, and so on)
Suitable Quality
Integration into Presentation
Conveyance of Ideas/Information

QUESTION/ANSWER SESSION (SCALE OF 1–10 POINTS) _____
Adequate Response
Language Usage

F Reading Articles on Presentations

Read an article in a business publication that deals with presentations. List three to five suggestions covered in the article that would help you and your classmates become better presenters.

TITLE OF ARTICLE _____

MAGAZINE OR JOURNAL _____

PUBLISHER _____

DATE OF PUBLICATION _____

PAGE NUMBER _____

SUGGESTIONS FOR MAKING EFFECTIVE PRESENTATIONS:

1. _____
   _____

2. _____
   _____

3. _____
   _____

4. _____
   _____

5. _____
   _____

G Annoying Speaker Attributes

By becoming aware of speaker attributes that interfere with your concentration during a presentation, you can develop a list of things *not* to do while presenting. Think about speakers you have heard recently either in person or on television or radio. Without identifying any of the speakers, list any speech qualities or nonverbal gestures that distracted you from the content of their messages.

_____
_____
_____
_____
_____
_____
_____
_____
_____
_____
_____
_____
_____

H Introducing a Speaker

Select a person whom you know (an instructor, parent, businessperson, campus administrator, and so on). Write a brief, three-paragraph introduction that would be appropriate to use if you were introducing that person as a speaker at a campus event. Be prepared to rehearse your introduction before your class. *Remember:* Reading your introduction insults your audience.

PARAGRAPH 1

_____

_____

_____

_____

_____

PARAGRAPH 2

_____

_____

_____

_____

_____

PARAGRAPH 3

_____

_____

_____

_____

_____

I Sound Alikes

Choose the word in parentheses that correctly completes each sentence. Write the word in the space provided. ✓

1. You should be able to (adapt, adept) to your new software with little training.

   1. _____ _____

2. At what age can (miners, minors) fly alone?

   2. _____ _____

3. Will you (right, write) the customer and let him know that the merchandise will be shipped within 10 days?

   3. _____ _____

4. The bank robbers stole an undisclosed (some, sum) of money and valuable coins.

   4. _____ _____

5. You should buy a smoke detector, which is a small, inexpensive (device, devise) that can save lives and property.

   5. _____ _____

6. James Durbin, the arresting officer, read the charges (allowed, aloud).

6. _____ ____

7. Are you (liable, libel) for charges made on your credit card after it was stolen?

7. _____ ____

8. Flu shots were offered to all of our (personal, personnel).

8. _____ ____

9. Please pay all invoices before July 1, the beginning of our (fiscal, physical) year.

9. _____ ____

10. Admission fees will be (waived, waved) for senior citizens.

10. _____ ____

J Attention-Getting Openings and Closings

Assume that you are speaking to a group of students at your alma mater. The purpose of your speech is to convey to these students some of the basic educational requirements for the field in which you have been working for over a year. (Select the field of your choice.) Suggest three different attention-getting ways to open your talk and three different ways to close your talk.

1. Opening: _____

_____

_____

_____

Closing: _____

_____

_____

_____

2. Opening: _____

_____

_____

_____

Closing: _____

_____

_____

_____

3. Opening: _____

_____

_____

_____

Closing: _____

_____

_____

_____

 **USING**
INFORMATION PROCESSING

A Selecting Appropriate Software for the Job

For each of the following situations, identify the type of software from the list that would be most appropriate for completing the job.   ✓

1. Merging names and addresses for use with a form letter.
   a. Database software
   b. Desktop publishing software
   c. Spreadsheet software
   d. Word processing software   1. ____ ____

2. Organizing a list of patients' names and addresses.
   a. Database software
   b. Desktop publishing software
   c. Spreadsheet software
   d. Word processing software   2. ____ ____

3. Preparing a flier for an upcoming company event.
   a. Database software
   b. Desktop publishing software
   c. Spreadsheet software
   d. Word processing software   3. ____ ____

4. Projecting revenue and expenses for a new product.
   a. Database software
   b. Desktop publishing software
   c. Spreadsheet software
   d. Word processing software   4. ____ ____

5. Drafting a letter to a client regarding a recent order.
   a. Database software
   b. Desktop publishing software
   c. Spreadsheet software
   d. Word processing software   5. ____ ____

6. Updating inventory records.
   a. Database software
   b. Desktop publishing software
   c. Spreadsheet software
   d. Word processing software   6. ____ ____

7. Creating an electronic inventory of products.
   a. Database software
   b. Desktop publishing software
   c. Spreadsheet software
   d. Word processing software   7. ____ ____

B Organizing Information in a Database

You have been asked to organize a database with the name, address, telephone number, and total amount of year-to-date purchases for the top seven corporate customers for your company. Using the information given, list the company names in alphabetical order in the database form that follows. Provide headings for each column of information in the database. Use Figure 9.2 on page 429 of your textbook as a guide.

Information for the database:

Northeast Nutrition Center; 14 Delaware Square; Quincy, MA 02171;
   617-555-6299; $21,325

Boston Community Healthcare Center; 652 Knightsbridge Drive;
   Boston, MA 02215; 617-555-0257; $42,000

McBride Manufacturing; 39 Bleeker Street; Boston, MA 02115; 617-555-3091;
   $57,432

Paulson Legal Services; 325 Newborough Street, Suite 6; Dorchester, MA 02124;
   617-555-2114; $33,056

Caulder and Sons, Inc.; 1657 Riverside Drive; Boston, MA 02126; 617-555-8622;
   $28,580

Hightstown Database Systems; 114 Waterworks Drive; Quincy, MA 02168;
   617-555-9236; $26,140

Hightower Financial; 5632 Plymouth Way; Boston, MA 02127; 617-555-8870;
   $37,439

C Using Word Processing Features

You have typed the following draft of a memo. Before you circulate the memo, you need to make corrections using the spelling checker, grammar checker, and the cut-and-paste feature of your word processing program. Write your corrections on the lines provided. ✓

Our senior vice president, Alana Hensley, and myself is
confident that this acquisition will strengthen our
reputation as the premier publisher of educational
software programs. Your probably aware that on August 21
Hanson Publishing Company acquired Glenacre Software
Design, making Hanson the nations largest publisher of
educational software programs. As a result the of acquisition,
a number of staff members form Glenacre will be joining
our present staff.

_____ ____
_____ ____
_____ ____
_____ ____
_____ ____
_____ ____
_____ ____
_____ ____
_____ ____

If you wolud like more information on the details of
this acquisition visit the company's Intranet home page on
the World Wide Web.

_____ ____
_____ ____
_____ ____

D Editing Practice

Underline any errors in the following sentences, and write your corrections on the lines provided. Write *OK* for any sentence that is correct. ✓

1. Despite price increases, unit sales dropped off in the first quarter, furthermore, sales dollars also decreased.

1. _____ ____

2. All the print advertisements were developed by Roxanne Cunningham, the chief copywriter for Lester, Bruce, & Ellis.

2. _____ ____

3. "Do you have any questions about the new customer service procedures," asked Danielle?

3. _____ ____

4. According to the chart, each container should have no more than 5 grams of potassium and should cost $.95.

4. _____ ____

5. Ms. Sizemore plans to retire at the end of November, she will then move to North Carolina with her family.

5. _____ ____

6. By Mon. or Tues., the prices for the various cruise packages should be posted on the Internet site.

6. _____ ____

7. One keynote speaker, Marlon Westfield, has been delayed at the airport; therefore we will adjust the schedule to allow him time to reach the convention center.

7. _____ ____

8. For our May 15th conference, the Messrs. Cullen have invited Sen. Hanby to give the keynote address.

8. _____ ____

9. More information is provided see pages 463 through 498, for those individuals who wish to do further research.

9. _____ ____

10. Rosemary would like to register for the afternoon sessions at the conference, she says that she is already familiar with the material covered in the morning sessions.

10. _____ _____

11. Ms. O'Neil, a former accountant with our Company, now manages her own CPA firm.

11. _____ _____

12. Tanya, do you know whether Ms. Cortez has announced whom will get the leading role in the community theater production?

12. _____ _____

13. Either Betsy or Terry have been assigned to complete the Danville project during Malcolm's absence.

13. _____ _____

14. As you probably already know Mr. Barbarino is in Boston signing a contract for their advertising campaign.

14. _____ _____

15. One of the reasons why the shipment was delayed, is that we didn't have three of the five items that were ordered.

15. _____ _____

16. Some of the customers with whom I spoke are quite satisfied with the performance of their new cars.

16. _____ _____

17. Because we had ordered more than 50 picnic baskets we received an additional discount of 5 percent.

17. _____ _____

18. Ms. Belton will be in Colorado on business all next week, furthermore, she will be on vacation the following week.

18. _____ _____

19. Yes Mr. Milligan, I charged the batteries for your cellular phone and for your laptop computer.

19. _____ _____

20. Sean has already spoke with us about his ideas for renovating the warehouse.

20. _____

 **USING
TELECOMMUNICATIONS**

 Telephone Communication

You work as an administrative assistant at a firm that employs 22 people. You and one other administrative assistant handle all incoming telephone calls. To better handle telephone calls, you investigate the advantages and disadvantages of using a voice-mail system in the office. Based on your findings, you decide to recommend to the office manager that a voice-mail system be used. List the advantages and disadvantages of voice mail that you would mention in a memo to the office manager.   ✓

ADVANTAGES OF VOICE MAIL

1. _____
   _____
   _____   1. _____
2. _____
   _____
   _____   2. _____
3. _____
   _____
   _____   3. _____
4. _____
   _____
   _____   4. _____
5. _____
   _____
   _____   5. _____
6. _____
   _____
   _____   6. _____

DISADVANTAGES OF VOICE MAIL

1. _____
   _____
   _____   1. _____
2. _____
   _____
   _____   2. _____
3. _____
   _____
   _____   3. _____

B Using Voice Mail

As an accountant for Dalton Manufacturing, your job responsibilities include meeting with colleagues at other sites and attending professional conferences. You use voice mail to track calls you have received and to respond to callers. In the space provided, compose a voice-mail greeting or a message for each of the following situations.

✓

1. A greeting for internal calls (calls from inside the same building):

_____

_____

_____

_____

_____   1. ____

2. A response to a message from Shirley Kwan, one of your colleagues. Shirley had left a message asking if you would attend an organizational meeting on Thursday, June 10. You will be out of the office from June 8 through June 11 at a conference. You will return to the office on June 12.

_____

_____

_____

_____

_____   2. ____

3. A greeting for outside calls. This greeting will be used for calls received while you are attending the conference from June 8 through June 11.

_____

_____

_____

_____

_____   3. ____

C Selecting Technologies

For each task described, select the appropriate technology from the list. Write the letter of the correct answer in the space provided.

✓

1. Transmit a copy of a printed document for receipt the same day.
   a. audio teleconferencing
   b. e-mail
   c. fax machine
   d. Internet
   e. pager
   f. videoconferencing   1. ____   ____

✓

2. Conduct a meeting in different locations using the telephone only.
   a. audio teleconferencing
   b. e-mail
   c. fax machine
   d. Internet
   e. pager
   f. videoconferencing   2. _____ _____

3. Conduct a meeting in different locations using audio, graphics, and video.
   a. audio teleconferencing
   b. e-mail
   c. fax machine
   d. Internet
   e. pager
   f. videoconferencing   3. _____ _____

4. Send a written message from one location to another using a computer network.
   a. audio teleconferencing
   b. e-mail
   c. fax machine
   d. Internet
   e. pager
   f. videoconferencing   4. _____ _____

D Using E-Mail

E-mail provides a quick, convenient way to communicate information. The following draft of an e-mail message is longer than it needs to be. Rewrite the message to make it clear and concise and no longer than 30 words in length.

> The July inventory report shows that we have over 250 backorders for our Model XT5 laser printer. Based on the product release form I received on June 15, this item should have been in stock at the warehouse on June 18. Please check with Jim Karey in inventory control regarding the status of this product. (52 words)

_____
_____
_____
_____
_____
_____
_____
_____
_____
_____

E **Searching the Internet**

Your instructor has asked you to search the Internet to locate sites on the World Wide Web that would be of interest to fellow students at your college. Working with a classmate, locate one site for each of the following items.

1. Locate the home page for a business-related organization. Write the Web address for the site in the space provided. Provide a one-sentence description of the information the site offers.

   _____

   _____

   _____

   _____

   _____

   _____   1. _____

2. Locate the home page for a newspaper or a periodical that covers business-related issues. Write the Web address for the site in the space provided. Provide a one-sentence description of the information the site offers.

   _____

   _____

   _____

   _____

   _____

   _____   2. _____

3. Locate the home page for a United States government site that provides information that is related to your career field. Write the Web address for the site in the space provided. Provide a one-sentence description of the information the site offers.

   _____

   _____

   _____

   _____

   _____

   _____   3. _____

SECTION 9.3 CONSIDERATIONS FOR COMMUNICATING ELECTRONICALLY

A Factors to Consider in Communicating Messages

From the choices listed with each item, identify the factor that is most important to
consider in communicating the message. ✓

1. Mailing a sales letter to potential customers in a five-state area.
   a. confidentiality   b. volume   c. message intensity   1. _____ _____

2. Sending a copy of a contract to a client.
   a. feedback capacity   b. personalization   c. quality   2. _____ _____

3. Notifying eight employees at the same site of a change in the time for a meeting
   tomorrow.
   a. volume   b. time and speed   c. formality   3. _____ _____

4. Submitting a bid for a building project to a city official.
   a. confidentiality   b. personalization   c. formality   4. _____ _____

5. Sending patient records to the hospital in preparation for upcoming surgery.
   a. quality   b. message complexity   c. cost   5. _____ _____

6. Distributing copies of the annual report to all shareholders.
   a. quality   b. feedback capacity   c. formality   6. _____ _____

7. Informing a client of a change in the travel itinerary for an overseas trip that
   begins in two days.
   a. quality   b. time and speed   c. formality   7. _____ _____

8. Sending an e-mail message to a colleague to confirm that you received information
   sent by that person.
   a. time and speed   b. confidentiality   c. formality   8. _____ _____

9. Distributing copies of the agenda for a board meeting.
   a. time and speed   b. volume   c. formality   9. _____ _____

10. Submitting an employee's performance appraisal to the Human Resources
    Department.
    a. formality   b. message complexity   c. feedback capacity   10. _____ _____

B Transmitting Messages by Various Modes

For each of the following tasks, decide which communication technology is most
appropriate for the situation. Not all choices will be used.

audio teleconference   letter sent overnight delivery
e-mail   letter sent U.S. mail
envelope marked "Confidential" voice mail
fax   teleconference   ✓

1. A customer has not paid an invoice from last month. The
   payment is now 10 days past due. You need to inform the
   customer that payment is due.   1. _____ _____

2. You are in charge of the company blood drive to be held this Friday, two days from today. You need to send a reminder to all those who have volunteered to donate blood.

2. _____ ____

3. As a realtor, you are working with a client to finalize the paperwork for purchasing a property. The client is out of town from Monday through Thursday this week and she must review certain paperwork before the closing on Friday. You receive the paperwork on Monday.

3. _____ ____

4. While traveling on business, you make last-minute changes to your itinerary in order to attend an additional meeting. Although it is after business hours, you need to inform your administrative assistant of your change in plans.

4. _____ ____

5. You are in charge of conducting a meeting with colleagues located in California, Texas, and Minnesota. The purpose of the meeting is to discuss a complicated project that will begin in two weeks. Due to budget cuts, no money is available for travel.

5. _____ ____

6. To maintain the deadline for a project, you need to send confidential documents to an attorney in another city as soon as possible.

6. _____ ____

C Recognizing Homonyms

Some of the following sentences contain homonym or pseudohomonym errors. Underline the incorrect word and write the correct word on the space provided. Write *OK* for any sentence that has no error. ✓

1. The writer of the article sited several authoritative sources.

1. _____ ____

2. Given the complexity of the evidence, the district attorney herself persecuted the case.

2. _____ ____

3. She made a conscience effort to complete the report on time.

3. _____ ____

4. We least another office that is more conveniently located.

4. _____ ____

5. I would advice you to get a second opinion on the proposed design.

5. _____ ____

6. You will need to be discrete in handling this sensitive court case.

6. _____ ____

7. The company health insurance plan covers employees' minor dependents.

7. _____ ____

8. You may be libel for damages if someone has an accident on your property.

8. _____ ____

9. We will device another plan to replace the old one.

9. _____ ____

10. Prior to selling their house, Brian and Elain Karteris had its value appraised.

10. _____ ____

SECTION 10.1   PLANNING MESSAGES

A   Direct Approach

Based on the information given, compose a message that uses the direct approach. Begin with the most important point, continue with supporting information, and close with an upbeat ending.

SITUATION

     As a reservations manager at Hospitality Suites Hotel and Convention Center, you are writing to Mr. Jay Gould regarding arrangements for the Tri-State Literacy Council Convention next month. You are pleased to inform Mr. Gould that Hospitality Suites is able to accommodate his request for special displays for the convention. Write the body paragraphs for a letter to Mr. Gould. ✓

_____

_____

_____

_____

_____

_____

_____

_____

_____

_____

_____

_____

_____

_____

_____

_____

_____

_____

_____

_____

_____

_____

_____

_____

_____

_____

B Indirect Approach

Using the information given, compose a message that uses the indirect approach. Begin the message with a buffer that presents background information, continue with reasons and explanations, present the bad news, and end with a buffer.

SITUATION

As a graduate of Athens University, you have been invited to speak at the upcoming alumni weekend at the school September 16–17. Although you would like to attend, you have other commitments. However, you would be willing to participate in another event at a later time. Write the paragraphs for a letter that turns down the invitation.

✓

C Persuasive Approach

Using the information given, compose a message that uses the persuasive approach. Begin the message with an attention-getting opening, follow the opening with information that generates the reader's interest, continue with additional information to create a desire on the reader's part, and close by asking the reader to take the desired action.

SITUATION

As a sales representative for CIT Cable, you are writing a sales letter to potential customers. In the letter your goal is to encourage recipients to sign up for Internet Cable Access service that provides Internet access using a television. To persuade customers to sign up for the service, you plan to describe these benefits: a $22-a-month subscription fee, unlimited Internet access, and convenient hookup using existing television cable. Your company is the only cable service in the city offering this service, and the price is very reasonable. The $22-a-month subscription fee is an introductory offer that is only in effect until December 1.

D Improving Message Content and Presentation

Revise the following paragraphs from a memo so that the message is clear, concise, correct, and courteous. Write your corrections in the space provided. If a line is correct, write *OK*.

✓

This year as last year, once again, we have the opportunity _____ ____

to help build a strong comunity. Your participation in the _____ ____

United Way Campaign provides much needed funding for _____ ____

teen counseling, summer camp for children from low-income _____ ____

familys, job training for unemployed adults, and much more. _____ ____

If you would like to please review the attached brochure _____ ____

that lists more than 30 agencies and programs in our _____ ____

community that benefit from you gifts to the United Way. _____ ____

Last year, United Way agencies assisted more then _____ ____

5,000 people in our community, and the need is growing. _____ ____

Due to cutbacks in goverment programs, agencies such as _____ ____

the United Way are often the only source of aide for _____ ____

many people. _____ ____

Help us reach this year's goal of $50,000—a goal that _____ ____

we can reach. However, we need your help to make this _____ ____

goal a reality. Look at the attached flier regarding _____ ____

contribution options. All contributions are tax-deductible _____ ____

and the company will match every dollar of employee _____ ____

contributions you give. _____ ____

E Special Formatting Techniques

In a phone conversation on April 3, your supervisor, Ronald Plate, asked you to give him a list of the monthly sales figures for January, February, and March for the four top-selling salespeople. The salespersons and the sales figures are: T. James—$26,293, $28,394, $29,938; B. Larson—$26,123, $28,284, $29,743; C. Larson—$28,837, $29,384, $30,839; N. Peterson—$25,384, $27,394, 28,192. Using some of the special formatting techniques discussed in Section 10.1, write the body paragraphs of the memo. List the salespeople starting with the person with the highest sales over the three-month period.

✓

_____
_____
_____
_____
_____
_____
_____
_____
_____
_____
_____
_____

SECTION 10.2   PLANNING MEMOS

A Planning a Memo

You are writing a memo to your supervisor, Angelina Weber, informing her of a proposed change in the budget for a project you are working on. Using the information in the following list, write a memo that contains a statement of purpose, a message, and a statement of future action.

- You and the project coordinator, Jim Wade, have reviewed the budget for the Allen project and have determined that more money is needed for travel.

- You and Jim will need to travel to Memphis at least once a month for five months to meet with the client. Current travel budget is $1,900; you propose increasing the travel budget to $4,800.

- Attached to the memo is a copy of the current budget and a copy of the revised budget.   ✓

_____

_____

_____

_____

_____

_____

_____

_____

_____

_____

_____

_____

_____

_____

_____

_____

_____

_____

_____

B Subject Lines for Memos

The following subject lines for memos are too wordy. Rewrite each subject line to be more concise.   ✓

1. The Policy of Anderson Industries Regarding Employee Use of Company Computers

_____   1. ____

2. New Procedure Instituted by Human Resources for Enrolling in the Medical Plan

_____ 2. _____

3. Orientation Meeting for New Staff Members in All Departments Hired in September

_____ 3. _____

4. Recent Promotion of Monica Sellers to Head of the Pathology Lab

_____ 4. _____

5. Code of Ethics for the Company That Applies to All Employees

_____ 5. _____

C Critical Thinking Skills

In the space provided, write the body of a memo using information from the following paragraph. Include a statement of purpose, a message, and a statement of future action.

SITUATION

You have worked at the Discus Manufacturing Company for one year. Recently you read an article in an industry magazine on a new manufacturing technique that you feel could be a cost-saving measure for the company. The article mentions a seminar on the new technique that will be held in St. Louis on March 20. The cost for the seminar is $80 plus travel expenses (round-trip plane ticket $200), hotel expenses (approximately $65), and food expenses (approximately $30). To request approval to attend the seminar, you must write a memo to your supervisor that explains the reasons for attending the seminar, identifies the benefits of the seminar for you and the company, and estimates what the expenses will be. The deadline for registering for the seminar is February 20.

_____

_____

_____

_____

_____

_____

_____

_____

_____

_____

_____

_____

_____

_____

_____

_____

_____

_____

_____

 **SECTION 10.3**   MEMO TYPES AND PARTS

 Standard Memo Format

Revise the following memo, correcting any errors in format and style.

Memo To: Jana Hansen

FROM: Mrs. Greta Savage

Date: 7/12/<YEAR>

SUBJECT: Payroll Change Effective August 1

Dear Jana:

Beginning Friday, August 1, payroll checks will be distributed twice each month instead of only once. The checks will be available on the first and the fifteenth of each month.

Employees may choose to have their checks automatically deposited. If they choose automatic deposit, they should complete the necessary forms in the Human Resources office.

Employees requested both of these changes. Please keep me informed on the feedback you receive on these two changes.

Enclosure
rg

✓

_____
_____
_____
_____
_____
_____
_____
_____
_____
_____
_____
_____
_____
_____
_____
_____
_____
_____
_____
_____
_____

Your supervisor, Lee Helton, has asked you to type a memo with the following information and to include a distribution list with the following names: Roselle Jones, Heather Livingston, Holly Bardoe, Joe McArthur, and Mark McDaniel. Include reference initials and an enclosure notation.

This month the employee insurance policy needs to be revised for the upcoming contract ratification. Since you served as a member of this committee for the last contract, the union thought we would again ask for your assistance with this matter.

Several concerns about the current insurance policy have been brought to my attention recently. Attached is a copy of the concerns I have received from other employees. Please review this information and arrange for a time to meet with the other members of your committee to discuss possible solutions.

If you are unable to serve on this committee, please let me know by the end of this week so I can locate a replacement.

✓

Writing a Memo

Following the guidelines on pages 473–476 of your textbook, write a memo based on the following situation. Use the standard memo format for plain paper.

SITUATION

As the manager for the clothing department at Kenson Department Store, you need to write a memo informing all employees of a new clothing line for fall. You will attach a brochure on the new clothing line to the memo. To encourage sales, the store is holding a one-month sale on the new line. In addition, the store is offering an incentive to employees in the form of bonuses for the two top salespersons for the month. If employees have any questions they should contact you by the end of the week. Include the file name of the memo (newcloth.doc) in your memo.

✓

_____
_____
_____
_____
_____
_____
_____
_____
_____
_____
_____
_____
_____
_____
_____
_____
_____
_____
_____
_____
_____
_____

D Outdated Expressions and Redundancies

Underline any outdated expressions or redundancies in the following sentences, and write your revisions on the lines provided. ✓

1. James wants to form a team that can cooperate together to complete the project.

2. In the event that the results of the blood tests are inconclusive, we will have to run more tests.

3. Please advise us as to the date on which you plan to move into the building.

4. At the present time, all of our customer service representatives are busy.

5. Michelle advised us as to the date when we could expect to receive our first paychecks.

6. Will you kindly stop by my office when you return from lunch.

7. Due to the fact that Mr. Sharp is in Tokyo, Ms. Napier will conduct the meeting.

8. From past experience, we know that a successful international trade show takes months of preparation.

9. At next week's meeting, we will continue on with our discussion of the proposal to construct a new warehouse.

10. We were surprised to learn that the consultant submitted the same identical studies to both companies.

11. Implementing the plan to consolidate our offices is our chief main goal for next year.

12. Jesse needs to face up to the fact that the sales estimates are too ambitious.

13. I trust that you will agree with my recommendations regarding the new computer system.

14. For the record, your comments on the allegations are duly noted.

15. It has been our customary practice at the clinic to ask all patients to sign in at the reception desk.

16. Would you kindly notify the team members of a change in our next meeting date.

17. We plan to meet up with our colleagues from Arizona at the national convention.

18. If you need clarification on the issue, refer back to your notes from the last board meeting.

19. Most of the surveys distributed to our key clients will be sent via overnight mail.

20. Herewith is the contract request form that you asked about.

1. _____ ____

2. _____ ____

3. _____ ____

4. _____ ____

5. _____ ____

6. _____ ____

7. _____ ____

8. _____ ____

9. _____ ____

10. _____ ____

11. _____ ____

12. _____ ____

13. _____ ____

14. _____ ____

15. _____ ____

16. _____ ____

17. _____ ____

18. _____ ____

19. _____ ____

20. _____ ____

SECTION 10.4 LETTER PARTS AND FORMATS

 Block Style Letter

Format the following letter using the block style. Include all the necessary letter parts, such as a salutation and a complimentary closing. Use your name in the closing.

Current date/ Mr. Alexander Veach/Remodeling Specialists/ 473 Rockway Drive/ Beachtown, ME 34595

As we discussed on the phone yesterday, I have decided to use ceramic tile instead of linoleum for the floor in the upstairs bathroom. Also, the existing sink will be replaced with a two-sink vanity.

Enclosed are the samples for the ceramic tile and a diagram showing the proposed pattern for the tile floor. Once you have a chance to review these plans, please call and leave a message on my answering machine regarding the time frame for completing this project.   ✓

_____
_____
_____
_____
_____
_____
_____
_____
_____
_____
_____
_____
_____
_____
_____
_____
_____
_____
_____
_____
_____
_____
_____
_____
_____

B Modified-Block Style Letter With Indented Paragraphs

Format the following letter using the modified-block style with indented paragraphs. Supply all necessary letter parts.

Current date/Mr. Frank Eberle/Alvena Consulting/132 Chambon Avenue/Toronto, Ontario M4T 2Z8/CANADA/Subject: Task Force Candidates/SINCLAIR ADVERTIS-ING, INC./Natalie V. Powers, Vice President/c: Roger Durban

Frank, it was a pleasure to meet with you in Toronto last week to discuss our partnership on the North Star project.

Based on our discussion, the next step is to establish a task force to review the existing advertising campaign. At your suggestion, enclosed is a list of the names of account managers here at Durban and Associates who have the expertise needed for such a high-profile project. Also enclosed are samples of their work. I believe you will agree that any of these candidates would be an asset to the project.

Once you have had a chance to review the enclosed materials, please call me at 313-555-9263 to discuss your recommendations for the task force.

✓

✓

_____
_____
_____
_____
_____
_____
_____
_____
_____
_____
_____
_____
_____
_____
_____
_____
_____
_____ ____

C Proofreading Practice

Underline any errors in the following sentences, and write your corrections in the space provided.

✓

1. Three-fourths of the completed surveys has been tabulated. 1. _____ ____

2. Brenda said that the employees who have the expertise in that area are Larry and her. 2. _____ ____

3. As we had expected, the production manager assigned the inventory analysis to Nicholas and myself. 3. _____ ____

4. The new computer system, which includes laser printers and scanners in each department, has not been used to their full potential. 4. _____ ____

5. According to the results of the informal survey, a number of employees is requesting a change in our policy regarding performance reviews. 5. _____ ____

6. All of the labels for the CD-ROM discs should be forwarded to Gilmore and Associates, which are the assembler of those packages. 6. _____ ____

7. Kenneth Dolby and Pam Burnett have doubled the sales in their territory; they obviously work very well with one another. 7. _____ ____

8. You will view the situation different, Jennifer, when you have a chance to review the results of the survey. 8. _____ ____

9. Will the new county courthouse be located opposite to police headquarters? 9. _____ ____

10. With only one week remaining until the deadline, it looks like we will be able to finish the report on schedule. 10. _____ ____

D Personal-Business Letter

Write a short personal-business letter in the space provided. To make your letter realistic, write to an actual person or a company. For example, you might write to a company requesting a catalog.

✓

_____

_____

_____

_____

_____

_____

_____

_____

_____

_____

_____

_____

_____

_____

_____

_____

_____

_____

_____

_____

_____

_____

_____

_____

_____

_____

_____

_____

_____

_____

_____

_____

_____

_____

_____

_____

_____

_____

_____

SECTION 10.5 STATIONERY AND ENVELOPES

A Formatting Envelopes

Format a No. 6 3/4 envelope addressed to Ms. Joan Yamaguchi/1493 E. Douglas
Avenue/Veedersburg, IN 49583. Use your return address for this envelope. Type both
addresses in capital and lowercase letters.

Format a 6 3/4 envelope addressed to Scott Linsek, Business Department Chair/ Highland
College/ 7438 N. Main Street/ Old Towne, MI 94858. Use a Certified mailing notation
for this envelope. Type the address in all-capital letters.

ABS Publishing Company
14 Bindery Avenue
Houston, TX 77089

B Clear Sentences

Rewrite the following sentences to make sure they communicate the meaning clearly.   ✓

1. The new contract took effect yesterday that we voted on.

   _____

   _____   1. ____

2. To get the most benefits from the training program, hours should be spent every day in practicing.

   _____

   _____   2. ____

3. Howard gave me the name of the car dealer where you can have the engine checked out.

   _____

   _____   3. ____

4. In displaying the slides, the lights were turned off.

   _____

   _____   4. ____

5. Before closing the software program, the document should be saved to the hard drive.

   _____

   _____   5. ____

6. We only need to complete one more order.

   _____

   _____   6. ____

7. To show growth in sales, illustrations were used by the sales manager.

   _____

   _____   7. ____

8. Driving to the meeting, my truck got a flat tire.

   _____

   _____   8. ____

9. To find the mistake, the assistance of a bookkeeper will be needed.

   _____

   _____   9. ____

10. By using high-quality stationery, letters will look more attractive.

   _____

   _____   10. ____

SECTION 11.1 INFORMING

A Making an Announcement

Prepare an announcement about the relocation and grand opening of a florist shop from one street location to another in your city. Include all necessary details.

✓

_____
_____
_____
_____
_____
_____
_____
_____
_____
_____
_____ _____

B Creating a Flier

Create a flier appropriate for posting on a bulletin board about a meeting of a student organization. In the spaces provided, identify the who? what? where? when? why? how? or how much? to include on the flier.

✓

1. *who* _____
_____

2. *what* _____
_____ _____

3. *where* _____
_____ _____

4. *when* _____
_____ _____

5. *why* _____
_____

6. *how* _____
_____ _____

7. *how much* _____
_____ _____

C Clear Sentences

Rewrite the following sentences to make sure they communicate clearly.   ✓ ●

1. Hanging in the closet, I saw that the coat had become wrinkled.

_____

_____   1. _____

2. Martin sent me the name of the consultant where we could find out what our company's problem is.

_____

_____   2. _____

3. To show sales growth, charts were used by the sales manager.

_____

_____   3. _____

4. The new rates became effective August 1 that were approved by the utility board.

_____

_____   4. _____

5. To assure success in your courses at school, a number of hours each day will be required for study.

_____

_____   5. _____

6. Leaving the office, my car seemed to be acting up.

_____

_____   6. _____

7. Before putting the tax forms in the mail, signatures will need to be added.

_____

_____   7. _____

8. Opening the window, the sky looked very dark and stormy.

_____

_____   8. _____

9. Under the stack of books, I noticed the folder that I had been looking for.

_____

_____   9. _____

10. Whenever thinking carefully, the correct telephone numbers can usually be remembered.

_____

_____   10. _____

SECTION 11.2   REQUESTING

A   Complete Requests

You work in the Reservations Department of a major New York hotel. Today you receive the following request:

> Dear Reservations Manager:
>
> Next month I will be in New York on business and would like to book a room. Please let me know the cost and availability of rooms.
>
> Sincerely,

List some of the important details omitted from this letter. Then write the letter that should have been written, supplying all details needed to make the request complete.

Details omitted:
1. How many guests?
2. Dates the room will be needed?
3. Type of room preferred?
4. What time will the guest be arriving?

Sample Letter

_____
_____
_____
_____
_____
_____
_____
_____
_____
_____
_____
_____
_____
_____
_____
_____
_____
_____
_____
_____
_____

B Precise Sentences

The following sentences are imprecise. Rewrite them, supplying any details needed to make them specific.

✓

1. Please send me information about your company.

_____

_____

_____

_____

_____ 1. ____

2. Do you have a vacancy at your resort during spring break?

_____

_____

_____

_____ 2. ____

3. Please send the video dealing with effective people skills.

_____

_____

_____

_____

_____ 3. ____

4. I wish to order a copy of the book on how to build children's toys.

_____

_____

_____

_____

_____ 4. ____

5. As I am interested in investing in the stock market, I need brochures.

_____

_____

_____

_____ 5. ____

6. May I use your company library in the near future?

_____

_____

_____

_____ 6. ____

✓

7. We are interested in having our class reunion at your banquet hall. Would you be able to accommodate us?

_____

_____

_____

_____

_____   7. ____

8. Will you be able to complete the work on schedule?

_____

_____

_____

_____

_____   8. ____

9. I am interested in starting a garden. Please send me brochures you think will be helpful.

_____

_____

_____

_____

_____   9. ____

10. What magazines do you recommend that I subscribe to?

_____

_____

_____

_____

_____   10. ____

C Selecting the Best Sentence

In each of the following groups, one sentence is best in terms of spelling, grammar, and punctuation. Identify that sentence and write its identifying letter on the line provided.   ✓

1. a. Hernandez is an energetic resourceful young man.
   b. On the original memo, note the number of copies to be made.
   c. Mary should have went to the bank, but she forgot.
   d. Although late, the car seemed to be running out of gas.   1. ____ ____

2. a. The Society of Scholars celebrates it's 25th anniversary Monday.
   b. Do not use a comma to join separate distinct thoughts.
   c. The person with whom I spoke advised me to call you.
   d. Perhaps the fact that your account is overdo has slipped your mind.   2. ____ ____

3. **a.** Dr. Harrison will be glad to see you at ten a.m. on June 12.
   b. Olivia as you know will make the presentation.
   c. Jennings speaks Russian doesn't he?
   d. A booklet containing instructions comes in the box with the recorder.

3. _____   _____

4. **a.** Paula has a degree from Ohio University.
   b. Her specialty is copywrite law.
   c. We spent nearly $30 at the charity bizarre.
   d. The reporter revealed that he had not interviewed
   Terry Flowers the athlete.

4. _____   _____

5. **a.** Diane will be the principle presenter at the conference in Toronto.
   b. Sergio found his notes laying beside his computer.
   c. Harrison bought tickets for his brother and I.
   d. Your article in *The Morning Star* was very well written.

5. _____   _____

D Writing Claim Letters

The Daily Dispatch, 800 West 64 Avenue, Toledo, Ohio 46059, has billed you for a month's delivery of both daily and Sunday newspapers. You ordered only the daily newspaper, however, and that is all you have received. Your bill is for $7.20 for 24 issues of the daily newspaper and $6 for 4 Sunday issues. Write a letter to Mr. Sinclair Jackson, Circulation Manager, and request a correction to your records.

✓

_____

_____

_____

_____

_____

_____

_____

_____

_____

_____

_____

_____

_____

_____

_____

_____

_____

_____

_____

_____

_____

_____

_____

_____

_____

 **SECTION 11.3**   RESPONDING TO REQUESTS _____

A Thinking Positively

Using positive words can lighten the burden of answering a problem request. In the left column is a list of negative words. Study each word in this list, and in the right column, write a positive word (or short phrase) to replace each negative word.   ✓

Negative Words	Positive Words
1. cheap	**1.** _____ _____
2. complaint	**2.** _____ _____
3. careless	**3.** _____ _____
4. liable	**4.** _____ _____
5. biased	**5.** _____ _____
6. stubborn	**6.** _____ _____
7. neglect	**7.** _____ _____
8. failure	**8.** _____ _____
9. problem	**9.** _____ _____
10. mediocre	**10.** _____ _____

B Saying No Tactfully

Analyze the following sentences. Then, on the lines provided, rewrite the sentences so that they say no more tactfully.   ✓

1. Our company's policy against providing free multiple copies will not permit us to grant your request.

_____

_____

_____

_____

_____   **1.** _____

2. Although we contributed in the past, we are not going to this year.

_____

_____

_____

_____   **2.** _____

3. You neglected to tell us what finish you wanted on your bookcase.

_____

_____

_____

_____ **3.** _____

4. You are not qualified for this position because you do not have the necessary skills.

_____

_____

_____

_____

_____ **4.** _____

5. I do not have time to speak to your organization on February 23.

_____

_____

_____

_____

_____ **5.** _____

6. We cannot send 20 brochures because our supply is low.

_____

_____

_____

_____

_____ **6.** _____

7. The fact that you did not follow the proper instructions for caring for your hair dryer means that we will not replace it.

_____

_____

_____

_____

_____ **7.** _____

8. When our equipment-leasing agreement with you expires, we will take our business to someone who does what they promise.

_____

_____

_____

_____

_____ **8.** _____

✓

9. You did not tell us when you expect to arrive; therefore, we are unable to book your room at our hotel.

_____

_____

_____

_____

_____

_____   9. _____

10. You sent a check for the wrong amount; you sent $12.50 by mistake instead of $15.20.

_____

_____

_____

_____

_____

_____   10. _____

C Sentence Improvement

Correct and improve the following sentences taken from answers to requests. Write your revisions on the lines provided.

✓

1. If you had taken time to read the user's manual, you would not have troubled us with these unnecessary questions.

_____

_____

_____

_____

_____   1. _____

2. Under separate cover, please find our catalog of recent date in which the items about which you request information are described and priced.

_____

_____

_____

_____

_____   2. _____

3. The costs of printing and mailing catalogs are skyrocketing, and unless you place an order you won't be receiving our catalog again.

_____

_____

_____

_____   3. _____

4. This letter is an acknowledgment of your request of March 15, in which you asked us to refund you $7.95 in delivery charges paid by you. In compliance to this request, therefore, our check in the amount of $7.95 will be forwarded to you at an early date by our cashier.

_____

_____

_____

_____   **4.** ____

5. In your letter, you prevail upon us to ascertain the date of shipment for your order. In compliance with this request, we can certainly assure you that your order will be shipped in the very near future.

_____

_____

_____

_____   **5.** ____

D Be Sales-Minded

The Association of Office Mangers has asked you to speak at its monthly meeting on February 15. The topic is to be streamlining office systems. Because of a major project due February 10 and because you didn't receive the invitation until January 26, you do not think that enough time remains for you to prepare a good speech. Write a letter of refusal to the chairperson, Marjorie Pinnell, 938 West Magnolia Street, Smithville, VA 24070. Make a suggestion of another topic about which you would be prepared to speak, or tell her about Harriet Evanston, a collegue of yours who gave a similar talk at another meeting.

_____

_____

_____

_____

_____

_____

_____

_____

_____

_____

_____

_____

_____

_____

_____

_____

_____

_____

E Error Hunt

Underscore all the errors in the following adjustment letter, and write your corrections in the spaces provided. For each line that has no error, write *OK*.   ✓

Ms. Marietta Johnston   _____ _____
7190 Colorado Blvd   _____ _____
Lincoln, Nebraska 68505   _____ _____

Dear Ms. Johnston: _____ _____

    Thank you for your letter of August 29th in which   _____ _____
you mentioned faulty performance features of your new   _____ _____
Regal Vaccum Cleaner, which you bought from us resently. _____ _____

    As you will recall, our service represenative examined _____ _____
your machine and found several mechanical defects. The   _____ _____
sucsion was malfunctioning and causing dust to escape   _____ _____
from the tank. We discovered a small split in the hose   _____ _____
where the hose fits into the tank. Its now operating   _____ _____
properly so you should have no dust escaping   _____ _____
unneccesarily from the hose.   _____ _____

    If you should experience any farther problems,   _____ _____
Mrs. Johnston, please let us know immediatly and we will _____ _____
take care of the matter for you as quickly as possible. _____ _____
During future visits to our store, please enjoy this coupon _____ _____
for a 10 percent discount off any merchandise. Just   _____ _____
remember—Sloan's is hear to serve you.   _____ _____

Sincerly yours,   _____ _____

F Plurals and Possessives Review

In the blank provided, indicate the correct plural or possessive form of each word enclosed in parentheses.   ✓

1. My (boss) hotel reservation needs to be changed.   1. _____ _____

2. Mr. Smith gave Henry a box of monogrammed
   (handkerchief).   2. _____ _____

3. The proposal was supported by all the (analysis) that
   were submitted.   3. _____ _____

4. The two (solo) sung by Mary were accompanied by John. 4. _____ _____

5. The three (editor-in-chief) presented the plans for the
   new year.   5. _____ _____

6. Safe investments can be made in public (utility).

6. _____ ____

7. (Men) clothing can be purchased at a 30 percent discount today.

7. _____ ____

8. Doctor Marelli is a person (who) experience is highly regarded.

8. _____ ____

9. Even though the computer was on, (it) speakers were turned off.

9. _____ ____

10. The (bunch) of bananas were arranged neatly on the counter.

10. _____ ____

11. Our (attorney) recommended that we decide against running the editorial in next Sunday's newspaper.

11. _____ ____

12. (Louise) and (Marcus) offices were relocated to the annex facility so they could share office space with other marketing managers.

12. _____ ____

13. One (salesperson) suggestion was to increase the discount on all purchases over $75.

13. _____ ____

14. Based on the testimony of three (plaintiff), both defendants engaged in fraudulent activities regarding the sale of the property.

14. _____ ____

15. The new Med-Flight emergency services will handle trauma calls for six (county) in the tri-state area.

15. _____ ____

16. Seven members of the city council voted to consider funding the construction of a sports arena by selling (security).

16. _____ ____

17. Our day care center is licensed to accommodate up to 28 (child) for each age group.

17. _____ ____

18. The doctors consulted on the test results and they came up with two different (diagnosis).

18. _____ ____

19. All sales (representative) laptop computers provide access to the company's inventory system.

19. _____ ____

20. The (man) basketball team will travel to Tennessee by bus; the (woman) basketball team will travel to Missouri by plane.

20. _____ ____

SECTION 11.4 PERSUADING

A **Targeting Audiences**

For each product or service listed, determine the audience(s) you would target. Select your audience on the basis of such factors as age, geographical location, income, occupation, or lifestyle.

1. Four-in-One, a multipurpose software program

_____
_____
_____
_____
_____   1. ____

2. Bug Off!, an insect repellent lotion

_____
_____
_____
_____   2. ____

3. *Ski Land and Sea*, a new monthly magazine

_____
_____
_____
_____   3. ____

4. Office Galore, a new office supplies store

_____
_____
_____
_____   4. ____

5. Henrietta, a line of classic, yet stylish, women's clothing sold through professional consultants by appointment

_____
_____
_____
_____   5. ____

B Planning a Sales Letter

A new business networking group is being organized to meet the needs of men and women in the community who need additional opportunities to meet other people with similar challenges and concerns involved in promoting and growing their small businesses. As the newly appointed marketing chairperson of this new group, you have been asked to write a letter that would be mailed to small businesses listed in the Yellow Pages and members of the local chamber of commerce. The purpose of your letter is to persuade people to attend the organizational meeting and become charter members and pay the dues and initiation fee. Plan the letter by writing two appropriate sentences for each category indicated below. The two sentences should work together to form a paragraph.

✓

1. Attracting Attention

   a. _____
   _____
   b. _____
   _____
   _____

1. ____

2. Establishing a Relationship

   a. _____
   _____
   b. _____
   _____
   _____

2. ____

3. Appealing to Buying Motives

   a. _____
   _____
   b. _____
   _____
   _____

3. ____

4. Persuading Someone to Act

   a. _____
   _____
   b. _____
   _____
   _____

4. ____

5. Providing the Opportunity to Act

   a. _____
   _____
   b. _____
   _____
   _____

5. ____

C Identifying Sales Appeals

Read the following sales appeals to identify the specific want or need to be satisfied in each case. Write that want or need in the space provided.

✓

1. Imagine not being able to read this letter. If you would like to help someone learn how to read, please send a contribution to the Literacy Guild today.

   _____   1. _____

2. Late getting home from work and a family to feed? Healthy Gourmet is at your rescue with a five-course meal; just call when you leave the office and dinner will be delivered to your door soon after you arrive home.

   _____   2. _____

3. We can put you in the driver's seat of a new luxury Executive sedan in a truly elegant color.

   _____   3. _____

4. Look great while you take your walks through your neighborhood! Wear Jean Hinson sportswear in colors that come alive with movement.

   _____   4. _____

5. The SafeCo security system protects your home and loved ones from vandalism and break-ins.

   _____   5. _____

6. The Beauty Sleeper ensures that you will awaken each morning ready to face the day.

   _____   6. _____

7. Put your money where it can work best for you—Marston Investments, Inc.

   _____   7. _____

8. Shop at Jo-Mart—where your dollar gets you more!

   _____   8. _____

9. The Energy Glider will give you the muscle toning and breathing ease you need and will make that waistband feel more comfortable.

   _____   9. _____

10. See the latest and greatest movies while you enjoy your evening meal at Flicks and Feast.

   _____   10. _____

11. Install a new Enviro-Clean air purifier today to make your home virtually dust free. This patented system all but eliminates the need to vacuum.

   _____   11. _____

12. Treat yourself to a relaxing, revitalizing all-day spa at our new facility on Westmoor Boulevard—you'll be glad you did!

   _____   12. _____

D Revising for Improvement

Rewrite the following paragraph from a sales letter to give it more of a you-attitude and to correct mechanical errors.

> The Athenian Mutual Life Insurance Early Retirement Policy is designed to help people have enough money for retirement at age fifty-five. To accumulate enough money, savings can mount up quickly. Please find the information card that is enclosed and fill it out. One of our representatives will call to set an appointment to discuss how you can begin accumulating savings for after you quit work.

✓

_____
_____
_____
_____
_____
_____
_____
_____
_____
_____
_____
_____
_____
_____
_____
_____
_____
_____
_____
_____
_____
_____
_____

E Writing Collection Letters

Each of the following statements appears in a separate letter in a series of five follow-up collection letters. Based on the firmness of the wording, identify the order in which the following statements would appear in the series of five follow-up letters.

a. In order to avoid a letter from our attorney, please send us your check for $528 no later than March 1 for the balance of the money owed on the living room set you purchased from our Nottingham store.

b. The holidays have come and gone, and I am certain our statement for the $528 balance on the living room set you purchased from our Nottingham store must also have "come and gone." That's why I am enclosing another statement; please be sure to mail your check in time for it to reach us by January 15.

c. Didn't you receive the statement from us a few weeks ago? We thought we would have received your $528 check by now. If you have a problem paying the total amount, please call me at 1-800-555-2340 to arrange for installment payments.

d. It is imperative that you pay the $528 balance of your account no later than February 1. Avoid further damage to your credit rating and mail your check today.

e. Please mail your $528 check today. I know the fact that we haven't received it on time must be due to an oversight on your part.

✓

1. ____   1. ____

2. ____   2. ____

3. ____   3. ____

4. ____   4. ____

5. ____   5. ____

F Editing Practice

Underline any errors in the following sentences, and write your corrections in the space provided. Write *OK* for any sentence that is correct.

✓

1. Christine Whitley, former state senator from Cincinnati, is a Senior Partner with the law firm of Duncan, Dodge, and Dilbert.

   1. _____ ____

2. My supervisor, Dave Lawton, knows more about those remediation systems than any engineer in the company.

   2. _____ ____

3. If two-thirds of our stockholders agrees with the proposed merger, the board of directors will move forward with the plan.

   3. _____ ____

4. More than likely it was he who ordered the screen saver program to be used on all network computers.

   4. _____ ____

5. Both Laurice and Paul have extra copies of the new requisition forms; ask any of them if you should need copies of the forms.

   5. _____ ____

6. Although learning how to use new software will be challenging, I'm looking forward with using an integrated software package.

   6. _____ ____

7. According to company policy, no employee can engage in consulting work without he or she first gets permission from management.

   7. _____ ____

8. Read the first chapter, "Marketing for Results", for an overview of the marketing process.

   8. _____ ____

9. Most of our customers in the L.A. area have signed up for the conference on Tues., February 10.

   9. _____ ____

10. The Manufacturing Department will be hiring 6 additional employees to deal with the increase in production.

    10. _____ ____

The following is a draft of a first follow-up collection letter. Improve the writing in the letter based on your knowledge of the collection process.

Dear Mr. Montefiore:

To date you have not responded to the two statements that we have sent you. This letter is our reminder that the balance due on your account is $121.50.

If for some reason you believe our statement to be in error, please let us know at once. If other circumstances exist that prevent you from paying, please write or call me at 1-800-555-2781 to explain and arrange a payment plan. Otherwise, please send us a check for $121.50 to clear your account. A preaddressed envelope is enclosed for your convenience in responding.

Sincerely yours,

_____

_____

_____

_____

_____

_____

_____

_____

_____

_____

_____

_____

_____

_____

_____

_____

_____

_____

_____

_____

_____

_____

_____

_____

_____

_____

_____

 **SECTION 11.5** PUBLIC RELATIONS LETTERS

A Creating Goodwill

Assume that you work for Crafts Galore, a popular store that merchandises all kinds of craft supplies. Because the need for more space has forced you to relocate, you must draft a letter letting customers know about the plan to move. Use your imagination to write a lively, interesting message to Crafts Galore customers to share the news with them—and retain their goodwill, of course. Include any details that will add realism to your letter. Write your message in the space provided.

✓

_____

_____

_____

_____

_____

_____

_____

_____

_____

_____

_____

_____

_____

_____

_____

_____

_____

_____

_____

_____

_____

_____

_____

_____

_____

_____

_____

_____

_____

B Promoting a New Business

Think of a business enterprise that interests you—one that you might like to start someday. In the space below, write a PR letter in which you introduce yourself and announce the nature of your business. Your aim, of course, is to establish positive public opinion and to attract customers.

✓

_____
_____
_____
_____
_____
_____
_____
_____
_____
_____
_____
_____
_____
_____
_____
_____
_____
_____
_____
_____
_____
_____
_____
_____
_____
_____
_____
_____
_____
_____
_____

Attracting New Customers

Assume now that five years have passed since you established your business that you announced in exercise B. An industrial park, new housing communities, and a retirement village have opened in your area, increasing the entire business community's potential for new customers. In the space below, write a PR letter designed to attract new customers to your business and to persuade them to join your other satisfied customers.

✓

_____

_____

_____

_____

_____

_____

_____

_____

_____

_____

_____

_____

_____

_____

_____

_____

_____

_____

_____

_____

_____

_____

_____

_____

_____

_____

_____

_____

_____

_____

_____

D Polishing the Public Image

Assume that you work for Western Gas & Electric Company. Read the following sentences from letters to be sent to WG&E customers, and revise them so that each helps build a favorable image of WG&E.

✓

1. Your electric bills are high because your home appliances are energy hogs.

   _____

   _____

   _____   1. ____

2. You are hereby informed that Western Gas & Electric will sponsor a free concert of Oceanside Symphony Orchestra to celebrate our donation to the Symphony Fund on Wednesday evening, April 8, at 8 o'clock.

   _____

   _____

   _____   2. ____

3. By scheduling more of your power usage during off-peak hours, money can be saved as well as avoiding "brownouts."

   _____

   _____

   _____   3. ____

4. As part of our mission to educate the public about energy conservation, we have enclosed a most informative pamphlet.

   _____

   _____

   _____   4. ____

5. To continue paying healthy dividends to our stockholders, we have applied to the State Utilities Commission for a rate increase.

   _____

   _____

   _____   5. ____

6. Now, for the very first time in our history, you will be afforded the opportunity of spreading your utility payments over a 12-month period.

   _____

   _____

   _____   6. ____

7. May we in the Customer Service Department take the liberty of offering our congratulations upon the occasion of your forthcoming marriage to Peter Rumboldt?

   _____

   _____

   _____   7. ____

8. Everyone knows that we are in business to make a profit, but we still wish to be of service to you.

   _____

   _____

   _____   8. ____

 SOCIAL-BUSINESS
COMMUNICATIONS

 Writing Thank-You Letters

You have worked for Magna Industries for three years. Recently, when the manager of your department retired, you were promoted to his job. As a result, many of your friends and coworkers sent you congratulatory notes, two of which are shown here. In the space provided, write a thank-you letter for each.

1. The first letter is from Joanie A. Bennett, president of Magna Industries.

Congratulations on your promotion to manager of Direct Mail—and welcome to the Magna management team!

Since you joined Magna three years ago, you have certainly developed a reputation for communicating expertly with customers and solving their problems quickly and satisfactorily. As manager of Direct Mail, you will be in an even better position to ensure customer satisfaction—a very important factor for Magna's future success!

All of us at Magna are confident that you will be a superlative manager and that you will have a most successful career with the company. We look forward to working with you and your staff. Please let me know, of course, whenever I may be of help to you.

✓

_____

_____

_____

_____

_____

_____

_____

_____

_____

_____

_____

_____

_____

_____

_____

_____

_____

_____

_____

2. The second letter is from James Richenberry, the national sales manager for Magna. During your three years with the company, Jim has become a friend and a valued business associate. You work closely with Jim and his staff on a daily basis, and your mutual cooperation has proved to be very effective.

Congratulations! I am really happy—but not at all surprised—to hear the good news about your promotion to manager of Direct Mail.

As a sales manager, I certainly value strong customer relations. Therefore, I appreciate all your efforts to communicate effectively with our top customers and to provide all customers with fast, efficient service. It's been a pleasure working with you!

My best wishes to you in your new position. I know that you will do a superb job, and I very much look forward to working more closely with you.

Sincerely,

✓

_____

_____

_____

_____

_____

_____

_____

_____

_____

_____

_____

_____

_____

_____

_____

_____

_____

_____

_____

_____

_____

_____

_____

_____

_____

_____

B Proofreading for Errors

Use your proofreading skills to correct the errors in the following letter. Underline the errors, and write your corrections on the lines provided. Write *OK* for any line that has no error.   ✓

Congradulations! You, indeed, deserved the recent   _____ ____
promotion to senior vice president. Several of your   _____ ____
colleages have spoken to me in the past about you achieving   _____ ____
so much in the short time since you arrived at Smith's.   _____ ____

If I may be of help as you begin your new position   _____ ____
just let me know. You will acomplish much, I am sure,   _____ ____
in your new leadership roll.   _____ ____

By the way, do you still plan to attend the annual   _____ ____
fall conferance of The Association for Business   _____ ____
Communication.   _____ ____

Yours truely,   _____ ____

C Handling Invitations

Practice your skill at handling invitations by completing the following assignments.

1. As chairperson of the entertainment committee for Magna Industries, you must prepare the committee's formal invitation to the company's annual dinner dance. In the space below, print the invitation precisely as you want it to be printed. (The reception begins at 7 o'clock in the evening and will be followed at eight o'clock by dinner. The evening's events are to take place on Saturday, May 20, in the Lincoln Room at the Springfield Manor Hotel.)   ✓

_____
_____
_____
_____
_____
_____
_____
_____
_____
_____
_____
_____
_____
_____
_____

2. You received a formal invitation from Mr. And Mrs. Richard Juarez to attend their dinner party on Friday, November 10. In the space below, write your reply *accepting* their invitation.

✓

_____

_____

_____

_____

_____

_____

_____

_____

___

3. In the space below, write a reply to the invitation from Mr. and Mrs. Juarez indicating that you *cannot* accept their invitation.

✓

_____

_____

_____

_____

_____

_____

_____

_____

_____

___

 FORM PARAGRAPHS,
FORM LETTERS, AND TEMPLATES

 Advantages and Disadvantages of Using Form Letters

You work for a travel agency that is planning to use form letters for a large mailing to promote various vacation and weekend getaway packages. Your supervisor has asked you to identify the advantages and disadvantages of form letters, and to present your findings at the next staff meeting.

List five advantages of using form letters.   ✓

1. _____
   _____   1. ____
2. _____
   _____   2. ____
3. _____
   _____   3. ____
4. _____
   _____   4. ____
5. _____
   _____   5. ____

List three disadvantages of using form letters.

1. _____   1. ____
2. _____   2. ____
3. _____   3. ____

B **Types of Form Letters**

Based on the advantages you listed in exercise A above, the travel agency has decided to use form letters for different situations. For each of the following situations, select the type of form letter from the list that would be most appropriate.

   a. Form letter
   b. Form letter with variables
   c. Letters with form paragraphs   ✓

1. Notifying potential customers about upcoming cruises.   1. ____   ____

2. Responding to a job applicant's interest in employment with the travel agency.   2. ____   ____

3. Enclosing tickets for a client's upcoming trip.   3. ____   ____

4. Outlining a proposed travel itinerary for a client.   4. ____   ____

5. Requesting information in order to update a client's travel profile.   5. ____   ____

C Preparing a Letter With Form Paragraphs

As the assistant to the personnel manager at Palm City Plastics, you handle all correspondence with job applicants. To streamline the process, you use form paragraphs. Maria Lavelle, a job applicant, has sent an application letter and résumé to the personnel manager. The personnel manager has asked you to send a letter to Ms. Lavelle requesting that she complete an application form and provide the names of three references. An interview will be scheduled once the information is received.

Select the form paragraphs from the following list that you would use for the body of the letter. In the spaces provided, write the numbers of the form paragraphs you would use. List the numbers in the order that the paragraphs would appear in the letter.

1. Thank you for your interest in employment with our company. We would be delighted to discuss career opportunities with you.

2. Business trends will not permit us to hire additional employees at this time. However, we do anticipate position openings in several specialized areas within the next three to six months.

3. The qualifications shown on the résumé you recently sent impressed us. Would you please stop by our office to complete an application form. Please include the names and addresses of three references on the application.

4. We were quite impressed by the qualifications you listed on the application form you recently completed. Would you please submit a résumé. Also, please include the names and addresses of three references.

5. As soon as we receive the information requested, we will call you to arrange a mutually convenient time for an interview.

6. Thank you for your interest in our company. We look forward to hearing from you.

7. We will keep your application on file and notify you if a suitable position becomes available in the future.

8. Although your qualifications are impressive, we have decided to hire a candidate whose qualifications best match those of the position for which you interviewed. If you would like, we will keep your application on file and contact you should any openings become available in your area of interest.

9. Several months have passed since you first completed an application with us. If you would like us to keep your application on file, please contact the Personnel Office at the number on the letterhead.

_____
_____
_____
_____
_____
_____

Writing Form Letters

As the administrative assistant to the president of Dresden Baskets, one of your important responsibilities is responding to routine correspondence for the president, Brian Dresden. You compose letters and Mr. Dresden signs them. Because of the volume of similar routine correspondence, you decide to use form letters. Write form letters, form letters with variables, or letters with form paragraphs for each of the following situations.

✓

1. Write the body paragraphs of a form letter that can be used to respond to consumers' requests for free catalogs. Enclose the free ten-page catalog with the letter.

_____

_____

_____

_____

_____

_____

_____

_____

_____

_____

_____

_____

1. _____

2. Write the body paragraphs of a form letter, with variables, that responds positively to requests from local charitable organizations for contributions. Variables will be the receiver of the contribution (for example, the Central Iowa Literacy Council) and the amount of the contribution.

_____

_____

_____

_____

_____

_____

_____

_____

_____

_____

_____

2. _____

3. Write form paragraphs that can be used to respond to requests for plant tours. Write a paragraph to cover each of the following items:

    a. A goodwill opening paragraph.

_____

_____

_____

_____

_____   **a.** _____

    b. Daily tours are conducted Mondays through Fridays from 9 a.m. to 4 p.m. from April through November. Groups are limited to 25 participants.

_____

_____

_____

_____

_____   **b.** _____

    c. Tours can be arranged by calling Jenny Briand at 1-800-555-4252.

_____

_____

_____

_____

_____   **c.** _____

    d. Dresden Baskets Factory Store, across the street from the plant, is open from 9 a.m. to 4 p.m., Monday through Saturday. A variety of baskets and other gift items are available.

_____

_____

_____

_____

_____   **d.** _____

    e. A goodwill closing paragraph.

_____

_____

_____

_____

_____   **e.** _____

 **SECTION 12.1**

THE IMPORTANCE OF
GOOD CUSTOMER SERVICE

A Remembering Key Points

Using the Key Points in Section 12.1 in your textbook, complete the items that follow.   ✓

1. Customer service is the performance of activities or services for the purpose of
   ensuring _____.   1. _____

2. Outstanding service helps a business _____ current customers and
   _____ new ones.   2. _____

3. _____ customers are people outside your organization who
   purchase your goods or services.   3. _____

4. An _____ customer is someone within your own organization who
   depends on products, supplies, or services that you provide.   4. _____

B Customer Service Statements

Circle *T* if the statement is true and circle *F* if the statement is false.   ✓

1. If you represent a company in any capacity, the customer will believe that you
   can help him or her with a need or a concern.   1. T F _____

2. You should treat customers, within the guidelines of company policy, the way you
   would want to be treated.   2. T F _____

3. Customer service is a function that should exist only when a customer
   complaint arises.   3. T F _____

4. Customer satisfaction occurs when the customer's needs are met and when
   the customer feels valued by the company.   4. T F _____

5. Making customers feel valued instills the feeling that their business is
   appreciated, that they will be treated with respect, and that their business will
   receive conscientious attention.   5. T F _____

6. Top management's involvement with customer service isn't necessary because
   the responsibility for customer service rests exclusively with employees who
   come in direct contact with the customer.   6. T F _____

7. Many companies derive much of their new business through referrals
   (often called recommendations) from their satisfied customers.   7. T F _____

8. Improving relationships between internal customers can help a business run
   more smoothly.   8. T F _____

9. Company personnel deal with external customers only through face-to-face
   contact.   9. T F _____

10. The following is an example of a situation involving an external customer:
    A supply room associate delivers surgical dressings to a nurse.   10. T F _____

C Turning Ill Will Into Goodwill

The following items contain negative statements or questions. In the space provided, rewrite each item making it more positive and thus more customer oriented.

✓

1. I can't help you until you do a better job of explaining your complaint.

   _____

   _____   1. ____

2. It wasn't my idea to do it this way; the higher-ups ordered it.

   _____

   _____   2. ____

3. What's your gripe?

   _____

   _____   3. ____

4. Don't blame me; the company bigwigs suggested that policy change.

   _____

   _____   4. ____

5. Don't you understand what I'm trying to tell you? Listen this time; I'll repeat the procedure.

   _____

   _____   5. ____

6. Unless you have the warranty information, I can't help you get your videocassette recorder repaired.

   _____

   _____   6. ____

7. Hold on a minute while I look on the computer. Your account information should be on file somewhere in our records.

   _____

   _____   7. ____

8. All lines are busy. No one can take your call now. Stay on hold or hang up and call us back.

   _____

   _____   8. ____

9. I'll need the model number, purchase date, and reason for the return before we can give a refund.

   _____

   _____   9. ____

10. You should have noticed the defect in the fabric when you bought the item. We can't let everyone return items just because they have a little wear and tear.

   _____

   _____   10. ____

MAINTAINING GOOD CUSTOMER SERVICE

A Recalling Key Points

Using the Key Points in Section 12.2 in your textbook, complete the items that follow.   ✓

1. Maintain continuous _____ with customers to reinforce the
   _____ between your company and the customer.   **1.** ____

2. Employees who come in contact with customers should be knowledgeable about the
   _____ or _____, as well as company
   _____.   **2.** ____

3. Your company is _____ to customers if you make it easy for
   them to conduct business.   **3.** ____

4. When a customer speaks, _____ attentively.   **4.** ____

5. Any employee who comes in contact with a customer directly or indirectly can influence
   that customer's perception of _____ and its _____
   and _____ .   **5.** ____

6. Customer service should be an ongoing function in which employees anticipate
   _____ and implement _____.   **6.** ____

B Meeting the Public

Items A–J contain some commonsense rules for meeting the public. Statements 1–10
violate one or more of these rules. In the space provided next to each statement, write
the letter of the rule or rules that were violated.   ✓

Rules:

A. Give prompt attention to all callers.

B. Greet callers pleasantly.

C. Don't let personal business interfere with greeting the public.

D. Screen callers before permitting them access to executive offices.

E. Be courteous at all times, even though the caller may annoy you.

F. Do not reveal company secrets.

G. Keep within your authority.

H. Make refusals tactfully.

I. Show eagerness to be of assistance.

J. If the person whom a caller wishes to see is busy, let the caller know how long he
or she will have to wait.

Statements:

1. "No, Mr. Odubu can't see you without an appointment."   **1.** ____ ____

2. "Mrs. Sandifer is arranging a deal with a Japanese investor."   **2.** ____ ____

3. "I'm sorry, but it's not my job to look up information for customers."   3. _____ _____

4. Receptionist to visitor: "What do you want?"   4. _____ _____

5. Receptionist: "I think it will be OK for you to read the report that is on Mr. Godfrey's desk."   5. _____ _____

6. "Mr. Agler is at the bank trying to get a business loan for the company."   6. _____ _____

7. Visitor (who is a stranger): "May I see Mr. Torres?" Receptionist: "Sure, first door on your right."   7. _____ _____

8. Sales representative to customer: "I'll be with you as soon as I finish this inventory report."   8. _____ _____

9. Administrative assistant on the telephone: "...so I said to Frank, I can't go to the movie with you; I have to work tonight and then he said... Hold on a minute, Lisa..." (turning to a visitor who has just approached) "I'll be with you just as soon as I finish this call."   9. _____ _____

10. "I realize you have an appointment, Mr. Austell, but Ms. Adams is busy right now."   10. _____ _____

C Maintaining Customer Contact

Cathy Sheldon has been a sales representative for Acme Medical Supplies for eight months. She personally calls on the same customers at least once every three weeks. Most of the supplies that she sells can be bought from her competitors; thus, she strives to maintain a high level of customer service as her competitive edge. What should Cathy do in each of the following situations to maintain customer contact?

1. While Cathy is traveling, she receives an e-mail message from her home office telling her that her most important client wants to talk with her about some supplies that are urgently needed within two days. It is about 3 p.m., and Cathy is about an hour's drive from the client or about an hour's drive from her home. Cathy is tired and wants to go home. What should she do?

_____

_____

_____

_____

_____

_____

_____   1. _____

2. Cathy called one of her clients, Mr. Tyler, early this morning. Mr. Tyler's assistant told Cathy he was at the hospital with his wife who was delivering their first child. Cathy's company has a policy against expensive gifts, but she felt that she should acknowledge the birth in some way. What should Cathy do?

_____

_____

_____

_____

_____

_____

_____   2. _____

✓

3. Cathy received an e-mail message from a customer who buys very few supplies from her each month. The customer asked if Cathy's company might contribute a door prize for an upcoming company picnic. Cathy has never had this particular type of situation arise. What should she do?

_____

_____

_____

_____

_____

_____

_____

_____

_____

_____   **3.** _____

4. When Cathy checked her voice mail, she had a message from a customer canceling his appointment that afternoon due to a death in his family. Cathy is concerned about this situation because this customer had previously indicated that he would place his first order with her this afternoon. What should Cathy do?

_____

_____

_____

_____

_____

_____

_____

_____

_____

_____   **4.** _____

5. When Cathy returned a telephone call to one of her customers, the customer told Cathy that the supplies that she shipped for next day delivery had not arrived today. The package should have arrived by 2 p.m., and it is now 3 p.m. What should Cathy do?

_____

_____

_____

_____

_____

_____

_____

_____

_____   **5.** _____

D Proofreading Practice

Proofread the following paragraphs from a letter. Underline any errors and write your corrections in the space provided. For each line that has no error, write *OK*.

✓

Dear Mr. Early: _____ ____

Thank you for returning the registration card for you _____ ____
new Browser Monster software. As a registered user, you _____ ____
have access to our technical support staff 24 hours a day. _____ ____
The enclosed brochur explains how to reach us by _____ ____
telephone, fax, or e-mail should the need arise. _____ ____

In addition to technical support, all registered users will _____ ____
recieve a monthly newsletter packed with tips for using _____ ____
your Browser Monster software for Internet searchs, _____ ____
e-mail, and more. _____ ____

If you have any quesitons, please contact me at the _____ ____
address and telephone number on the letterhead. _____ ____
Insuring customer satisfaction is our goal. _____ ____

Sincerely, _____ ____

SECTION 12.3   IMPROVING CONTACT WITH CUSTOMERS

A Key Points

Using the Key Points and the OOPS! features in Section 12.3 in your textbook, complete the items that follow.   ✓

1. Every visitor should receive _____ and _____ treatment.   **1.** _____

2. Ignoring a customer who is waiting _____ for assistance while you are on the phone can cause the customer to react to you and your firm in a _____ way.   **2.** _____

3. Both _____ and _____ contacts a customer has with your firm are important in either _____ or _____ good customer relations.   **3.** _____

4. Sending a fax addressed "To whom it may concern" to a company that is a potential customer will _____ the likelihood of a _____ response—or any response.   **4.** _____

B Talking With Customers

Circle *T* if the statement is true and *F* if the statement is false.   ✓

1. Anyone who greets visitors or answers telephone calls can have a significant impact on a customer's perception of a firm.   **1.** T F _____

2. Immediately recognizing a visitor's presence is not necessary or expected in today's fast-paced world.   **2.** T F _____

3. If a customer treats you rudely, you should respond in the same way.   **3.** T F _____

4. Explaining a delayed appointment to a visitor and giving the visitor an estimated waiting time would be an unwise course of action.   **4.** T F _____

5. You should always relate all details when explaining to a customer why your supervisor is late for the customer's appointment.   **5.** T F _____

6. When transferring calls, you should (if technically possible) make sure that the extension to which you are transferring the call was answered.   **6.** T F _____

7. Maintaining a respectful, courteous tone in speaking with customers can reduce problems such as customer frustration and hostility.   **7.** T F _____

8. When you make a commitment to a customer, make sure that you follow through on it.   **8.** T F _____

9. When answering a call for others, you should offer to help the caller or to transfer the call to someone who can help.   **9.** T F _____

10. If a caller wants to speak to someone who isn't available, you should tell the caller to call back later.   **10.** T F _____

C Talking With Customers

Reword the following unprofessional responses to telephone calls. Make sure they convey a positive image of you, your supervisor, and your company.   ✓

1. Mr. Brandon has been gone for over three hours. It took him longer to trade cars than he thought it would.

_____

_____   1. _____

2. Mr. Brandon doesn't answer his extension. I don't know where he is. I know he is here today because I saw him when we took our coffee breaks about 10:30.

_____

_____   2. _____

3. Mr. Brandon isn't back from lunch yet. He's been gone for almost two hours so I think he will be back soon.

_____

_____   3. _____

4. Mr. Brandon hasn't come in yet this morning. I wish he would tell me when he is going to be late.

_____

_____   4. _____

5. Mr. Brandon is running so far behind with his appointments this morning that he asked me to hold all of his calls. I don't know when to tell you to call back.

_____

_____   5. _____

D Using Your Electronic Thesaurus

Use the thesaurus in your word processing program to find one synonym and one antonym for each of the following words.   ✓

	SYNONYM	ANTONYM	
1. encourage	_____	_____	1. _____
2. obstinate	_____	_____	2. _____
3. difficult	_____	_____	3. _____
4. expensive	_____	_____	4. _____
5. proficiency	_____	_____	5. _____
6. astute	_____	_____	6. _____
7. homogeneous	_____	_____	7. _____
8. conscientious	_____	_____	8. _____
9. lawful	_____	_____	9. _____
10. truthful	_____	_____	10. _____

 **RESPONDING TO CUSTOMER SERVICE NEEDS**

A Key Points

Using the Key Points in Section 12.4 in your textbook, complete the items that follow. ✓

1. The goal of customer service procedures is to _____ customer dissatisfaction and to take _____ action when problems occur.

   1. ____

2. Be sure to _____ your company's customer service policies or procedures.

   2. ____

3. The obvious solution to customer complaints is _____ action.

   3. ____

4. Sometimes _____ that is intended to simplify customer service increases customer frustration.

   4. ____

B Creating a Company Policy

You work for Alexander's Appliance Store, a family-owned company that sells and repairs small kitchen appliances such as toasters, coffee makers, and microwave ovens. Your store is experiencing a large volume of returned merchandise. Most of the returned merchandise wasn't defective when purchased, but it has been damaged by carelessness and improper use. Often times, the warranty has expired. Write a company policy for returned merchandise. ✓

1. _____
   _____
   _____   1. ____

2. _____
   _____
   _____   2. ____

3. _____
   _____
   _____   3. ____

4. _____
   _____
   _____   4. ____

5. _____
   _____
   _____   5. ____

6. _____
   _____
   _____   6. ____

C Customer Service Representative

Describe several characteristics that a customer service representative should exhibit in responding to dissatisfied customers in person, by letter, and by telephone. Use complete sentences.

✓

_____

_____

_____

_____

_____

_____

_____

_____

_____

_____

_____

_____

_____

_____

_____

_____

_____

_____

D Handling a Customer Complaint

As the manager of the Customer Service Department at Metropolis Power Company, you received a letter from a customer complaining about the way repairs to his electrical service were handled.

In his letter, the customer related that the electric meter that monitors electricity usage attached to the back of his home crackled and shot sparks, resulting in a power outage.

The customer called the Metropolis Power Company's customer service number and got the following response: "If you are using a touch-tone phone, press 1 now. If this call is about a bill, press 2 now. If this call is about establishing service, press 3 now. If this call is an emergency or life-threatening call, press 4 now."

Concerned that his house might burn or that children playing nearby might be in danger, the caller pressed 4 and heard the following message: "All of our lines are busy; please hold; your call will be answered within 1 minute." The call was not answered within 1 minute but took almost 5 minutes. The Metropolis operator who took the call said that someone would call the customer within 45 minutes. No one called within 45 minutes so the distraught customer called back. The response was as follows: "Someone will call you." No one from Metropolis ever called back, but the service crew arrived 2 hours after the initial call had been made. Power was restored within 2 additional hours.

As manager of the Customer Service Department, you feel that the customer's call was not handled properly and want to prevent this same type of incident from happening again. There were no other emergencies at that particular time. Upon investigating the incident, you discover that the service crew members were making routine checks on their service route and were away from the two-way radio in their truck. In addition, the service crew took their lunch break, which delayed their receiving the call for at least an hour.

List at least five suggestions for improving the way this call was handled.   ✓

1. _____
   _____
   _____
   _____
   _____
   _____   1. _____

2. _____
   _____
   _____
   _____
   _____
   _____   2. _____

3. _____
   _____
   _____
   _____
   _____   3. _____

4. _____
   _____
   _____
   _____   4. _____

5. _____
   _____
   _____
   _____   5. _____

E Responding to Customers

1. A bank customer went through the drive-through window of her local bank after 5 p.m. on Friday and made a deposit of $1,000. Early Monday morning she needed $200 in cash, wrote a check, and returned to the same drive-through window.

The teller responded, "Mrs. Rousseau, this check isn't any good. There aren't enough funds in your account. It's against the law to write bad checks."

Mrs. Rousseau realized immediately what had happened—her deposit made late Friday evening had not been posted to her account—but she was offended at the teller's response.

What should the teller have said to Mrs. Rousseau?

_____

_____

_____

_____

_____

_____

_____

_____

1. _____

2. Mr. McCallister received his monthly bank statement and noticed that his balance showed that he had $28,000 more than he actually had. He immediately called his bank and in his haste made an accusation, "You made a mistake on my bank statement." The teller was offended by the accusation and responded, "Mr. McCallister, we use computers to record all customer transactions, and computers don't make mistakes." Mr. McCallister was somewhat cynical with his reply, "Good! I assume then that the extra $28,000 in my account is mine. Thanks."

Mr. McCallister immediately hung up the telephone and waited impatiently. An apologetic teller called back to report that someone made the deposit without using a preprinted deposit slip and mistakenly wrote Mr. McCallister's account number, which was one digit different from the other customer's number.

What should have been the teller's response to Mr. McCallister's accusation?

_____

_____

_____

_____

_____

_____

_____

2. _____

SECTION 13.1 GATHERING
INFORMATION FOR REPORTS

 **Types and Purposes of Reports**

Identify the type of report that would be written in each of the following situations. On
the line to the right of each description, write the choice that best identifies the type of
report: informative, analytical, justification, feasibility, or proposal.   ✓

1. You are asked to report on the steps you have taken
   toward completion of an assignment.   1. _____ ____

2. Your company is interested in identifying a company
   that can do some computer programming to handle your
   monthly sales analysis. You ask three companies to
   submit information.   2. _____ ____

3. A salesperson has just shown you a new copier; you
   write a report to your supervisor explaining reasons why
   purchasing the new copier is a good idea.   3. _____ ____

4. Should the marketing department go ahead with plans to
   promote the new product now although the schedule for
   its release is a month behind? You believe they should go
   ahead and you want your reasons known to the vice
   president of marketing.   4. _____ ____

5. You have just been handed completed questionnaires that
   your instructor had students in all the business
   communication classes complete. You have been asked to
   report on the results.   5. _____ ____

6. You are serving as chairperson for the annual fund-raiser
   of the Business Leaders organization in your school. At
   the monthly meetings you are asked to present a written
   report on the preparations completed.   6. _____ ____

7. All travel agents in your office are required to compile a
   monthly report of the customer service requests they
   receive from clients.   7. _____ ____

8. The hospital where you work is exploring the possibility
   of opening outpatient surgery centers in several suburbs
   of the city the hospital serves. As a member of the
   oversight committee, you are asked to prepare a report
   that explores the benefits and drawbacks of this plan.   8. _____ ____

9. Your supervisor, the manager of patient services, is asked
   to prepare a report for the hospital board that explains
   the reasoning behind the plan to develop outpatient
   surgery centers.   9. _____ ____

10. Construction on the first outpatient surgery center began
    two months ago. The facilities manager of the hospital is
    asked to write reports on a regular basis regarding the
    pace of the construction.   10. _____ ____

B Gathering Information

Select a topic of your choice related to a hobby, your current job, or a possible future career. State your topic clearly. Then, using one or more of the following indexes— *Readers' Guide to Periodical Literature*, the *Business Periodicals Index*, or *The New York Times Index*—develop a list of a minimum of ten secondary sources about your topic. These sources should be from publications that are no more than three years old. If you have access to on-line services, you may select sources you find in an Internet search. Be sure to capture the following information for each source:

- author
- title of article
- title of periodical
- date of publication
- page numbers

The latest indexes may be available only on electronic versions in some libraries.

✓

1. _____

2. _____

3. _____

4. _____

5. _____

6. _____

7. _____

8. _____

9. _____

10. _____

1. ____

2. ____

3. ____

4. ____

5. ____

6. ____

7. ____

8. ____

9. ____

10. ____

Reliability of Sources

Select one article from the sources identified in exercise B. Prepare a one-page report
about the reliability of the information in the article based upon the following criteria:

1. Does the source provide current information on the topic?
2. Is the source reliable? Why or why not?
3. Is the information pertinent to your topic?
4. Is the author an authority on the subject? What evidence do you have?
5. Does the author identify his or her opinions? ✓

_____

_____

_____

_____

_____

_____

_____

_____

_____

_____

_____

_____

_____

_____

_____

_____

_____

_____

_____

_____

_____

_____

_____

_____

D **Survey Questions**

Critique each of the following questions based upon its value for use in a questionnaire intended for customers in the student cafeterias. Write your answers on the lines provided. The questionnaire will be used to determine the favorite foods of students who eat meals in the student cafeterias on campus.

1. Rank the following foods in order of your preference with 1 being the most liked and 5 being the least liked:

   ____burgers   ____casseroles

   ____salads   ____deli sandwiches

   ____pizza

   _____

   _____

   _____   1. ____

2. What foods do you least like that you have seen served in the campus cafeteria?

   _____

   _____

   _____   2. ____

3. Do you like desserts? ____ Yes ____ No

   _____

   _____

   _____   3. ____

4. What foods do you suggest that the cafeteria serve in the future?

   _____

   _____

   _____   4. ____

5. How often do you eat in the cafeteria?

   ____most days   ____never

   ____2-3 times a week   ____other; please specify: _____

   ____once a week

   _____

   _____

   _____   5. ____

Primary Sources

Develop a questionnaire of 10 questions that could be used to survey students on your campus about one of the following topics:
1. Electronic textbooks
2. Four-day school week
3. Study habits
4. Living on campus or off
5. Speech course requirement   ✓

1. _____
   _____
   _____   1. ____
2. _____
   _____
   _____   2. ____
3. _____
   _____
   _____   3. ____
4. _____
   _____
   _____   4. ____
5. _____
   _____
   _____   5. ____
6. _____
   _____
   _____   6. ____
7. _____
   _____
   _____   7. ____
8. _____
   _____
   _____   8. ____
9. _____
   _____
   _____   9. ____
10. _____
   _____
   _____   10. ____

F Conducting and Analyzing the Survey

Using the questionnaire developed in exercise E, survey the students in one of your classes. Tabulate the responses and prepare a two- to four-page analytical report on your findings. In the space provided, list the findings you will write about in your report.

_____

_____

_____

_____

_____

_____

_____

_____

_____

_____

_____

_____

_____

_____

_____

_____

_____

_____

_____

_____

_____

_____

_____

_____

_____

_____

_____

_____

_____

SECTION 13.2 TECHNOLOGY AND REPORTS

A Using Keywords to Search for Information

For each of the following topics, list two keywords you might use for an Internet search on that topic.

✓   ✓

1. ethical behavior in business

_____ _____   _____ _____

2. speaking in public

_____ _____   _____ _____

3. small businesses

_____ _____   _____ _____

4. job search

_____ _____   _____ _____

5. conflict resolution

_____ _____   _____ _____

6. purchasing a home

_____ _____   _____ _____

B Searching the Internet for Information

Using the tips for an Internet search found on pages 578 and 579 of your textbook, conduct a search on one of the following topics:

- interviews
- public speaking
- job skills
- negotiation
- cultural diversity
- voice quality

In the spaces provided, write the topic you selected and at least four keywords to use in your search. If you do not have Internet access, conduct a search of print materials.   ✓

Topic:

_____ _____

Keywords used for search:

1. _____   **1.** _____
2. _____   **2.** _____
3. _____   **3.** _____
4. _____   **4.** _____

Locate four sources of information on the topic. (If you do not have Internet access, conduct a search of print materials in the library.) For each source you locate, provide the following information.

✓

Name of the source (Internet site or the title of the publication):

1. _____
   _____   1. ____
2. _____
   _____   2. ____
3. _____
   _____   3. ____
4. _____
   _____   4. ____

Brief description of the information provided by each source:

1. _____
   _____
   _____
   _____
   _____
   _____
   _____   1. ____
2. _____
   _____
   _____
   _____
   _____
   _____   2. ____
3. _____
   _____
   _____
   _____
   _____
   _____   3. ____
4. _____
   _____
   _____
   _____
   _____
   _____   4. ____

Date the Internet site was accessed or date the publication was printed:

1. _____   1. ____
2. _____   2. ____
3. _____   3. ____
4. _____   4. ____

SECTION 13.3 REVIEWING ARTICLES AND
DOCUMENTING SOURCES

 A **Working Bibliography**

Using 3" x 5" cards, prepare bibliography cards for sources on one of the topics from
the list in exercise 13.2 A in the workbook. Prepare at least one bibliography card for
each of the following sources:
- Book
- Magazine article
- Publication copied from the Internet
- Reference book
- Dictionary
- Newspaper

B **Note Taking From Sources**

Select one article on the topic you selected for exercise 13.3 A above, and prepare two
note cards using the guidelines on page 582 of your textbook. ✓

Documentation Formats

From the bibliography cards you prepared in exercise 13.3 A on the preceding page, select three cards. Prepare three separate 3" x 5" bibliography cards in each of the three formats described on pages 583-584 in your textbook: Chicago Style, APA Style, and MLA Style. Use a different card for each of the three documentation formats.

 Documenting Electronic Sources

Review the information given on pages 584-585 of your textbook on preparing citations from electronic sources. If you have access to the Internet, look up a source dealing with one of the topics given in exercise 13.2 A in your workbook. Locate three of the four types of sources listed in the chart on page 585 of your textbook. Create a bibliography card for each source using 3" x 5" cards.

 Proofreading Practice

Proofread the following memo. Underline any errors and write your corrections in the space provided. Assume that people's names are correct. For each line that has no error, write *OK*.

✓

MEMO TO:	Brent Anderson	_____	____
FROM:	Marsha Blevin	_____	____
DATE:	May 5, <YEAR>	_____	____
SUBJACT:	Ticket Sales for Fall Concert Series	_____	____

Begining with the upcoming Fall Concert Series, we will
be offering patrons a variety of options for purchasing
tickets. Patrons may purchase tickets for individual
concerts, for a block of 3 two 5 concerts selected by the
patrons or for the entire series.

We plan to mail a brochure to all currant season ticket
holders in July that details this ticket options. In
additoin, we will use a direct-mail campaign to target
members of the Metropolitan Performing Arts Patrons
whom are not already season ticket holders.

Please plan to met with me on May 15 at 1 pm to review
our plans for the promotional announcements for the
Fall Concert Series.

SECTION 13.4 WRITING INFORMAL REPORTS

A Specific Subjects

Below are general subject lines used in informal reports. For each, write a revised subject line that tells the reader more specifically what the report is about. Add details if necessary.

✓

1. SUBJECT: Products

SUBJECT: _____   1. _____

2. SUBJECT: Openings

SUBJECT: _____   2. _____

3. SUBJECT: Profit

SUBJECT: _____   3. _____

4. SUBJECT: Donations

SUBJECT: _____   4. _____

5. SUBJECT: Readings

SUBJECT: _____   5. _____

B Writing an Unsolicited Informal Report

Your condominium complex has been having difficulty with motorists driving too fast. The posted speed limit is 15 miles an hour; however, you suspect that some residents and guests have been driving up to 40 miles per hour. Although no serious accidents have occurred to date, people walking and children riding tricycles have almost been struck by speeding traffic. You are aware of the success experienced in some similar complexes with the addition of speed bumps. Write an informal report to Jeff Bankston, the president of the association, giving several statements of concern by other residents with whom you have spoken. Mention several other condo complexes that have added speed bumps, and include other information you wish the president to share with the association board.

_____

_____

_____

_____

_____

_____

_____

_____

_____

_____

_____

_____
_____
_____
_____
_____
_____
_____
_____
_____
_____
_____
_____
_____
_____
_____
_____
_____
_____
_____
_____
_____
_____

 Tone and Organization

You are the manager of the community softball team, which is financially supported by Community Bank and Lawton's Foods. The team includes both men and women. Using an appropriately informal tone, rewrite the following report to the presidents of both the bank and the food store. Organize the information properly into paragraphs.

We have finished a 10-game season in the Jackson City League, with 6 wins and 4 losses, coming in third place in the League. Twenty residents reported for the opening of the season: fourteen served as starters, 6 served as substitutes. Last year we had 21 people on our softball roster. Assisting me as manager was Janie Henry, an accountant. Our home games were played every Tuesday evening at 7 p.m. at Macrae Field. We appreciate the support of all the fans who attended the games in our support, but we hope even more will attend next year. Next year would it be possible to post the game schedule at both Community Bank and Lawton's Foods and run the schedule in the suburban papers. Having copies available to each player to hand out to family and friends would be helpful too. Doing so might improve attendance. This year new equipment purchased from funds from Community Bank and Lawton's Foods included 8 new uniforms, a dozen softballs, 6 bats, one bench, 2 fielders' gloves, and a new catcher's mitt. Based on the condition of our equipment at the end of this season, we will need a budget of $1,200 for next year. May we count on you for this support?

✓

_____
_____
_____
_____
_____
_____
_____
_____
_____
_____
_____
_____
_____
_____
_____
_____
_____
_____
_____

D Unsolicited Report

Think of a way of improving the operation or facilities of your school. For example, maybe you have an idea for increasing student attendance at school events, or maybe you have an idea for improving campus security. In the space provided, write a one-page unsolicited report describing your idea. Explain why you think a specific improvement is needed and how you think it should be implemented. Direct your report to the staff person who has authority to put your idea into effect. Route your report through your instructor.

✓

_____
_____
_____
_____
_____
_____
_____
_____
_____
_____
_____
_____
_____

_____

_____

_____

_____

_____

_____

_____

_____

_____

_____

_____

_____

_____

_____

_____

_____

_____

_____

_____

_____

E Revising Sentences From Reports

The following sentences were selected from reports. If a sentence is correct, write *Correct* in the space below it. If a sentence has any errors, rewrite the sentence, correcting each error.

1. Everyone accept Ms. Applegate has approved the reccommendation.

_____   1. ____

2. Mr. Alexander, whom I met at the Conference of Communicators, has become someone whose opinions I have come to trust.

_____   2. ____

3. Ms. Marzetti will screen perspective employees for the position.

_____   3. ____

4. The principle rules are posted on the bulletin board.

_____   4. ____

5. One of the things we have discovered is that it's product is far superior.

_____   5. ____

SECTION 13.5 WRITING FORMAL REPORTS

A Preparing to Write Formal Reports

Complete each sentence by writing the name of the correct report part in the space provided.

✓

1. The _____ tells what the report is about, who prepared it, and when it was prepared.

1. ____

2. The _____ shows where the principal elements of a report are located within the report.

2. ____

3. The _____ provides background information such as who requested the report, why the report needed to be prepared, and how the report was developed.

3. ____

4. The _____ gives the reader a quick overview of what the report contains.

4. ____

5. The _____ gives all the details of the report—all the factual material and the sources of these facts.

5. ____

6. The _____ lists the findings and makes recommendations based on these findings.

6. ____

7. The _____ indicates the books and periodicals that were used in preparing the report and provides other information supporting the material in the report, such as tables, charts, questionnaires, and letters—all of which may be referred to as exhibits.

7. ____

B Defining the Purpose and Scope

A common fault of many report writers is making the scope of a report too general or too vague. Revise the following report titles to make each more specific and meaningful, as in the example shown. Add details as necessary.

Sample: Advertising

　　　　Television Prime-Time Spot Advertising Rates

✓

1. Job Performance

_____

1. ____

2. Retirement

_____

2. ____

3. Birthdays

_____

3. ____

4. Jogging

_____

4. ____

5. Study Habits

_____

5. ____

C Organizing the Report

Prepare an appropriate outline for a report on one of the topics in exercise 13.5 B in the workbook.

✓

D Objective Reporting

A business report should be written in an objective manner, with personal opinions and attitudes kept to a minimum. Revise the following sentences to eliminate the use of personal and subjective references.

✓

1. I feel that all the staff members should receive further training in all aspects of communication.

_____

_____

_____

_____   1. _____

2. I think the members of the senior class will agree that instruction is needed on completion of placement documents.

_____

_____

_____

_____   2. _____

3. In our opinion, the bank should be open until 7 p.m. every weekday evening and on Saturday mornings for the convenience of customers.

_____

_____

_____

_____   3. _____

4. Most of us believe that the combination locks need to be replaced.

_____

_____

_____

_____   4. _____

5. It seems that the reorganized floor plan is proving effective.

_____

_____

_____

_____   5. _____

6. In my opinion, the use of spreadsheets will make it easier to compile our monthly sales report.

_____

_____

_____

_____   6. _____

Proofreading for Grammar Errors

Underline any grammar errors in the following paragraphs. Write your corrections in
the space provided. For each line that has no error, write *OK*.   ✓

Mr. Justin Simone, our management consultant has   _____ ____

completed an analysis of the employer morale survey   _____ ____

conducted March 14. He reports that 95 % of our   _____ ____

employees responded.   _____ ____

On Tuesday, April 20, at 10:00 a.m. in the main   _____ ____

conference room, Mr. Simone will present the results of   _____ ____

the survey. He will distribute copys of teh full report and   _____ ____

a summary of the findings to each attendee. In addition,   _____ ____

Mr. Simone will interpet his findings and present   _____ ____

reccommendations for improvement.   _____ ____

KEEPING MEETING RECORDS

A Meeting Vocabulary

In the space provided, write a definition of each term as it applies to a business meeting of an organization. Use a dictionary as needed.

✓

1. Quorum

_____

_____   1. _____

2. Agenda

_____

_____   2. _____

3. Motion

_____

_____   3. _____

4. Carry

_____

_____   4. _____

5. Chairperson

_____

_____   5. _____

6. Preside

_____

_____   6. _____

7. Record

_____

_____   7. _____

8. Call to order

_____

_____   8. _____

9. Table

_____

_____   9. _____

10. Minutes

_____

_____

11. Adjourn

_____

_____

12. Second

_____

_____

B Recording the Minutes

As the recorder for the Student Volunteers Association, you must prepare the minutes of yesterday's meeting from the notes that follow. Prepare formal minutes of the meeting.

1. Date, time, place: September 28, <YEAR>, 5 p.m., Regal Conference Room

2. Chairperson: Sam DePew, President

3. Call to order & quorum: Call to order at 5:10; quorum established (30 percent required)

4. Present: R. Ball, L. Crenshaw, J. Toombs, M. Robbins, K. Fischer, P. Lucas, J. Shaw, V. Christie

5. Absent: V. Owen, O. Williamson, J. Riffle

6. Approvals: Minutes of the May 25 meeting; treasurer's report; audit report

7. Committee reports: Bylaws, Membership, Program

8. Unfinished business: Fund-raiser: Motion by Shaw, chairperson of Ways and Means Committee, to raffle a summer weekend stay in Cincinnati and tickets to Kings Island; sale of $5 tickets to begin Nov. 1. Profits to go to Ronald MacDonald House. Carried.

9. New business: Motion to accept the invitation of the Monroe Community Leaders' Association to have a Student Volunteers representative speak at their November 15 meeting with Robbins to speak. Seconded and carried. Motion by Lucas to contribute $500 to the United Way. Motion seconded and failed.

10. Tabled: Discussion of Spring Garage Sale until January meeting.

11. Adjournment: 6:25 p.m. Next meeting scheduled for October 18 at
Pizza King at 6 p.m for member recruitment.

✓

C Proofreading Minutes

Underline any spelling errors in the following sentences from the minutes of meetings. Write your corrections on the lines provided. Write *OK* for any sentence that has no spelling error.

✓

1. Hernandez anounced that the annual fund-raising campaign will be held in May.

   1. _____ ____

2. Their were no additions or corrections to the minutes of the April 13 meeting.

   2. _____ ____

3. The board reccomended increasing the deductible on the employees' health insurance.

   3. _____ ____

4. O'Leary thanked Johnson for serving on the Personnal Committee.

   4. _____ ____

5. Isaacs complemented the employee council for it's work on the flextime survey.

   5. _____ ____

6. Hinderman reported that salary adjustments should appear on the October 30 payroll check.

   6. _____ ____

7. Crandall moved that the seperate statement of principle on loan payments should be formulated.

   7. _____ ____

8. Davidson pointed out that the miscelaneous expenses included the purchase of a desktop copier for the student lounge.

   8. _____ ____

9. The next meeting is scheduled for Feburary 10 at 4 p.m.

   9. _____ ____

10. Owens presented a calender of activities for the winter months.

    10. _____ ____

11. The motion was seconded and carried that the audit report be excepted.

    11. _____ ____

12. Morgan submitted the fourth-quarter sales figures for discussion.

    12. _____ ____

13. The group agreed that members' relatives should not be illegible to receive the scholarship.

    13. _____ ____

14. The company selected to do the printing job was Deminsion Graphics.

    14. _____ ____

15. There being no farther business, the meeting was ajourned.

    15. _____ ____

SECTION 13.7   PREPARING NEWS RELEASES

A   **Analyzing a News Release**

You are the President of a large civic organization that is sponsoring a benefit dinner dance to raise money for the orphanage in your community. Your public relations chairperson has resigned, and you requested the secretary of the organization to draft a news release for your approval, which is shown below.

> The Johnsburg Civic Club is in the process of planning its annual dinner dance. To get tickets, which cost $50 each, you can mail your check for the total amount to Jennifer Polaski, National Printing, Inc., 448 West Madison, Nomesville, OH 48999. If you have questions, please call 614-555-8000.
>
> As you may know, the Johnsburg Civic Club has put on this event every year for the past 15 years. The money brought from sale of the tickets is used for the benefit of all the orphaned boys and girls at the Children's Village on State Route 31. If you wish to help with this most worthy cause, be sure to get your tickets ordered before the deadline of August 26.

✓

1. Compose four alternative titles for this news release.

    a. _____

       _____

    b. _____

       _____

    c. _____

       _____

    d. _____

       _____   **1.** _____

2. Write three different opening sentences for the news release.

    a. _____

       _____

       _____

    b. _____

       _____

       _____

    c. _____

       _____

       _____   **2.** _____

B · Function of the News Release

In the space provided, write *Yes* for each situation that is an appropriate subject for a news release. Write *No* if the situation is inappropriate.   ✓

1. A major corporation within a mid-sized city has determined that the location for its new building will be in the new industrial complex north of the city.

   1. _____ _____

2. An opening exists for a new human resources manager at XYZ, Inc.

   2. _____ _____

3. Marshall McCabe is completing 25 years with the Green Company.

   3. _____ _____

4. Employees of Educational Publishers spent each Saturday in May painting and repairing houses in the flood areas of the southern part of the state.

   4. _____ _____

5. The college will be closed for spring vacation during the week of March 19.

   5. _____ _____

6. Jefferson McHenry, chief executive officer of a multinational corporation, will be retiring at the end of the year after 17 years in the position.

   6. _____ _____

C · Writing News Releases

In the space provided, identify the who, what, when, where, and why in the opening paragraphs of the following news releases: ✓

1. The Johnsburg Civic Club is in the process of planning its annual dinner dance. To get tickets, which cost $50 each, you can mail your check for the total amount to Jennifer Polaski, National Printing, Inc., 448 West Madison, Nomesville, OH 48999. The dinner dance will be held on September 15 from 7 to 11 p.m. at the Regency Inn.

   Who: _____

   What: _____

   When: _____

   Where: _____

   Why: _____   1. _____

2. Laura Ison, president of Ison & Associates, has been named chairperson of the Omaha Downtown Council's Board of Directors for the coming year. She will succeed Ronald Wilson III, executive vice president of Brotherhood Insurance.

   Who: _____

   What: _____

   When: _____

   Where: _____

   Why: _____   2. _____

3. Texas Barbecued Ribs plans to open ten restaurants in Eastern Europe over the next seven years to expand into new markets.

   Who: _____

   What: _____

   When: _____

   Where: _____

   Why: _____   3. _____

4. Los Angeles-based Health 2100 Corporation disclosed Thursday that it plans to open a chain of exercise centers across the United States in the next year. According to company spokesperson Margaret Saks, the centers will be for men and women age fifty or older who feel uncomfortable working out in regular health centers.

Who: _____

What: _____

When: _____

Where: _____

Why: _____   **4.** _____

5. As part of a cost-saving program, Little Fritters, Inc., the nation's leading maker of salty snacks, will announce layoffs Monday that will hit the Nashville area hardest. Layoffs will take place immediately.

Who: _____

What: _____

When: _____

Where: _____

Why: _____   **5.** _____

6. Marvel Computer Training in Oklahoma City is opening a new training center on Ardmore Boulevard on August 15. The training center will maintain a staff of 10 full-time and 6 part-time instructors who will conduct courses for business and industry computer personnel.

Who: _____

What: _____

When: _____

Where: _____

Why: _____   **6.** _____

7. Central Carolina Power and Light is implementing a new energy reduction program for all customers in the Piedmont region beginning April 1. The program is intended to encourage customers to conserve electricity and is open to all residential and business customers of Central Carolina Power and Light.

Who: _____

What: _____

When: _____

Where: _____

Why: _____   **7.** _____

8. Donna Marcell, the former city attorney for Columbia, Missouri, has been appointed the new attorney general for the state effective immediately. She was appointed by the governor to fill the remainder of the term of Thomas Daimler, who was recently elected to the state supreme court.

Who: _____

What: _____

When: _____

Where: _____

Why: _____   **8.** _____

D **The Form of the News Release**

Revise the draft of the news release shown in exercise 13.7 A in the workbook.

_____

_____

_____

_____

_____

_____

_____

_____

_____

_____

_____

_____

_____

_____

_____

_____

_____

_____

_____

_____

_____

NAME_____ DATE _____ SCORE ____

 COMMUNICATING
IN THE JOB SEARCH_____

 Analyzing Yourself and the Job

In the left-hand column, describe your career goals, education, skills, experience,
and personal characteristics. Then locate a specific job opening that interests you. In
the right-hand column, describe the education, skills, experience, and personal
characteristics required for the job. Decide whether the two columns match.

My Career Goals   ✓   Job Openings   ✓
_____   _____
_____   _____
_____ ____   _____ ____

My Education Thus Far   Education Required
_____ ____   _____

Degree/Expected Graduation Date   _____

_____ ____   _____ ____

My Skills   Skills Needed
_____   _____
_____   _____
_____   _____
_____   _____
_____   _____
_____ ____   _____ ____

My Experience   Experience Required
_____   _____
_____   _____
_____   _____
_____   _____
_____   _____
_____ ____   _____ ____

My Personal Characteristics   Personal Characteristics Required
_____   _____
_____   _____
_____   _____
_____   _____
_____ ____   _____ ____

B Considering Job Factors

Circle the factor or factors in each group that would be most important for your ideal job. On the blanks provided, explain why the factor or factors is important to you.

1. Company

small	national
medium	international
large	values
local	purpose—goods or services

_____

_____

_____

_____   _____

2. Location

large city	willing to relocate within 500 miles of home
small community	willing to relocate within 1,000 miles of home
rural setting	willing to relocate within the United States
easy commute from home	willing to relocate internationally
accessible by public transportation	

_____

_____

_____

_____   _____

3. Job Content

variety of tasks	limited amount of responsibility
limited number of tasks	work directly with customers, clients, and the public
high degree of responsibility	limited interaction with customers, clients, and the public

_____

_____

_____

_____   _____

✓

4. Supervision

close   democratic

minimal   supportive

authoritarian

_____

_____

_____   _____

5. Work Area

office   noisy

outdoors   private

quiet   open

_____

_____

_____   _____

6. Schedule

flexible hours   days

regular hours   nights

full-time   job share

part-time

_____

_____

_____   _____

7. Rewards

financial   level of challenge

fringe benefits   opportunity to use skills and talents

opportunity for advancement   sense of helping others

sense of accomplishment   additional education and training provided

_____

_____

_____   _____

8. Fringe Benefits

health insurance   child care

dental insurance   paid vacation

vision insurance   stock options

disability insurance   company car

retirement package   parking space

_____

_____

_____

_____

9. Coworkers

work closely with others   develop friendships outside of work

work independently   limited social interaction with coworkers

develop friendships with coworkers

_____

_____

_____

_____

10. Work-Related Travel

local (none overnight)

national

international

overnight travel—several nights per week but home on weekends

moderate overnight travel, up to five nights per week

extensive travel—traveling two or three weeks at a time including weekends

_____

_____

_____

_____

C Assessing the Job Market

List specific sources of information in your community you can use to find out about job opportunities. Include people, agencies, newspapers, and journals.

✓

1. _____   1. ____
2. _____   2. ____
3. _____   3. ____
4. _____   4. ____
5. _____   5. ____
6. _____   6. ____
7. _____   7. ____
8. _____   8. ____

D Classified Advertisements

Clip one classified advertisement from the newspaper that describes a job that interests you. Paste or tape the advertisement in the space provided. Based on the advertisement, describe what you would write about each of the following items in your application letter. Write your answers in the space provided.

✓

Advertisement:

____

Education:

_____
_____
_____
_____   ____

Experience:

_____
_____
_____
_____   ____

Personal qualifications:

_____
_____
_____   ____

E Describing Job Experience

Write a description of your most recent or your current job. Use at least four of the action verbs that appear in the Memory Hook on page 625 of your textbook.

✓

_____

_____

_____

_____

_____

_____

_____

F On-Line Employment Search

Search the Internet and the World Wide Web for job postings in your career area. Print one of the job postings and paste or tape it in the space provided.

G Preparing a Technologically Friendly Résumé

Using the guidelines on pages 629–631 of your textbook, prepare a technologically friendly résumé to send in response to the job posting you clipped in exercise E. Adapt the résumé you prepared in item 5 of the Practical Application on page 635 of your textbook.

✓

_____
_____
_____
_____
_____
_____
_____
_____
_____
_____
_____
_____
_____
_____
_____
_____
_____
_____
_____
_____
_____
_____
_____
_____
_____
_____
_____
_____
_____

H Completing an Application Form

Complete the application form on the next page. Read and follow all directions carefully.

Satellite Communications Company

An Equal Opportunity Employer

Personal Data

Company use only	Date _____
	Interviewer _____

Applying For Position As _____ Salary Desired _____ Date Available _____

Date Applied _____

Name: _____
              (Last)   (First)   (Middle)

Address: _____
           (Street)   (City)   (State)   (Zip Code)

Telephone No. _____ Social Security No. _____ U.S. Citizen? _____
         (Area Code)

Who referred you to us? _____

Educational Data

SCHOOLS	NAME OF INSTITUTION	ADDRESS	MAJOR	COURSES TAKEN	No. Yrs. Attended	Yr. Grad.	Degree
HIGH SCHOOL OR EQUIVALENT							
COLLEGE							
OTHER							

Employment Data   Begin with most recent employer.

NAME OF COMPANY	ADDRESS	YOUR POSITION and DUTIES	DATES	SALARY RECEIVED	SUPERVISOR'S NAME	REASON FOR LEAVING
			From	Start $		
			To	Finish $	TITLE	
			From	Start $		
			To	Finish $	TITLE	

References

NAME	ADDRESS	TELEPHONE NUMBER

 **SECTION 14.2**

THE EFFECTIVE
EMPLOYMENT INTERVIEW

A **Researching a Prospective Employer**

Select a local firm for which you would like to work. After checking as many sources of
information as are available to you, answer the following questions. ✓

1. What type of ownership or organization (sole proprietorship, partnership, or
   corporation) does the firm have?

   _____

   _____   1. _____

2. What are the principal goods sold or the services provided?

   _____

   _____   2. _____

3. How long has the company been in business?

   _____

   _____   3. _____

4. Where is the home office located?

   _____

   _____   4. _____

5. How many people are employed at the local office?

   _____

   _____   5. _____

6. Does the firm have offices in other states? If so, which ones?

   _____

   _____   6. _____

7. Does the firm have offices outside the United States? If so, where?

   _____

   _____   7. _____

8. Who are the company's chief competitors?

   _____

   _____   8. _____

9. Is the company involved with the community? How?

   _____

   _____   9. _____

10. From what sources did you obtain this information?

    _____

    _____   10. _____

B Preparing Questions to Ask the Interviewer

You have been invited to interview for a position with the company you identified in exercise A. Based on the information you compiled in exercise A, prepare three questions to ask the interviewer.

✓

1. _____
   _____
   _____
   _____   1. _____

2. _____
   _____
   _____
   _____   2. _____

3. _____
   _____
   _____
   _____   3. _____

C Anticipating Interview Questions

To prepare for a job interview, develop answers to the following questions that are often asked at interviews.

✓

1. What are your strongest points?

   _____
   _____
   _____
   _____   1. _____

2. What are your weakest points?

   _____
   _____
   _____
   _____   2. _____

3. Why did you select this particular course of study?

   _____
   _____
   _____
   _____   3. _____

4. Why would you be a good candidate for this position?

   _____
   _____
   _____
   _____   4. _____

D Interview Quiz

Circle *T* if the statement is true and *F* if the statement is false.   ✓

1. Effective interview planning begins many days before the actual interview.   **1.** T F _____

2. Confirm your appointment for an interview about one week before the scheduled interview.   **2.** T F _____

3. Do not ask directions to the company location because it makes you look uninformed.   **3.** T F _____

4. You should allow a minimum of 30 minutes extra for travel delays.   **4.** T F _____

5. In an employment interview, the person being interviewed is usually considered as the seller.   **5.** T F _____

6. One goal of a job interview is to find out if the job fits your career plans.   **6.** T F _____

7. Chew a stick of gum during the interview to make sure that your breath is pleasant.   **7.** T F _____

8. You should bring at least three copies of your résumé to the job interview.   **8.** T F _____

9. Preparing a résumé takes the place of completing an application form.   **9.** T F _____

10. After spending 15 minutes or so in the interviewer's office, you should rise and terminate the interview.   **10.** T F _____

11. If the interviewer asks about controversial issues, you should waste no time in aggressively expressing your opinion.   **11.** T F _____

12. When you are leaving a bad employment situation, you should respond in a positive manner if encouraged to speak about your former supervisor or employer.   **12.** T F _____

13. If you are invited to eat lunch or dinner while being interviewed, you may relax because mealtime is not a part of the interview consideration process.   **13.** T F _____

14. Personal appearance is of little significance during most job interviews because the interviewer is only interested in your experience and skills.   **14.** T F _____

15. Being qualified for the job guarantees that you will get it; thus, you should take every rejection personally.   **15.** T F _____

E Another Interview Quiz

In the answer column, write the letter that corresponds to the best answer to each of the following questions.   ✓

1. Which one of the following ways would *not* be appropriate for finding out the exact name and title of the interviewer?
   a. Telephone and ask the interviewer.
   b. Ask the receptionist.
   c. Ask the interviewer's assistant by telephone.
   d. Find out from the person who referred you to the interviewer.   **1.** _____ _____

2. Which of the following is the best reason for finding out in advance all you can about the company?
   a. You may know someone who works there.
   b. The information will help you to decide whether the company is a good place to work.
   c. You can impress the interviewer with your knowledge.
   d. Once you learn about one company, you have an accurate picture of all similar companies.

   2. _____ _____

3. It is a good idea to prepare some questions to ask the interviewer. Which of the following questions would you be *least* likely to ask?
   a. What are the duties required in this position?
   b. What are the opportunities for advancement?
   c. Does the company provide for further education?
   d. How long have you been with the company?

   3. _____ _____

4. Which one of the following is *not* a reason for bringing copies of your résumé to a job interview?
   a. Your résumé will provide details you need in filling out an application form.
   b. Rereading your résumé will refresh your memory about your background and experience.
   c. Your interviewer or interviewers may not have a copy of your résumé.
   d. You can make the interview more efficient by reading your résumé to the interviewer.

   4. _____ _____

5. There are three reasons why it is important that you arrive early for the interview. Which one of the following is *not* one of those reasons?
   a. You will feel less stress because you didn't have to rush in at the last minute.
   b. You will have extra time in which to complete the application form.
   c. You will have an opportunity to freshen up before you are called into the interviewer's office.
   d. It is inconsiderate to keep the interviewer waiting because you are late in arriving.

   5. _____ _____

6. While waiting in the reception room for the interviewer, the applicant should:
   a. Review the résumé.
   b. Take the initiative in engaging the receptionist in conversation.
   c. Comb his or her hair.
   d. Walk around the room.

   6. _____ _____

7. An interviewer for a publishing company asks you this question: "Why do you think you should be hired for this position?" Which of the following replies is the most appropriate?
   a. "I'm a hard worker and I thrive on challenges."
   b. "I like people."
   c. "Your offices are only about two miles from my home."
   d. "I always read your magazine, and I think the work would be fun."

   7. _____ _____

8. When you are asked by the interviewer to talk about yourself, which of the following would you be *most* likely to omit?
   a. Your aspirations in your career.
   b. The subjects you took in school that related to the job.
   c. Your social and leadership activities in school.
   d. Your marital status and religion.

   8. _____ _____

✓

9. Which answer would you choose when an interviewer asks, "What salary would you consider to be fair for this position?"
   a. "I understand that the beginning salary for this position is $1,200 a month. I would hope to receive such a salary."
   b. "I think I'm worth whatever the salary is for this position."
   c. "I would leave the matter of salary to your judgment."
   d. "I don't know."   9. _____   _____

10. With which of the following statements do you disagree?
    a. Face the interviewer and speak directly to him or her.
    b. Speak slowly and distinctly.
    c. When asked about your skill in communication, simply say, "Okay."
    d. Be honest with your interviewer when asked about your previous experience.   10. _____   _____

F   International Countries and Cities

In the space provided, write the correct spelling of each international country or city that is misspelled. If the item is correct, write *OK* in the space.

✓

1. Switserland, Rome, Stockholm, Haiti   1. _____ _____

2. Florence, Berlin, Uruguay, Israel   2. _____ _____

3. Jamaica, Estonia, Beijing, Phillipines   3. _____ _____

4. Montreal, Johannesburg, Vienna, Tokeyo   4. _____ _____

5. Eygpt, Cologne, Mexicali, Portugal   5. _____ _____

6. Peru, Barsellona, Tanzania, Latvia   6. _____ _____

7. Frankfurt, Honduras, Grease, Kyoto   7. _____ _____

8. Turkey, Cairo, Bogotá, Bolivia   8. _____ _____

9. Edinburg, Munich, Toronto, Moscow   9. _____ _____

10. Ireland, Jerusalem, Brussels, Kenya   10. _____ _____

11. Ontario, Casablanca, Paraguay, Ukrain   11. _____ _____

12. Pakistan, Dominican Republic, Calcuta, Afghanistan   12. _____ _____

13. Mongolia, Thayland, Nagasaki, Guatemala   13. _____ _____

14. Hanoi, Perth, Malaysia, Australea   14. _____ _____

15. Winnipeg, Greenland, Panima, Buenos Aires 15. _____ _____

16. Dublin, Sweden, Helsinki, Austria   16. _____ _____

17. Manchester, Romania, Seyria, Nigeria   17. _____ _____

18. New Guinea, Bangladesh, Amman, Poleland   18. _____ _____

19. Venezuela, Budapest, Jordan, Algeria   19. _____ _____

20. Argentina, Warsaw, Luxemburg, Seoul   20. _____ _____

G Proofreading Practice

Proofread the following letter and underline any errors. Write your corrections in the space provided. If a line is correct, write *OK*.   ✓

Ms. Irena Madison _____ _____

Human Resources Directer _____ _____

Huntington Publishing _____ _____

14 Starliner Drive _____ _____

Huntington, WV 28310 _____ _____

Dear Ms. Madison _____ _____

Please consider me an applicant for the positoin of _____ _____

associate editor advertised in the June 5 edition of _____ _____

the *Huntington Gazette*. _____ _____

In May I graduated from West Virginia University with _____ _____

an Bachelor's of Arts degree with a major in English. As _____ _____

you can see on my enclosd résumé, my concentration _____ _____

was in English education, specifically grades 6 through 12. _____ _____

My coursework, combined with the student's teaching I _____ _____

completed in the Huntington schools, offers I an insight _____ _____

into the educational needs of students and teachers for _____ _____

who you publish materials. _____ _____

The position of asociate editor with Huntington Publishing _____ _____

is very appealing to me. If you would like to contact me _____ _____

regarding an interview please call me at 304-555-7823. _____ _____

Sincerely, _____ _____

 COMMUNICATING
AND YOUR CAREER

 Accepting a Job Offer

You have received a letter from JPT Financial Services offering you a position as a financial consultant. The letter outlines your terms of employment and specifies that you will begin work three weeks from today (current date) when in-house training for the licensing exam will begin.

Write a letter to Ms. Alicia Charpentier, Human Resources Director, accepting the position and confirming the first day of employment. Transmit the letter by fax. The company is located at 828 Coconut Avenue, Honolulu, HI 96815-3824. Use the block-letter style with standard punctuation. Use the current date and your own return address. Type and print the letter if you have access to a computer.

✓

_____

_____

_____

_____

_____

_____

_____

_____

_____

_____

_____

_____

_____

_____

_____

_____

_____

_____

_____

_____

_____

_____

_____

_____

_____

_____

_____

B Declining a Job Offer

You recently accepted employment as a graphics designer with Wilson Graphics, Inc., but two days later received a much better offer (higher salary, better benefits, and more opportunity for advancement) from Champion Graphics, Inc.

Write a tactful letter to Mr. W. F. Wilson of Wilson Graphics, Inc., letting him know that you have accepted another job. Use the block-letter style with open punctuation. The address is 3826 Balsam Court, Covington, KY 41017-3826. Use the current date and your own return address. Type and print the letter if you have access to a computer.

_____

_____

_____

_____

_____

_____

_____

_____

_____

_____

_____

_____

_____

_____

_____

_____

_____

_____

_____

_____

_____

_____

_____

_____

_____

_____

_____

_____

_____

_____

_____

C Writing an Interview Follow-Up Letter

You applied today for the position of administrative assistant to Mr. Alex Tyler, the plant manager of Tyler Manufacturing Company, Inc. Mr. Tyler interviewed you personally because he needs to fill the job as soon as possible. You really want the job and can begin work immediately because you are attending night school.

Write Mr. Tyler an interview follow-up letter using the modified-block style (indented paragraphs) with standard punctuation. The company address is 1806 Tyler Avenue, Ogden, UT 84404. Use the current date and your own return address. Type and print the letter if computers and word processing software are available.

✓

_____

_____

_____

_____

_____

_____

_____

_____

_____

_____

_____

_____

_____

_____

_____

_____

_____

_____

_____

_____

_____

_____

_____

_____

_____

_____

_____

_____

_____

_____

D Writing a Letter of Resignation

You have been an office assistant at Schaeffer Real Estate Company for three years and have been attending night school. Graduation is in two weeks. You have been offered and have accepted the position of office manager at Metrolina Regional Medical Clinic at a significant increase in compensation. Metrolina has recruited two additional physicians, which will increase your responsibilities and your income. One of your career goals is to get a masters degree in business administration, and Metrolina has agreed to reimburse you for tuition and books while you are working on this degree.

Write a letter of resignation using the modified-block style (block paragraphs) with standard punctuation to Mrs. Adrianna Tomlin, Schaeffer Real Estate Company, 389 Butternut Ridge, Anderson, SC 29621. You and Adrianna are personal friends. Address her by her first name in the salutation. Your contract letter specifies a three-week notice. Use the current date and your own return address.